DIRECTIONS

New Zealanders Explore the Meaning of Life

DIRECTIONS

New Zealanders Explore the Meaning of Life

NEVILLE GLASGOW

Dear Steve,

On each birthday one needs new directions for the next year. We hope these will prove useful.

Love from Sophie and Franc.

SHOAL BAY PRESS

Dedication

This book is dedicated to the memory of three
great New Zealanders, Sir Guy Powles, Dr Fraser
McDonald and Dr Eru Pomare, all of whom have
died since the original interviews were broadcast,
yet who continue to inspire us by the way they gave
their lives meaning, purpose and direction.

First published in 1995 by
Shoal Bay Press Ltd
Box 2151, Christchurch

ISBN 0 908704 30 5

Cover photograph: *Banana Palm Leaf*, by Neville Glasgow

Production and design by Orca Publishing Services Ltd
Printed by GP Print Ltd
Distributed by Macmillan New Zealand Ltd, 6 Ride Way,
Albany Industrial Estate, Auckland, Fax (09) 4156 659

Contents

Acknowledgments

I first wish to thank those people or their families who have allowed their stories to be included in this book. To open up one's life in this way takes a certain amount of courage and I wish to acknowledge that. I want to say also what a heartwarming experience it was to talk again with people I had interviewed, sometimes six or seven years ago, and to pick up immediately the intimacy and friendliness we had established during the original interview.

I acknowledge also the financial contribution of National Radio, which made a generous contribution towards the cost of transcribing the interviews and continues to play the *Directions* series as part of its role as a public radio network reflecting New Zealand's identity and culture.

To Sharon Crosbie, general manager of New Zealand Public Radio, and Gavin McGinley, production director of National Radio, go my grateful thanks for their encouragement and support. My thanks also to publishers Ros Henry and David Elworthy, and writer and friend Alison Gray, for their support and enthusiasm for the project.

To Lloyd Geering goes my gratitude, not only for writing the foreword, but also for the way he has inspired me and thousands of other New Zealanders with his honesty, sincerity and courage, sometimes in the face of intense criticism.

The painstaking job of transcribing the interviews was done by Brenda Watson and Faith Beard. The photographs were, in many cases, chosen or supplied by the interviewees themselves as favourites or expressing something about who they are.

To Diana, who gave me loving support for many years and continues to remain my friend, my thanks – also to my 'support group': my family and extended family, Rob and Angie, Debbie and Phil, Kathy and Lyndon, Ruth and Red, Miriam and Joanne, who died in 1985. She was our 'rebel' but in the last years of her life she always ended her long overseas telephone conversations with, 'I love you, Dad.'

To Helen, my wife, partner, friend and companion in life's adventure, thank you for your love, patience and encouragement, which play such a large part in giving my life joy and meaning.

Foreword

Professor Lloyd Geering

It is an honour and privilege to be invited to write the foreword to this collection of personal interviews by Neville Glasgow, whom I have now known for thirty years, as student, colleague and friend. Using his own personal skill as an interviewer who can empathise with his subjects, he has brought us into personal contact with many well-known New Zealanders whom otherwise we would never have the opportunity of meeting. With gentle probing he has encouraged them to tell us their own story and to express their own reflections on the meaning of life.

The telling of stories is quite basic to us humans and may even be said to have provided the foundation for the evolution of human culture. The fascination which stories hold for children, from the time they take their first steps into language, most probably reflects that long period in our cultural past when story-telling provided the growing edge for human culture. Each tribal group expressed its identity in the cycle of stories it created and transmitted from generation to generation. Those stories introduced each new generation to an understanding of the way the world operated and what was expected of them.

In ancient Greece the name for these stories was the word that has given us our word 'myths': originally it simply meant stories told by word of mouth. A particular feature of those ancient myths, of course, is that they were stories of the gods. It is that very fact that enables us to appreciate the extreme importance of stories to this very day. As our ancient forebears had come to understand reality, it was the gods and not humans who wielded all the power, held all the keys and generally controlled all significant events. What puny humans could do, by comparison, was hardly worth talking about. So it was the stories of the gods that explained why the world is as it is, who we humans are and why we are here.

It was mainly in the first millennium BCE (Before the Common Era) that human stories began to be felt to be of at least some comparable importance. Thus came to birth the telling (or writing) of human history, particularly among the Hebrews and the Greeks. History is the telling of the human story and it is no accident that 'history' and 'story' are both derived from the same Greek word, which meant something like 'human enquiry into'. It was at this point that history (the story of humans) began to be distinguished from myths (the stories of the gods).

Once established, the phenomenon of telling the human story began to play an even greater role in the evolution of human culture. The Jewish people have retained their identity over some 3000 years, and in the face of great odds, simply by retelling and continually celebrating their own story. The great civilisations founded on Buddhism, Christianity and Islam evolved, in each instance, around their own originating story – the Enlightenment of the Buddha, the life, death and resurrection of Jesus of Nazareth, the divine revelation of the Koran to Muhammad.

Modern secularisation has weakened the power of these great originating stories because it has increasingly turned our attention to this tangible world where human affairs are dominant. The stories of the gods are becoming increasingly displaced by the stories of humans. Indeed, some even point out that the continuing value to be found in the traditional stories of the gods (or God) is to interpret them as projections of the inner life of humans. In any case, secularisation has by no means brought an end to our dependence on story.

On the contrary, the telling of stories has exploded in the modern world. Novels, literature, biography, history, stories of current events have become a kind of cultural ocean in which we 'live and move and have our being'. There is no longer one simple story that we all share, like the Christian of the Muslim story; rather, we are in the midst of a bewildering medley of stories and they are nearly all human stories, rather than stories of the gods.

Thus we still live by stories. As the ancients told stories of the gods in order to structure the world in which they lived, so we tell human stories, some fictional and some from real life. We cannot really get away from the telling of stories. By stories we reach back to our roots in the past and by stories we try to look into the future. We often use stories on which to model our own lives or by which to measure the value or effectiveness of what we do. The daily news comes to us in the form of stories told by journalists. The decisions we make, and the opinions we hold, are often in response to such stories. Through all of these stories, in each day of our lives, we are weaving the story that constitutes our very identity.

One often hears people say, 'That is the story of my life.' The words frequently slip out as a throwaway line, which is not intended to have much depth. Yet this simple phrase is deceptively penetrating. The human existence of each one of us unfolds as a story, and it is only as we attempt to tell that story and to reflect on it, that we come to understand more clearly who we are, where we have come from, and where we are going.

Of course when we speak of our own story, it is always a story that is still awaiting its ending. None of us will ever be able to tell the whole of our own story, which is one reason why no one can ever write their own definitive biography. But once we have reached adulthood, and even more when we have passed mid-life, we are able to look back and recall, for better or for worse, the chief events of the story that has helped to make us who we are. Moreover, we can never go back and relive it differently, however much we would sometimes like to. As Omar Khayyam said:

The moving finger writes; and having writ,
Moves on; nor all they Piety nor Wit
Shall lure it back to cancel half a Line,
Nor all they Tears wash out a Word of it.

But though we can never change the past, we can always learn from it, as we can also learn much for our own benefit from the stories of others. As the story of each human life unfolds it has the possibility of becoming meaningful. One cannot speak about meaning without using words, for words are essential to the very concept of meaning. It is only because we humans are essentially products of human culture, which in turn has been made possible by the evolution of human language, that we can speak of the meaning of life and interpret human existence as the quest for meaning.

Neville refers to the work of Viktor Frankl, and his understanding of human existence as described as *man's search for meaning*. Frankl's experience led him to develop a form of therapy that he called 'logotherapy'; it may be roughly described as the attainment of psychic healing or wholeness by the creation of meaning. Whereas Freud concentrated on *the will to pleasure* and Adler on *the will to power*, Frankl became convinced that the primary motivation of humankind, and hence the basis of psychic health, is *the will to meaning*. Logotherapy simply attempts to assist the patient to find or create meaning in his or her life.

Whether or not we *consciously* think or talk about the quest for meaning is unimportant; but in so far as we humans live our lives seeking a sense of fulfilment, or purpose, or significance of some kind, this experience may be usefully described as our quest for meaning. What we make of our lives, by the many decisions we make, is in fact our own answer to that quest. And our answer is told in the story of our life.

There is no one simple and absolute answer to the quest for meaning; there are many answers. We may judge some to be better than others, but when we make that judgment we are doing so from the point where we stand. There is no absolute standpoint and it is as vain to search for some non-subjective and absolute point as it is dangerous to assume that our own standpoint is the one and only Archimedean point.

Yet it is from where each of us stands that we attempt to give the answer to the quest for the meaning of life. Not only is it a useful exercise for us from time to time to pause, recall our own past and reflect on our own story, but it is equally useful to listen to other people telling their own stories, for from them we commonly receive help, comfort, support and encouragement for our own continuing story.

No two stories are the same, for each of us weaves our own unique story. Just as there is no one clear and absolute answer to the quest for meaning of life, so it is in the quest itself, rather than in any one answer, that we find human existence to be worthwhile and significant. Each person's story is his or her own unique contribution to the long and complex story of the human species.

Introduction

Meaning is at the core of the creative process and of storytelling. It is both the goal and the attribute. When it is our own life story we are telling, or a story from our lives, we become aware that we are not the victims of random and chaotic circumstances; that we, too, despite our grief or feelings of insignificance, are living meaningfully in a meaningful universe. And, again, the response to our own story, as well as to the stories of others, is, 'Yes. Yes, I have a story. Yes, I exist.'

Deena Metzger, *Writing for Your Life*

The *Directions* radio series had its birth in 1988 when I submitted a proposal for a pilot series to National Radio. The first programmes started in December of that year and have continued in summer and winter series ever since.

Nearly eighty New Zealanders have now submitted themselves to the intimate scrutiny of their lives, values and beliefs that constitutes a *Directions* interview.

The interviews are very personal. They are generally conducted in the person's home and they traverse areas that are often reserved for one's most private conversations with friends or family – questions about life's meaning, about death, morality, religion, sexuality and spirituality, things that make us angry or sad or find hard to forgive, and things that inspire us, that help us to keep going or to celebrate.

I see my job as interviewer in this context as primarily that of a facilitator. I am there to facilitate the telling of a person's story of how they have found meaning in their lives. If I may borrow from the philosophy of one of the interviewers I admire, Michael Toms of New Dimensions Radio in the United States:

My contention is that if you give people a safe place to roam, by establishing trust, supporting them by being there as an attentive listener, and respecting their right to say whatever they want, however they want, the dialogue unfolds naturally in an atmosphere of mutual respect.

I've sometimes been criticised as a 'soft' interviewer by those critics who feel the only good interviews are those where there is blood on the floor. They say, 'Where are the hard questions?' All I can say is that some of the hardest questions we ever have to face are those about our sense of loss of a loved one, the memories of an abused or deprived childhood, our failures, our belief or lack of belief in a personal god, our personal values and beliefs and where they've come from and, perhaps the hardest one of all, 'Is my life meaningful or meaningless?' These are the questions people examine in *Directions*.

I continue to be amazed and humbled by people's courage and their willingness to talk about such issues honestly and frankly. It's not easy; sometimes it's costly and revealing.

In my original proposal for the *Directions* series in 1988 I suggested:

> *Life can be described as* man's search for meaning. *Not that most of us go around constantly asking, 'What is the meaning of life?' But most of us will ask, perhaps at a time of crisis, when someone we love dies, when we start a new career, fall in love, retire or become unemployed, maybe in a time of quiet reflection, 'What's it all about?' 'Who am I?' 'What am I here for?' 'What happens when I die?'*
>
> *These are questions about the nature of the human spirit or psyche. They deal with what some would describe as 'spiritual values'. We may or may not wish to describe them as 'religious' questions, but they are the great fundamental questions of all time. We seem to need, particularly in times of stress, to somehow make sense of our lives, to feel that our lives have meaning or purpose, a sense of direction. What the programme would do is talk with people whose lives reflect this. They may have things in common, but every story will be different.*

What the people in *Directions* have in common is that they are all 'creative' in the sense of reaching into their basket of talents, skills and experience and doing something with them.

Every story is different because every life is different. Our individual life story is our personal response to the challenges and opportunities that life as a whole presents to us. How we live out our lives, what we do with them, is the way we find or give meaning to our lives.

Psychiatrist Viktor Frankl, who survived years in Nazi concentration camps during World War II and is the author of *Man's Search for Meaning*, believes it is impossible to answer the question of an ultimate or universal meaning of life. For, he says, the meaning of life differs from person to person, from day to day, and from hour to hour:

> *What matters, therefore, is not the meaning of life in general, but rather the specific meaning of a person's life at a given moment. To put the question in general terms would be comparable to the question put to a chess champion, 'Tell me, Master, what is the best move in the world?'*
>
> *There is simply no such thing as the best or even a good move, apart from a particular situation in a game and the particular personality of one's opponent. The same holds for human existence.*

Frankl goes on to suggest that rather than our asking the question, 'What is the meaning of my life?' it is *we* who are asked. We are questioned by life. It is up to us to provide our own answer, and we can only answer the question in terms of our own lives.

A good friend has suggested that the *Directions* series is part of my own personal search for meaning. I guess that is true. Part of the reason I have been a journalist for the past twenty-five years, and for the past ten years a specialist in the areas of religion and spirituality, is that I am compelled passionately to pursue such questions as, 'How do people find meaning in their lives?' 'Why do people believe what they believe?' 'What's life all about?' Each of those questions is a personal one for me also. And every time I talk to people about such questions I have the chance to learn something as well.

That, coupled with the fact that I am an enthusiast – when I find out something new and interesting I have a need to tell others about it – is my main motivation for doing the *Directions* interviews. This is why I find the search for meaning so fascinating. This is why I am intensely interested in finding out how other people make their lives 'meaning-full'.

In *Directions* I talk with people about their story of their response to the challenges and opportunities that life has presented to them. I hear about their struggles and triumphs, their successes and failures, their times of joy and times of sadness, and I can share this with other people through the medium of radio.

In this book you can read the stories of some of the people who have inspired me by the way they have given their lives meaning, purpose and direction.

Fraser McDonald

Fraser McDonald

When psychiatrist Fraser McDonald died, in June 1994, one of his former colleagues described him as 'a very astute clinician and a great humanist'.

In the 1960s and 70s Fraser McDonald was well known as something of a media guru, speaking out about many areas of the national psyche. He may not have invented the term 'suburban neurosis' but he certainly brought it to New Zealanders' attention.

What is not generally known, however, is that much of his thinking about life and its purpose began on a hospital bed. In 1949, as a young doctor, Fraser McDonald contracted tuberculosis at a time when the life-saving anti-tuberculosis drugs were yet to be discovered.

FRASER McDONALD: In those days tuberculosis was a pretty deadly disease. I suppose the most significant thing as far as I was concerned was that I steadily got worse. No matter what they did I went down and down and down. I spent about three years in the sanatorium and I suppose the most important thing I learnt there was the awareness that I was going to die. That was a remarkably good thing to come up against. You have intellectual concepts about what life is all about, what your own life is all about, but I think it was there that I really started asking myself the hard questions about religion.

I had been brought up a Catholic – a very harsh and, I suppose, rigid type of Irish Catholicism that has a punitive God and is very much involved with sins of the flesh and all that sort of thing. When I was faced with the reality that I was probably going to die I had to think very carefully about questions like, 'Is this true or not true? What is my posture? What am I here for? What am I supposed to have been living for?' I think it was then that I realised that, whatever the rights and wrongs of that sort of Catholicism, it really just was of no interest to me at all. It was quite irrelevant and was of no help to me in having to face up to basically being dead.

So I think it was there that I lost my religion – if you lose religion. I have never really felt that it has had much relevance to me since then. Until that time I had been very much a good Catholic boy, but I think that because it really didn't help, it didn't mean anything, I realised that I would have to front up to being dead on my own. It really didn't matter what, or even if, a God existed. The fact of my dying was the paramount thing in my mind at this stage of the game and I was on my own.

17

I was confined to bed, and at one time I didn't put my foot on the floor for about fourteen months. I suppose what it did to me was make me realise that I really would stop living. And so I became very greedy to find out as much as I could about what life is all about, and what the world is about, and I read everything I could lay my hands on.

One of the few good things about a sanatorium is that you are lying there all day. You are not expected to do anything except lie there, so I could read my head off, and I suppose in a sense I almost did another university degree. I had just passed medicine and it was almost as if I did an informal BA with my reading. I plunged into everything, and of course in an isolated place like a sanatorium you are able to really follow up things very well. I ranged through a whole lot of Chinese philosophy and Indian and Greek and those sorts of things. I read extremely widely and fortunately I was a very fast reader. I remember Arnold Toynbee wrote a series, I think it was about a twelve-volume history of civilisation, and I read the lot. It was very interesting. I must be one of the few people who have read that right through, but this was to me a great education and I found it a very satisfying occupation.

However, it didn't still any of my fears about actually dying. Being a doctor I knew what was involved and of course I had treated tuberculosis. I had been working in tuberculosis wards where I caught the disease, so I knew very well how they died, and it was usually in a pretty messy fashion. They would die slowly and messily, with kidneys being gradually destroyed or tuberculosis pneumonia or tuberculosis laryngitis, which is one of the most painful illnesses you can get. They also used to die of severe haemorrhages from the lungs when the tuberculosis would leak into the arteries in the lungs and you would literally drown in your own blood. That was a major fear for me and it really developed into a bit of a neurosis. A frank neurosis!

When the lights went out I would lie down to go to sleep and I would suddenly get a terrible feeling as if there was something rushing up my trachea, and I immediately thought that it was blood, that this was it, that I was going to suffocate in my own blood, and I would sit up with my heart pounding in the middle of the night. That went on for months and months. Naturally, I didn't tell anybody. In those days a doctor was never supposed to have anything wrong with him. He was supposed to be fully in control of himself but I wasn't at all. I told myself these feelings were just signs of weakness but that didn't help me. It was pretty terrifying and it really only disappeared when I started to improve a bit.

I then had severe chest surgery. That was another very significant thing for me. In those days you had a thing called a thoracoplasty, which basically collapses the ribs in on your lung. That was pretty traumatic to my ego. I had been a pretty good-looking fellow before I got tuberculosis and I was quite proud of my well-developed physique. I used to play rugby, I was a hooker in the first fifteen at Silverstream and a great golfer and I loved physical activity. Of course my physique was ruined beyond all recognition by surgery. I wouldn't be seen dead in a swimsuit after that. Fortunately, it didn't interfere too much with my golf swing, for which I was quite grateful.

That was a watershed, having my ego lacerated like that, and it didn't do a hell of a lot for my confidence with women. At this stage of the game I was still supposed to be dying, but thoracoplasty stopped things more or less, and they finally decided that there really wasn't a great deal more they could do for me. I still had positive sputum – that is the germs in the sputum – but they decided to let me out of the sanatorium. They very generously said, 'You know, if you look after yourself very carefully you might live until you are forty-five.' In those days looking after yourself meant lying down and resting and becoming neurotically sure that you were not straining yourself. So, basically, from then on I really lived with the possibility of death.

But I think it also added a great seasoning, if you like, to my life. Because if you think you are going to die shortly, it has some bad effects but it also has some good effects. It makes you very appreciative of what is happening today; you really appreciate that this might be the last year that you see summer, or the last year that you see winter, or the last year that you are this well, this sort of thing. Unfortunately, it can also make you think too much in the short term rather than planning long term. So that was a bit of a problem.

I then went into the army to convalesce. In those days it was thought that mountain air was good for you, so I went to Waiouru as a medical officer and there, for some obscure reason, I started getting better. Even so, this feeling of futility remained with me, and I think my neuroticism stayed with me too.

I had always been quite interested in psychiatry and my own neurotic symptoms intensified that interest. I wanted to know what I could do about them and what they meant. I think that was what turned me into a psychiatrist, basically.

Having tuberculosis at that time had a bit of a stigma attached to it, didn't it?

Oh yes. Especially having a positive sputum. That made you a very 'dirty' person in the sense that you could never think of spontaneously kissing someone. You would want to hide the fact that you had tuberculosis and yet had shameful feelings about hiding the fact. There was always the possibility that you might give it to somebody. I suppose it was a bit like people with Aids these days. It was not as terrible as that, but something along those lines. There were those overtones about it.

That certainly affected me and made me feel very much an outsider, which I hadn't felt before then. That helped me in psychiatry, though, as in those days psychiatry was looked upon a bit as outside stuff. You were not a proper doctor!

When you thought death wasn't far away did you think about what was on the other side?

I felt that, given the immensity of the equation, any sort of human imaginings of what might be on the other side would be so pathetically childish and self-serving that they were hardly worth contemplating. I think my agnosticism developed at that stage. I felt, sure, there may be something but it's obviously going to be so different from what I or any human being could imagine that there is not much point in thinking about it. Also, once you are dead, you can't do a hell of a lot about it anyhow, so why worry about it?

I suppose I was obsessed with the dying process. I really wondered if I would be able to cope with it and that was what was filling my mind. To be dead would be almost a relief. Naturally, I always felt that if the dying process got too unpleasant I would kill myself. Being a doctor, I knew how I could do it pretty efficiently.

But, really, whatever happened I felt I would just have to live as best I could here. One couldn't do any more, anyhow. Whether there was a heaven or hell seemed irrelevant. I thought, this is the way I live and I'm living it the best way I know how. If that's not good enough, well, that's too bad!

All the reading you did in hospital – did it change your value system?

Very much so. It was then that I read a lot of, I suppose, semi-psychiatric things, you know, sort of psychological novels. In those days textbooks in psychiatry weren't very good. When I went through medicine there were, I think, about forty pages at the end of the textbook on medicine that were pretty simple-minded views about what psychiatry was. Really, the best textbooks on psychiatry were the great novelists, for instance the Russian novelists. I read all the great Russians and I felt I learnt more from Dostoyevsky, Gogol and Tolstoy than I ever did from any psychiatric textbook. Dostoyevsky in particular got me interested me in the workings of the human mind and, because I was a bit of a neurotic myself, that was what really changed my value system. I began to think psychologically and psychiatrically. There were things I wanted to know about the human condition in this world.

I also became very pantheistic in a sense, thinking of myself as being just another animal. Of course my medical training had taught me that humans were just other animals – similar to but different from dogs and cats. I never had any feelings that animals were inferior or anything like that. If you know the anatomy and the physiology of animals you are just amazed by the magnificence of it all.

So the difference is one of degree?

One of degree entirely, that was certainly the way I felt then.

What do you feel now?

I still feel the same, really. In comparison with, let us say, the mathematics of the galaxy or something like that, we are very little different from the animals around us – the dogs and the cats and the birds. And I am very conservation-minded now. I feel that our fate is linked with that of animals and plants: whatever fate is in store for them is in store for us.

Working at Porirua Psychiatric Hospital was another turning point?

I went there as a doctor. I mean, in those days psychiatrists were so rare that there were only about half a dozen in New Zealand. But they were screaming out for doctors. I had been in the army a couple of years, which I enjoyed very much, I must say. I had got married. I had no money and in those days Porirua Hospital offered good money, cheap housing and all sorts of goodies such as free vegetables, milk and meat. We intended to stay for about a year.

I had been, as I said, reading a lot of psychologically-oriented stuff. After I had been at Porirua a little while I was quite captivated by it all, and at the same time horrified by the conditions in which the patients lived. I felt I would be absolutely betraying them if I left before I had tried to do something about improving their conditions. The wards were at a level of disgustingness that I don't think people can have any concept of nowadays. The patients were like Belsen inmates, except that they were overfed instead of starved. They were dressed in awful dull, dirt-coloured uniforms of canvas and stuff.

They were just a seething mass of unrecognisable humanity. You would hardly think of them as humans – it was just quite appalling. There was no concept of their being treated as human beings at all. That, I think, was probably the most significant thing in my life. I was just trapped into staying with them until I could do something to make their conditions better.

So you wanted to change things?

Oh, absolutely. Very much. I had an automatic feeling of disgust that any human being should be treated like that. It made me feel that there had to be change. It wasn't that I wanted to. I felt that I had to.

The beds, for instance, in two of the women's wards were so close together that if I was called out at night to treat an emergency there was no room for me to walk.

I had to walk on the beds to get to the sick person, and if I stood on the floor I would be likely to stand in the pot that was used for their urine and faeces. There was a terrible feeling of hopelessness, of having to look after this appalling herd of difficult animals, and I found that totally repugnant.

I suppose one thing my Catholic upbringing had made me acutely – even excessively – aware of was the importance of the individual human being. In Catholicism, your tiniest action could mean that you would go to heaven or hell, so your actions were fearsomely important. One thing about the priests who taught me was that they cared desperately whether my mortal soul was saved or not. It was a passionate commitment for them to struggle against the devil, and to stop me from being flung into hell, because my soul was so important and every individual soul was so precious to God. Well, that stuck with me. That sort of thing has stuck with me very much.

The other thing about Catholicism is the priests and nuns who devote themselves to the service of the poor or the sick. That also stuck with me very strongly. Another thing that was indoctrinated into me was that if you have any talents they must never be buried. They must be used in the service of those less fortunate. Well, that was an absolute axiom, so that when I lost my faith, if you like, I never lost those sorts of things. You had an absolute duty to individuals; an individual was of supreme importance, and you had to see the vision of God in that individual. Even in the humblest of human creatures you had to see God.

While I was at Porirua Hospital I didn't believe in God and all that stuff, but there remained this feeling that here were these individuals who were utterly precious in the sight of God, if a God existed, and yet this was how they were being treated. I think those sorts of subconscious things drove me very, very hard.

There was a time in the 1960s when you become quite a guru in the media. You were speaking out about many issues – about New Zealand society, the New Zealand psyche, women's rights and men's rights. Was this a conscious decision you made to do this?

Yes, most certainly. I was very affected by my psychiatric training in Melbourne. There was a lot of talk in those days of the beginning of community psychiatry, about the fact that people were much more capable of helping themselves psychiatrically than had been thought. But people had to be informed about what caused psychiatric illness and what didn't, and what they could do to straighten up their lives and avoid obstacles. I was so horrified by what I'd seen in mental hospitals that I felt we would never get anywhere unless we did some preventative work.

I felt, basically, that while religions were helpful in many ways, they had all sorts of twists and distortions that made people sicker. For instance, I realised that stereotyped attitudes about maleness and femaleness made people sicker and that, really, these were a sort of psychiatric psycho-babble. In those days I was very optimistic. I felt that just by informing the community we could do an awful lot of preventative work. Then we might be able to have a manageable number of people in mental hospitals. They were totally unmanageable in those days: they were just seething masses. I think, too, it was also partly me working through my own resentments at my own religious upbringing.

You were at one time described as 'the guru of permissiveness'. What did do you feel about that?

I was never a guru of permissiveness, but what I did try to tell people was that they really should try to loosen up a bit and trust themselves, not be told by other people what to do. They were so often the best judges of what they should do with their lives, and especially about their roles as males and females. But I never at any stage advocated promiscuity. I think that is a very sick way to behave. I think it's a very exploitative way to behave and I always have.

I think exploitation of other people in any way is the sin. If there is going to be a sin, that is what sinfulness is: to treat other people with contempt or lightly or without respect. You can't have any sort of sexual relationship of any value with somebody if you're going to treat them with contempt or without respect. 'Wham bang, thank you, ma'am!' – that is ridiculous. I never ever recommended anything like that.

But I can remember what I did recommend. It came to a head when I was at Kingseat and I was treating women in the new suburb of Otara. I set up some outpatients' clinics at Middlemore Hospital because there weren't any. I had noticed that women were figuring hugely in the statistics of those coming into mental hospitals. These young married women with children were having the most terrible breakdowns and coming into hospital again and again. They would come in and get shock treatment for their suicidal depression, go out again, and after a few months they would come back in again. It seemed ridiculous.

You see, all the training in those days was very Freudian-based. It was believed that for a woman to have children was the absolute flowering of her as a person. That was the time when she should be most healthy, most satisfied, and here were these young women desperately wanting to kill themselves.

It was quite obvious, the terrible constraints of marriage in those days. My wife Jackie is very much a feminist, and when we were first married we read a lot of Simone de Beauvoir, and we were very keen on Sartre and existentialism and things like that. She also got hold of a copy of *The Feminine Mystique*, which we read eagerly, and we based our own marriage on it. We worked out a lot of things very early on in our own marriage as to the roles of wife and mother and husband. We had noticed that up until we had our first child we had been real mates, going out to parties together and rip-roaring around the countryside, dashing around in a sports car and God knows what. Suddenly she had a child and *boom!* Her life changed immeasurably and she was expected to be looking after this child twenty-four hours a day, seven days a week. She was now far from being an independent person.

This is really when we learnt all this stuff about suburban neurosis - that this was an intolerable role to suddenly hurl women into. They should be taught that it didn't have to be like that. All these women coming into mental hospitals were, in fact, just suffering the strains of living in a bad situation. Up until then they had been considered to have a constitutional weakness: they couldn't stand up to the glories of marriage because they were weak, or there was something wrong with them. There couldn't possibly be anything wrong with the institution of marriage.

It was then that I started speaking out, and I suppose it was at Otara that this was at its most horrifying. It was one of those suburbs in those days where they didn't have any kindergartens, where they didn't have any footpaths: it was all mud that the wives had to sort of push their way through. The only car they had, if they had one, the husband would take with him to work, leaving the wife out there gazing out of the window at these hostile neighbours she didn't know.

Of course they went mad in their thousands. Suicide attempts all the time. One day my social worker said to me, 'This is the last one from this street that's come,' and I said, 'What do you mean, the last one? We are only halfway through.' 'Oh no,' she said, 'everybody else in the street has been to your outpatients.' And I thought, my God, this is just too ridiculous for words. How can anybody say that these women have some sort of inherent defects? It was so obvious it was this dreadful environment.

I think I was always quite strongly of the opinion that what you do with your environment is terribly important for your mental health. I really felt I had to speak out about it because of what I saw happening to the New Zealand institution of marriage. It was quite bad and sick-making.

There was a pathological pattern imposed on both women and men, but men got a bit of relief from it by going out to work and by someone putting money in their hand and saying, 'I value you so I pay you this amount of money.' Whereas the wife was pushed into a role of a little girl sitting at home and having to beg big daddy for some money for the groceries, with no stimulation, with feelings of failure, that she was no good as a mother. It was just dreadful. By changing the New Zealand pattern of marriage I felt we could prevent these women from having these suicidal depressions and terrible feelings of worthlessness.

Have things changed for the better for women?

I don't think they have, actually. I think there is a lot of lip-service being paid but it's not really a hell of a lot better. Unfortunately, what has happened is that some women have been allowed, in a sense, to take up the traditional roles of men – working and going to pubs and drinking and smoking flat out and having mates. But, you see, with a working wife, you still don't have most men really sharing the housework and childcare. In some ways it has been made worse in that the wife is expected to have a career, but also do the same amount of work that she used to do at home.

This creates for an awful lot of women terrible dilemmas about having children. It was never a dilemma for men to have children. Men could have children any time they felt like it. The money supply wasn't as good as it used to be and that was about it. But for women to have children it's still a major decision and a major disruption to their life.

There is to some extent more equality, but you don't see too many women chief executives of the big corporations. You don't see many women as heads of law firms or big finance houses. Until we see that we won't have true equality for women. I suppose I'd give one cheer for the feminist revolution but certainly not three cheers.

Here we are – two men talking about women's rights! We should be asking women, shouldn't we?

Yes, I know. And that's what made me shut up eventually. I began to think, why am I doing this? Women should be talking about this. They wanted me to go on the board of the National Council of Women and all sorts of women's rights organisations. But I felt I had done enough by pointing out the psychiatric aspects of it, which is my area of expertise. The only reason I suppose I concentrated on that was because it seemed to be the most acute and preventable problem at that stage of the game.

Men have plenty of problems of their own anyway, haven't they?

But of course. Men have their violence problems and their feelings of restriction and entrapment and their booze and their drugs and all their macho stuff.

So what is it about New Zealand society that seems to make it very difficult for men to be sensitive and truly human?

I think it is our pioneer background. It is also probably the macho traditions of all of the main cultures who settled New Zealand – the Irish, the Scottish, the English. All of them, especially the Irish and the Scottish, had traditions of very heavy-drinking macho men who really were, if you like, warriors, frustrated warriors who loved action, things like cutting down forests and breaking in farms. That was the role for men, and any of the softness and weepiness, that was the stuff for women.

It comes from our pretty militaristic traditions too, really. The only real traditions we have are military ones. I think it is fine all this stuff about Gallipoli, but those are about the only national traditions we have – warrior ones. We pride ourselves on our 'warriorness'. We don't pride ourselves on more gentle things like, for instance, the arts. It is the soldiers and the All Blacks, the action men, who are the male status symbols in New Zealand.

How important do you think the arts are for human growth?

Very important. Even before I met my wife Jackie, who's an artist, part of the education I had in the sanatorium very much impressed on me the fact that the artists are, if you like, our explorers of inner space who are testing out the boundaries, the frontiers of where humanity is going next. They are our teachers, who show us where and how our humanness can be expanded. I have the deepest respect for artists generally, and I think they are key people in our world. I feel it is so important for the human spirit; that a true appreciation of being involved in artistic creativity is essential for human health. If everybody was involved in that sort of creativity they would be very much more healthy than they are now.

Do you think everybody is creative?

I think everybody is creative. Everybody has potential. You know the old cliché: everyone has one book in them, everybody has one book of poems in them. Everybody's experience is unique, and it's gripping, and everybody's appreciation of the world is different. I must have heard literally thousands of life stories of the most intimate details of people's lives and I am never bored. Once people start talking to me about theories on psychiatry or anything I start yawning – to hell with that! But their own experience of their appreciation of life is a gripping work of art.

It is almost as if, if there is a purpose in life, we are here to create one work of art – ourselves. We have to create it, and everybody is in the process, whether they like it or not, of creating this one thing that is unique in the history of the universe. Now, that's a pretty important thing to do.

This interview was first broadcast on National Radio on 17 July 1990.

Dame Catherine Tizard

Dame Catherine Tizard, Governor-General of New Zealand, was Mayor of Auckland at the time this interview was conducted. She became Dame Catherine in the Honours List of 1985 and began her appointment as Governor-General in 1990.

Dame Catherine grew up in the small country town of Waharoa in the Waikato. Its main reason for existence was the large dairy factory where her father served as chief engineer.

She has spent much of her life in the public eye. 'Dame Cath', as many people know her, was formerly wife of Labour Cabinet Minister Bob Tizard. She has a strong sense of duty which stems, to quite a large extent, from her Presbyterian background.

DAME CATHERINE: My mother was a very rigid Presbyterian and Presbyterianism was the only faith in her view. My parents were Scots so that's not very surprising, but my father was not a believer at all. He never argued against Mum's beliefs, he just quietly didn't go to church and wouldn't be persuaded, and she didn't try to persuade him. She accepted his right to abstain. But I certainly went to Sunday School and then to Bible Class and when I came up to Auckland I joined St David's Presbyterian Church and sang in the choir and went to Bible Class.

Then I married a man who didn't adhere to any religion, got terribly busy and somehow the religious adherence just dwindled away and I found myself a few years later looking in a very detached way at the theology of Presbyterianism, at the theology of Christianity altogether, and saying, 'It just seems all so stupid, it just doesn't seem to make any sense.' But the impression left on my personality, the stamp of those early Presbyterian years I think was a pretty strong one just the same, particularly in terms of duty, of obligation, obeying the ethical commands of Christianity, doing the right thing. It left its mark.

Do you think you went to church and became involved in religious activities in those early years because you wanted to?

Oh yes, I wanted to all right. I was a very gregarious child – as I am a gregarious adult – and it was a gathering, a place to meet people. You were participating. It was a social group. I think that was very important, particularly coming from a small country town in the Waikato where there wasn't an awful lot of social life anyway. And I have to admit, churchgoing in Waharoa wasn't a very onerous obligation because it was only once every two weeks anyway. In later years I used to make quite an effort to get up to Matamata, a bigger town nearby, but again, I think a lot of it really was the social contact, being part of a group. I was an only child, too, so perhaps that was a motivating force – to be with other young people and have friends, to belong.

I wonder if you can remember what you believed at that time about such concepts as God and Jesus, heaven and hell?

I can remember quite clearly because at the Bible Class camps we used to go to there was a very strong evangelical spirit. People would get up and talk about the moment when the 'light on the road to Damascus' became their personal experience, and I kept waiting for some great revelation. I kept waiting for the blinding light. I kept waiting for the spiritual change that was going to make me one with the Lord. I remember saying to older women that I wanted to be a Christian. I really wanted to be one, and finally someone said, 'But if you want to be one and you follow, you are.' But that really didn't seem good enough for me. I wanted a revelation, so I think I kept looking for that revelation for some years until I became too busy with children to feel that this was any great gap in my life.

You once described yourself as being these days a 'liberal humanist'. Is that the label you prefer?

That'll do. I don't know exactly what these labels mean. I suppose that's fair enough. As I have got older I've stopped rejecting religion as I did. For many years I was quite cynical about it but as I have got older, as I have really listened to what the more modern theologians are saying, I've gradually mellowed. I followed the Geering affair for some years when Lloyd Geering was tried as a heretic in the Presbyterian Church and I have listened to his broadcasts and have often said to people, 'Well, if that is Christianity, then I am a Christian.'

But the rituals, the mysticism, the need to conform to other people's ideas of what Christianity is, accepting the miracles literally, the literal interpretation of the Bible, the refusal to accept anything other than the fundamentalist belief – that's what has stuck in my craw, I guess. And I guess I have just got a bit older and a bit more sophisticated and peeled off some of my prejudices and looked at the more subtle layers underneath. But I still don't feel the need to attend church or go through any rituals to express any personal belief.

If you asked me, 'Do you believe in God?' then I would have to ask you, 'Well, what is God, what is your concept of God?' You would have to explain that to me before I could say whether I believed in your God or not. I do believe in a God force inside myself but it doesn't seem to conform to anything that is laid out on Sundays in church.

What about when you die, do you think there's an after-life?

Not in the Christian sense, but I believe as a scientist there is so much unexplained that we have only just started to scratch the surface of what life is. I don't know whether there is any sort of after-life or not, but I don't believe that when I die I am going to go to the great city council in the sky or anything like that. Conversely, I don't believe that I am going to burn in hell. I think that your heaven or hell, part of it, is what you create for yourself.

You have said that your Presbyterian background contributed to a large extent to your sense of duty now. How do you work out what your duty is in any given situation?

That's an interesting question because a friend sent me a quote not long ago from Heinlein, the science fiction writer, and I came across it myself in a book that I was reading. I can't remember it all but it says something like, 'Do not confuse duty with what other people expect of you. Duty is what you expect of yourself.' That fitted in very well, that clicked with me, because it is very easy to perform to other people's expectation and think you are doing your duty.

In the end, whether there is an after-life or not, dying is a very lonely process. When you look back on your life and you know that your life is coming to an end, the test is, have you satisfied yourself within human limitations and, given all the mistakes we make along the line, have you done your duty to yourself? By doing your duty to yourself then I think you do your duty to society.

Do you have any heroes or heroines by whom you measure your duty to yourself?

One of the people whose philosophy in life always impressed me and, I think, clarified some of my own attitudes was Eleanor Roosevelt. She came from very blue-nosed Boston stock. Ladies of her generation did not do things independently, and they certainly didn't get involved in anything political. But when Franklin entered politics and Eleanor quietly started doing her own thing and offended her relatives and her circle, she just said something simple like, 'I'm sorry if what I do hurts your feelings but I must do what I believe to be right.'

That is quite a simple and, perhaps, almost naive statement, but it struck a chord with me. I can't perform in the way that other people think I ought to perform; I have to do what I believe is the right thing within my own limitations. And if what I do offends other people I am sorry, because I don't want to hurt other people's feelings, but I have to do it my way. I think that's what Eleanor Roosevelt was saying

– that you can't sit back and ignore what you perceive the needs to be, whether they are other people's needs or society's needs or, in my case, the things that the city needs. I have to fight for and work towards those things in the way that I think is right.

I guess that sounds very arrogant and I don't think I am an arrogant person because I try to listen to what other people say. I try to stay well informed, read, listen to other people's opinions, keep up with changing views on society and morality and things like that, but in the end you have to filter these things through your own perceptions and do it in your own way.

As mayor you have tried, I think, to keep what might be called 'a very open profile', is that right?

Yes. That's not particularly altruistic, though, it is quite a protectionist device. I am not a very private person – I mean, after all, my whole adult life has been spent to some extent in the public arena. I married very young and my husband contested his first election three months after we were married, so there has been public exposure all through my adult life. So I guess that, with my own fairly gregarious and outspoken nature, it has made it easy for me to lay my life out for public inspection.

The protective part of it is that if I tell the world about Cath Tizard, warts and all, then no one is going to come back and find skeletons in my closet. Having said that, of course, there are things in everybody's life that they are not going to tell in public, and we have all got those things. But, for instance, if I make a fool of myself or do something silly in public I am not going to try to hide it. Like the time I turned up at the Cathedral for a big funeral just after I was elected, and I sat there knowing that every eye was on the new mayor, and looked down at my feet and found that I had one brown and one maroon shoe on! So I thought, before somebody started whispering that this crazy woman who has just been elected wears odd shoes, I would turn it into a joke and use it against myself. I mean, that's the sort of thing I am saying. If I get in first then no one else can clobber me with it!

You have said that your mother told you when you were young that your tongue would get you hanged one day.

Oh yes, that's absolutely literal. My tongue gets me into a lot of trouble. It's probably getting me into trouble right now. Yes, I am far too quick on the lip and when I was younger we used to go to parties on Saturday night and I would have a few drinks and burble away, then I would spend Sunday thinking, 'Oh, my God, did I really say that? I hope she didn't misunderstand. I didn't really mean it to sound that way,' even to the point of ringing up someone and saying, 'Look, I am sorry I said such and such to you last night, I hope I didn't hurt your feelings, I didn't really mean it like that.' I went through years of shooting my mouth off and then going through remorse the next morning in one way or another.

By the time I got to about forty I stopped this self-flagellation because I suddenly realised that the people who had been my friends twenty years ago were still my friends, and that I was making new friends, and I thought, well, if they can live with my defects why can't I live with them? So I stopped this sort of introspection, which is not to say that it doesn't still happen occasionally. But yes, my tongue probably will get me hanged one day.

What makes you angry?

Spite, malice – I get very angry when people ring me up anonymously and abuse me or abuse my family, or they don't want to listen, or they have a set idea in their minds. I get very angry then and I want to lash back. People ring me up in the middle of the night and abuse me. I would love to know who they are so I can ring them back in the middle of the night. Bigotry makes me angry, closed minds make me angry. Coming back to religion again, the closed minds of some of the more stupid fundamentalist sects that say, 'This way is the only way. You can't deviate. You have to take the words of the Bible literally.' The sorts of campaigns that were mounted during the brawl over the Homosexual Law Reform Bill, the attitudes that surfaced on both sides of the argument, that makes me angry. It makes me sad too.

I find the older I get, the less rigid I become in my attitudes about a lot of things. If I'd had only one child I'd probably still be giving advice to people about rearing children. But, by the time I had four, I wasn't giving advice on how to rear children at all. I would pass on experience but I didn't tell them how to do it. I guess in lots of other parts of life that's become the pattern. I find I get less certain about my own rightness as I get older.

Since parting from your former husband, Bob Tizard, you have remained single – I presume by choice. Do you ever get lonely?

Well, actually no one's proposed to me since then! Yes, it is by choice, I am very happy being single. I am very lucky in that if I want an escort I have men friends who are happy to be dancing partners or escort me somewhere, but I don't often feel the need of it, so I suppose I have the best of both worlds. I am very glad to have no responsibilities in this job because it is an almost completely time-consuming job and to have no husband, no children, not even a dog or cat to feel responsible for gives me a great deal of freedom to do this job in the best way I can.

My loyalties are not divided and I am not torn in the use of my time so it is a really freeing thing. Sometimes I do get lonely, but you can also get lonely when you are married, and I had many years of great loneliness while I was still married – not just physical loneliness but, as Bob and I grew apart, mental and emotional loneliness. I would rather have the real physical loneliness of being a solo person than have to live with someone and be bitterly lonely.

Your father was a Labour Party supporter in the middle of the Waikato, which was really a National Party stronghold. What was that like?

Oh, that was probably my first experience of being odd man out, because in that little country town the only people who would admit to being Labour were our immediate neighbours. We lived in a dairy factory house in a street that was all dairy factory houses rented by the workers. The street has disappeared now. It was an awe-inspiring thing to go back and find that they had abolished my childhood, but I guess that happens to a lot of people. But, yes, certainly nearly all my friends' families were National and so therefore they were National. My mother was a very strong Labour supporter and her family were Labour too. Dad was a committed socialist so there was a lot of inner strength – there was no division in the family. All our immediate neighbours, as far as I know, supported Labour too, so our street was regarded as the 'Red Street' in those days.

I remember at school the headmaster tried to diffuse the political bitterness during the 1938 general election by having football matches. He wouldn't have Labour versus National, but all the National kids for some reason were called 'Peanut Butters' and the Labour kids were called 'Marmites', so we had Peanut Butter versus Marmite matches and it was all very obscure!

I do remember my father feeling many years later quite bitter towards a man who was his good friend but who snubbed him on election day for political reasons, and, although they continued to be friends and in later years regarded one another as oldest friends, he still remembered the day that George cut him dead for political reasons. My father also once led a strike at the dairy factory and was vilified by the people we knew round about, so that was a pretty good early lesson for me in swimming against the tide.

Would you describe yourself as a socialist now?

I hope so. I believe fundamentally in the sharing of wealth. If some people interpret socialism as bringing everyone down to the same level, not rewarding effort and initiative, I don't believe in that. That's not my view of socialism, but I do believe that if I pay a lot of income tax, that means I have a lot of income and some of it

Dame Catherine Tizard

should be shared for the greater good of society. I still want the reward of my own effort, but if I have a lot I think it is up to me to share some of it with other people who are not in a position to have a lot. I don't believe the Bob Jones philosophy of, 'I did it, I became a millionaire, therefore everyone in New Zealand can.'

To what extent do you feel we must be our sister's or brother's keeper?

To quite a large extent, but that doesn't necessarily mean Social Welfare handouts. I would rather see us being our sister's and brother's keeper in giving support and help and love and kindness to people before they get into the position of being dependent. You asked me earlier about the things that made me angry, and I guess one of the things I didn't say then was unkindness and indifference to other people's needs – the person who can turn away and pretend that she doesn't know that her next-door neighbour is at the stage of desperation where she is going to abuse her children. Someone who stands back and passes judgment and does not offer to help makes me angry. Yes, I believe we have a duty to be to some extent our brother's and sister's keeper, which doesn't mean you have to be a busybody and interfere in other people's lives.

You said once there's always part of you that wants to accept the challenge and part of you that wants security and comfort. How do you resolve that?

I don't know. It seems to resolve itself for me. I went through this when I stood for the mayoralty in 1983 and won. I didn't want to stand at that time. My marriage had broken up and the only thing that caused me any panic then was the economic future, mainly because I haven't got any sort of superannuation. I had a real panic about what I would do when I was old. So hanging on to my job and working for as long as I could to support myself was very important indeed.

To contest the mayoralty on a split ticket, possibly win it for three years, have to give up my job and then be out of a job at the age of, I don't know, fifty-six or something like that, was a real panicky thought. The temptation was to give it all away at that point. But there seemed to be a pressure tied up in the affairs of women that was carrying me on. It would have been cowardly to back away from that opportunity at that time. It wasn't that being mayor was all that important. I'd done it because of the women's issue in the first place.

The then mayor had run his course and the council was broken down politically at the time. I had to either have a go then or give it away forever because I would have had no political credibility thereafter. So things just came together. People were sitting in my house saying, 'You've got to stand. You can win this time.' I'd say, 'Oh, but I haven't got an organiser. I can't afford it. I haven't got the money.'

One of the women sitting there said, 'You have got an organiser. I'll do it! The money can be found, forget about it!' Then when both of those things happened how could I let her down? It just happened. I find quite often when I'm facing a hard decision between running for cover or accepting the next challenge, events take over and do it for me.

Being mayor isn't a particularly secure job if you look at it in the long term, anyway. What's after the mayoralty? What's the next job or task?

I don't know what's after the mayoralty and I certainly don't want to stay in this job to the point where people are saying, 'She's been there too long. She ought to go.' I would like one more term and after that I will have to re-evaluate my life and see what is ahead of me. I envisage a future in which I will work until the day I die. I mentioned the superannuation business. I have to keep on earning my living in one way or another. It may sound a strange thing to say, to talk about what you'll be doing when you're sixty or thereabouts, but one of the things I might like to do is just what you do. Some freelance broadcasting. I have had many offers of talkback work from different radio stations and perhaps some sort of part-time work in the public relations, media, speaking, writing area will be what I do in the future.

But that's another challenge for another day. At the moment I have probably the city's most interesting, stimulating, varied, rewarding job. People often say to me, 'Do you enjoy being mayor?' There aren't many of these jobs around. It's a great privilege that's entrusted to me by the people of Auckland. I'd be very ungrateful if I didn't enjoy it while I've got it.

You have always spoken out strongly about women's rights. I wonder where you feel women's rights have got to at this stage?

I think there has been enormous progress made in the last ten years. People talk cynically about the women's movement being over, but it has simply moved very largely from the rhetoric to the action level.

As a personal example – I would not be Mayor of Auckland unless there had been tremendous progress made in equality of opportunity for women. I hope I have in some way by example been part of that progress and certainly many people say to me, both men and women, that this is the case. All that happened was that I was given an opportunity to demonstrate in the local government field that women are just as capable of using their particular talents in a mayoralty as men are. They may be different talents and, after all, each person brings different skills to any job. This is happening right throughout the community. Where a few women are given the opportunity to show how their talents can operate in a particular field it paves the way for others. There has been more progress made in the last ten years than in the last ten centuries, and we just have to keep capitalising on that.

As a public person you get lots of labels. You have been described as a 'gadfly', an 'opportunist', 'publicity-hungry', a 'pragmatist'. Which one do you like the most and which do you hate the most?

I hate being pigeon-holed by people because I don't think any one label ever describes a person. Many conservative people, particularly men, see me as a mad radical socialist feminist, way out on some sort of extreme. It depends where you situate yourself on the political spectrum. My young radical friends see me as a middle-aged, middle-class, wishy-washy copout. So I don't see myself as being pigeon-holed in any way. People tell me they appreciate the fact that I am approachable and honest. I suppose, if I try consciously to follow any path in public life, I do try to stay honest. I try to be honest to myself and honest with the media, honest with the public and with people I work with - which is not to say that I don't do a little bit of political posturing from time to time. But I do try to stay fundamentally honest and straightforward.

If I had to put a label on myself it would probably be a rather funny pedestrian one. People often say to me, 'Oh, you are very sensible.' I don't think it is a bad thing to be thought of as sensible. So, you know, perhaps that's the one – in a very mundane way that does give me some pleasure.

This interview was first broadcast on National Radio on 5 February 1989.

POSTSCRIPT
Dame Catherine, now in her fifth year as Governor-General, feels her fundamental beliefs and values haven't changed, although, because the job has taken her out of political partisanship, it has made her much more tolerant.

She has also acquired a great deal more respect for 'provincial New Zealand', which, she says, is rather funny because that is where she came from. Dame Catherine says there is a tremendous amount of helping, neighbourliness and community effort that still goes on that is often not appreciated by city-dwellers.

She says there is still a great deal of 'get up and go', particularly in the smaller towns, despite the deluge of social, political and cultural change that all New Zealanders have had to endure in the last ten years.

DAME CATHERINE: They still come out and march for their local hospitals, and good on them. I'd be out there marching with them. They feel they've got to resist the speed of change and the lack of compassion in the economic changes we have gone through. But they are getting on with life just the same.

Dame Catherine believes New Zealand's 'gutsiness', its strength and ability, has increased in recent years. She is much more optimistic and hopeful about the future than she was when she came into office. About race relations, she says:

The whole of New Zealand must by now be aware of the validity, the justification, and the pain involved in Maori land grievances. They are real. They are not all ancient and historical – some of them are quite recent.

Dame Catherine is optimistic about the long term but believes there is a long road to travel.

We have allowed an underclass of poor, disaffected, angry and resentful Maori to become entrenched. It will take a generation or so and some very strong and positive action by a whole series of governments to bring about reconciliation.

Sir Guy Powles

Sir Guy Powles was one of New Zealand's most distinguished New Zealanders. Before his death in 1994 he served as lawyer, soldier, diplomat and this country's first Ombudsman.

Throughout his long years of service there was one standard, one value, one belief he always held on to.

SIR GUY POWLES: I have always been a believer in the rights of my fellow men and women and I've always liked people's rights to be furthered and protected. I've always done that to the best of my ability. During the last, the fourth part of my career I did exactly that as Ombudsman. In the other parts of my life I sort of headed that way too. In this respect one must, of course, refer to parental influence. That's where one gets a lot of things, from one's parents. Looking back I can see that I did get quite a lot. I got from my father, who was a distinguished soldier, this business of respect for the rights of others.

He was a sawmiller before he became a professional soldier?

He went sawmilling after he left Wellington College.

It's quite a change to go from sawmiller to professional soldier. Why did your father do that?

I think you have to consider those times in New Zealand. There was the famous visit of Lord Kitchener in 1911. Volunteers were called for and they were to be Mounted Rifles, Mounted Soldiers, and one of the great loves of my father's life was horses. Although he was married then and he and my mother were living in Opunake, he decided to go to this great opening camp they held at Takapau, up in Hawke's Bay .

As a result of that he applied to join the permanent staff corps and was accepted and enlisted as a captain. Then he proceeded as Captain Powles to run sort of area offices around Wellington and around the territory. He ran one from Palmerston North and then came back and ran one from Wellington.

He was in charge of the Wellington area at the time of the strike when they called out the Mounted Rifles, brought them down from the country with the horses and everything. The left wing regarded that as one of the great crimes. Unfortunately, my father was one of the prime organisers of that, acting under orders, of course.

He took his horse with him to World War I and kept it with him the whole time. He sent it to England when he went to France and then brought it back to New Zealand. He got a farm out at Te Horo and used to ride his old horse on the Te Horo farm after the war.

I think the soldier's life coupled with the horse life really appealed to him and he went away with the main body, as they called it, in 1914. He left me as a boy of nine and when he got back I was nearly sixteen. I'm sure it had an influence on my development.

My mother was a really remarkable lady – she was an extremely good mother for a growing boy. She was determined that I was going to be a lawyer. We lived in Tinakori Road and among her friends here in Wellington were lawyers' wives. She had a lot of sort of legal chit-chat that she collected from her friends and she used to retell it to me with great joy, filling me up with all sort of things for the future. 'You never know when you might need it' sort of idea. The result was that I never had any doubt as to what I was to do with my life. I was to go to university, get a law degree and practise law, and I had no qualms about that. I really embraced that with joy, that whole thing. I enjoyed my education very much.

You were a bit of a left-winger at Victoria University, weren't you?

I don't think so. No, I wouldn't say a bit of a left-winger. Perhaps I was a bit outspoken sometimes.

I note that you were a member of the Debating Society. Some people have described you as rather 'bolshie' at that time.

Oh well, that's what some people might have thought, but I wouldn't have thought that myself. After all, the Debating Society was a very good institution and comprised all sorts of views. As far as I can recollect we had members of Parliament and we used to have occasional Labour members such as Walter Nash come to speak to us. I would reject any suggestion that I had noticeably left-wing views when I was at university.

How would you describe your views at that time, then?

I think quite loyal and orthodox – not that left-wingers are not loyal – but no, I had quite orthodox views. You can see something of my views in those days by reading a chapter that I wrote for a book published by the Institute of International Affairs on contemporary New Zealand. It was written about 1926, perhaps a bit later. I think I held, even at that stage, the view that people had a right to speak for themselves, and I don't think I've ever forgotten that.

You seem to believe very strongly in the individual's right to dissent.

Oh yes. I've always agreed with that.

Where does this belief, this very strong belief, in the rights of the individual come from? Does it have a religious background, a philosophical background?

I don't really know. I don't think it has a religious background, not as far as I'm concerned. I think for me it started from parental influence, both my mother and my father.

I was talking to one of my father's old soldiers, one of his old batmen as a matter of fact, not long after the war, and he said, 'Your father's a just man. He's fair.' I said, 'What do you mean?' And he said, 'When you come up before him on a charge he'll always say, "Well, what have you got to say for yourself?".' I've never forgotten that. The defendant is always entitled to speak in his own defence, that sort of thing. And it's strange how valid that principle became during my Ombudsmanship. It's a very valid principle – used it many times.

One of those things you carry with you all your life?

Oh yes. Without a doubt.

You've virtually had four careers, haven't you? Lawyer, soldier, diplomat and Ombudsman. Have you moved easily from one to the other, has it simply happened by chance?

I think it happened by chance. By chance and necessity. It was an evolutionary process as far as I was concerned. When the 1939 war broke out Eileen and I had not long been married. Our youngest son Michael had just been born and we had an elder son, so I decided that overseas service was not for me at that time. I didn't think about pacifism or anything like that. I really wasn't thinking along those lines. I think I was quite willingly led by the sort of family tradition of doing your duty for king and country and so on. Several of my forebears in Britain had been officers.

What are your views now? I know you as a very strong worker for peace now, and yet you were a soldier.

I maintained the orthodox 'serve your country' attitude right through the whole of my four careers. It wasn't until the Foreign Affairs section that I had the first sort of jolt but I forgot it. I buried it.

What was that jolt?

I was asked by the secretary of External Relations whether I would be a member of the New Zealand delegation to the Far Eastern Commission. We were first to visit Japan and then afterwards I was to join the delegation at the Commission in Washington.

So I found myself in Tokyo with the New Zealand delegation in December of 1945. We were there five months after the capitulation and Japan was a downtrodden country. It was an extraordinary experience because I had heard such a lot about the Japanese and in my soldiering period in the Pacific I had been in armed conflict with them. I knew a great deal about the methods they used to conduct their war and that sort of thing. So the visit to Japan was a very strange one to me and I remember very clearly certain things that happened.

I remember we were driving in a car with a Japanese taxi driver. We were driving through Tokyo and a great deal of it had been burned. It was a dreadful sight and we came to a large place where there had obviously been extensive buildings and grounds. The Japanese taxi driver said in his broken English, 'School, school. Two thousand boys and girls, boys and girls. Two thousand. All killed, all killed.' And then he wept. I've never forgotten that, because Japanese don't often break down but he did. And he said, 'Surely the pilot could have seen them.'

We also saw Hiroshima and Nagasaki. We saw on the bridge over the river in Hiroshima, there on the concrete wall of the bridge, a burnt print of a man holding a little girl by the hand walking along the bridge. It was like a photograph printed on the concrete and it had been made by the heat, the tremendous heat that we know accompanies atomic explosions. These people had their photographs taken like that and then they vanished.

I went to Washington, where I was counsellor on the delegation. We attended the meetings and I also went to the British Commonwealth Japanese Peace Conference in Sydney with Prime Minister Peter Fraser.

But this business of the basic cause of the whole thing – I pushed it away. I didn't go into it at all until back in New Zealand when I had retired as Ombudsman. Dean Hurst at the Cathedral a few years later (about six or seven years ago) had a series of Easter lectures on nuclear weapons and I was invited to participate. I had plenty of time so I really studied it up and came to the conclusion that nuclear weapons were unlawful from the point of view of the United Nations and the treaties and so on, and that they were also contrary to the will of God. I've held that view ever since. Why I didn't get it before, I can't tell you. These things, once again, are chance and necessity, you see.

Would you describe yourself as a pacifist now?

Yes, undoubtedly. My wife and I are members of the Anglican Pacifist Fellowship,

Sir Guy Powles

the principle tenet of which is not to be associated with any organised preparations for war. It doesn't require you to be personally pacifist in the sense that you wouldn't hit anybody or anything like that. It doesn't go into that at all. It really requires you to be against war. In my more recent thinking that turned out to be the real thing to oppose. After all, the covenant of the United Nations says that very thing, something about the nations here gathered being determined to rid mankind once and for all from the scourge of war. That's been my view ever since.

You speak of nuclear weapons being against the will of God so you seem to believe in God in some way, or in the will of God. How do you discern this?

There are certain laws that could be regarded as the laws of God – certain dictates, commandments or whatever. I concluded that war was contrary to the laws of God in the sense that it was a deliberate and indiscriminate killing of unarmed people. I think there is a very strong church view on that. So, although the Anglican Church has wobbled around and they keep on bringing up this concept of a 'just war', in my own mind I've defeated that concept and I think that no wars are just.

Do you believe in a personal God?

No. I believe in what, perhaps, in shorthand, is called 'creative evolution'. In other words I believe in the evolution of the species as put forward by Darwin. I believe that as a fact. Yet Darwin explains how, but not why. Teilhard de Chardin has the idea that really attracts me most and that is the idea of 'creative evolution'. Evolutionists say the process of mankind emerges through chance and necessity, but I think there is something else sometimes. There is some influence, very difficult to say what, but there is some influence. It's very difficult not to say 'somebody', because we so like to personalise these sorts of things. But I believe there is some influence on the evolutionary process to push it in certain directions and so on.

Do you believe that your own life has had a purpose?

Yes, I think so. Not my life as a whole but certain sectors of it seem to have had certain sectional purposes and achieved certain sectional objectives. One could say, of course, that one's education and preparatory stage up till the time when one left university and went into the army had been a sort of preparatory, educational period. I don't think I exercised a great deal of influence when I was in the army in the early days, or when I became a junior practitioner of law in Wellington, but that was a developmental period as far as I was concerned.

The war years were rather difficult but I regard them as a period of personal training in a sense for what I was going to do later. On the whole, although there are many difficulties with army life, and there's the question of absence from family and that sort of thing, I didn't personally experience any great element of danger. I was in the artillery. The kind of island-hopping game that went on the Pacific didn't involve our unit in great aspects of personal danger. I can't think of any really important contribution that I made to the army or to the defence of New Zealand or anything like that other than to develop myself.

The time when you were High Commissioner of Western Samoa seems to have been a very significant and enjoyable part of your life.

I think I was appointed High Commissioner of Western Samoa because I came to Peter Fraser's attention at the Sydney peace conference I attended, so there's the effect of chance, you see. We lived in Western Samoa for eleven years and, looking at it dispassionately and without false modesty, I think I was substantially able to assist the Samoans to gain their self-government.

The right man in the right place at the right time?

That's right, that's what it was.

You have no feeling of being sent there?

No. You mean by ... ?

By some divine providence?

No, no. I was sent there by Peter Fraser!

I suppose it's easier for people like you who have had some influence on the affairs of mankind to believe that your life has some purpose. But has everybody's life a purpose?

Everybody's life? Yes, I think so. Not on a national scale, but everybody has a purposeful life, which means to be a good husband or wife or father or son and all that sort of thing, which helps in the development of being human.

So we have all, in a sense, been given a basketful of gifts and talents that we have available to use and it's our responsibility to use those creatively. Is it something like that?

You could put it like that. I wouldn't mind putting it like that, yes. Of course we mustn't overlook the fact that in everything you do, you learn and you add to it. I mentioned about my learning period in the army. It was in connection with what in those days they used to call 'man management', which of course is a term you couldn't use now. It would have to be 'people management'. But I learned a lot about that in the army, which stood me in very good stead when I was in Samoa as High Commissioner. How to talk with people, how to find out what they would like to do and how to get them to do it.

Did you seek the job of Ombudsman or were you asked to apply for it?

I was asked to apply for it, but there again, you see, it was one of these chance things. I was in India as High Commissioner for two years and while I was there the first Ombudsman Bill was introduced into Parliament. My son, who was practising law here, wrote to me and said, 'Dad, this is a job for you.' I had never heard anything about the development of this type of institution in law. I hadn't studied it; I didn't know anything about it. However, I came back to Wellington and a very good friend of mine put my hat in the ring.

There were several people wanting the appointment who were close politically to [Keith] Holyoake and the National Party. I had been away for seventeen years. In the last two years I had acquired a knighthood, so here I was, Sir Guy Powles, coming out of the bush, with no sort of bad connections. Nobody knew anything very much about me, and in a sense I was God's gift to the Ombudsman's office.

Because I had no connections of any kind it meant that I had remained rather isolated, but I had in fact always been a Labour supporter. I'm not talking about left-wing views; I was simply a supporter of the Labour Party branch in Karori.

The House was asked to nominate an Ombudsman by vote. That's the way it used to be done. I think it still is, but they've rather lost the strength of it. Holyoake had a list of four names and my name was one of them. He met Walter Nash, who was then Leader of the Opposition, in the corridor and said, 'Walter, these are our people for Ombudsman, have you got any suggestions?' Walter put his finger on my name and said, 'That's our man.' 'Okay,' said Holyoake, and he walked off, and that's how it was done.

You feel there's something of chance involved in that, do you?

Oh yes, yes. A lot of chance. You could also say of course that I got it of necessity because the office needed me to start it. To found it.

So it wasn't predestined in any way?

Oh, I don't think so. No.

What would you say was the chief talent you brought to the role of Ombudsman?

I think my clear, analytical brain. I could analyse cases and muster facts. I was a good lawyer. I believed that everybody must have his day. I started the office off with the understood sort of rule expressed to my investigating officers from time to time that the principle in this office is that the complainant is always right unless he's proved wrong. Some of them used to leap backwards when they heard that. But when you try it out in practice it makes a pretty good rule. Ombudsmen today, I think, still work on that principle, on the whole.

Shortly after your period as Ombudsman you made some very strong comments in a guest editorial for the 'Listener' about what you saw as the growing abuse of executive power. In fact you suggested we may be on the road towards 'a kindly fascism'.

Yes, I did. Yes, lots of people referred to it and I still think what I said was quite right.

Has this abuse continued?

On the whole I think it has.

With all the talk of corporate fraud and suchlike, some people are suggesting that there's a growing tendency in New Zealand towards an 'end justifies the means' sort of outlook. Do you go along with that?

I think that may be so and I'm very sad about it because there does seem to have been a falling-off of what one could call public morality. There were some dreadful things done by the financial people under the influence of the boom in the share-market. But of course I have to be careful because I'm now eighty-three and I don't want to seem like an old man grumbling because things have got away from me. I think they probably have, but there's nothing I can do about that.

Would you describe yourself as an optimist?

Yes, I would. I don't know whether it comes from one's way of life, standard of living or class, but I think I am an optimist. I think it's part of one's belief pattern because if you're not an optimist what are you doing here? You must hope for the better because if you think things are going to get worse then there's no hope at all. You've got to think that things are going to get better and we will benefit in the long run. I find that a much more satisfactory type of philosophy.

This interview was first broadcast on National Radio on 4 January 1989.

Dame Mira Szaszy

Dame Mira Szaszy is perhaps best known for her life-long fight for the rights of Maori women. She has done this as a welfare officer in the Maori Affairs Department, as a teacher and community leader, through the Maori Women's Welfare League and the Ministry of Women's Affairs. Now, though officially retired, she continues to work on many government and other committees.

Her qualities of leadership, her wisdom, her personal integrity and her contribution to Maoridom and the community as a whole were recognised when she was invested as a Dame in the 1990 New Year Honours.

With a Maori mother and a Yugoslavian father, Mira Szaszy grew up in the isolated and almost exclusively Maori settlement of Te Hapua. It was her early childhood experiences there that led her into the life-long role of what might be described as a 'reluctant fighter'; one who doesn't enjoy conflict but nevertheless is propelled into battle over issues she feels strongly about.

DAME MIRA SZASZY: It has something to do with my early beginnings. I was a fighter as a child – physically too – but somewhere along the line I was influenced by one of my Sunday School teachers. It was she who first told me of the life of Christ. His life, what he did, left a mark on me, on my soul perhaps. Somehow I related what he had done and his sufferings to my own experiences.

We were born into the Depression and extremely poor. Sometimes we had nothing to eat and I remember coming back from school and scratching in the garden for a carrot. I think it was through that that I became a Christian and came to believe in the Christian ethics, especially justice. Justice seemed to be the important thing in my mind – justice and truth and honesty. They have been the guiding principles in my life.

Are you still a Christian? Are you a churchgoer?

Yes, I am a churchgoer, though I do have questions. I go to the Anglican church because that's the church of my family, of my mother – certainly not my father – but I go to any church, and I think most of us do. Maori go to whatever is going on at the time we are there on the marae. We have these different denominations on the marae and they are all invited to participate or take part in the services. Maybe some of the interpretations that are coming through are not acceptable to me, and I stand aside in a way from being too close to those who profess certain theologies because I think I have my own understanding of the teachings of Jesus Christ.

Do you see any conflict between Maori spirituality and Christian spirituality?

Personally I don't. I can't see any difference at all. Maybe some of the early beliefs were not in line with the Christian beliefs, but the basics that we talk about, the universal values, seem to me to be the same in all groups, so I have no difficulties. Funnily enough, when I was teaching Maori studies many of my students – and they were university students – questioned this. How could I believe in Christian values and also my Maoritanga? My answer was that nobody, but nobody, can tell me that my people had no early historical connection with Christ before the missionaries came to New Zealand because they knew and understood love and expressed love. So how can it be so different?

One of the major events in your early life was the death of your mother when you were three. What effect did that have on you?

It had a traumatic effect on me. I recall the scene very clearly. It is my earliest memory but it took me a long time before I could talk to people about my inner feelings. I was reluctant to confide in people and I believe now that it was through that experience that I blamed my mother for leaving me when I needed her. I also blamed those who were there at the time who stopped me from going up to her. She was placed on the floor when she was dying and I tried very hard to get to her and I was taken away. I suppose the attitude was, 'She's too young for this kind of experience, take her away.' I think they asked for my eldest brother to go there but I remember staying at her feet.

My own introspective analysis is that from that moment on I couldn't trust anybody. I had to depend on myself from that point on. I was just a child needing my mother, needing to be close, maybe not understanding that she was dying but I knew or sensed that something was not quite right and I wanted to be close to her.

I think that feeling and that longing remained with me for a long, long time, because after that I seemed to migrate towards older Maori women, not women of my own age. I didn't have too many girlfriends but I always managed to establish a friendship with older women, sitting with them and talking with them and somehow being comforted in their presence. I think it is the result of that experience with my dying mother. I am searching for a mother figure.

Was Princess Te Puea one of your mother figures? Or a close friend?

To say so would be presumption on my part but when I became a social worker in Auckland the territory that was assigned to me included a part of the Waikato tribal area. Somehow, I am not sure how it came about, I decided that before I could operate in that area I must get permission from Te Puea. I went and talked to her about it and from that time on she gave me her blessing. Somehow something was established between us and I felt that she looked upon me as one her children, as it were. That was the kind of relationship we had. Te Puea and Dave, her husband, were really close friends.

I received a fellowship from the University Women's Association and went to Hawaii. Before I left she sent a complete Maori outfit for me, with a cloak and all. And one of the men, Mick Jones, sent me a message from them, a beautiful message in Maori. So those are the sort of gifts she gave me. When I came back and was in Wellington, Te Puea came to a ball that Maori Affairs was having (I was employed by Maori Affairs at the time). She arrived but she very ill and couldn't come in to the ball. So Dave, her husband, came in, and I went and sat in the car and chatted to her there. I began to shiver, so she told Dave to go and get her fur coat and give it to me. Later as I was leaving she said, 'Keep it,' so that was another gift. Those were the actions of a mother in a sense.

That wasn't all Te Puea did for me. Somewhere along the line a bishop was widowed and they were looking for a wife, as Maori are prone to do, and my name came up. Te Puea was present and she objected to it very strongly.

During your early childhood you were really very poor, and your father was away a lot. Who brought you up?

As I recall nobody brought me up. We just looked after each other. The older members of the family looked after the younger ones. We just survived and that was it. I particularly felt I was an independent person, even as a child.

At home at Te Hapua did you speak mainly Maori?

My father was Yugoslav but he didn't have other Yugoslavs around at the time when I was a child so he spoke Maori as well as English. Although we spoke English and Maori at home, in the community it was Maori all or most of the time. Of course, those were the days when we were not supposed to speak Maori in the school but I don't recall our teachers insisting on it as much as other people's teachers. I don't recall being told off or strapped for speaking Maori so I guess because of our isolation and our community it didn't really matter. We found no difficulty in picking up English, anyway.

You were a bright child in primary school but from a very poor family, so how were you able to come down to Auckland to Queen Victoria College?

47

My father had a shop at Te Hapua – we moved there when I was a baby. We had all the amenities – everything. We had a piano in the hall and beautiful furniture. But during the Depression everybody asked for credit, and so gradually he became bankrupt. He had to go away from home to look for work. All of us in the village were poor but we were particularly poor. Maybe it was because there was no mother there to do the things we needed as children.

I loved going to school and I loved reading and delighted in all I was taught. I read all the books I could get my hands on at school and this great interest in reading continued in later life also. I passed my exam, Proficiency in those days, and the teachers decided they were going to send me to school and Queen Victoria was the school that would accept Maori girls at the time. The teachers negotiated among themselves, and with people in Auckland and members of their own families, and they had it all arranged for me to go, with another girl from Te Hapua, to Queen Victoria.

But I needed a uniform – there's a list of clothing you must take with you to school – and these teachers set to and got some material. They made me a beautiful tunic out of the best serge they could get. So I went off with my beautiful tunic to Queen Victoria, together with the other girl, Mirimiri.

One particular teacher, Jean Archibald, took me to stay with her sister, a Mrs Latham, in Auckland, and Mirimiri to another sister, Mrs Holt. Mr Holt was at the time an associate professor of bookkeeping, something like that, at the university. Sam Latham was a lecturer in economics, so we landed in very good places as far as education is concerned. I think they paid for some of our expenses at school. We had Diocesan scholarships but there were other needs that they subsidised. I think we were very lucky people.

I spent three years at Queen Victoria but I did not really receive the kind of education I should have because they didn't teach certain subjects and they didn't have courses for Matriculation. So after the third year I had to leave and I did intensive study at a Christian college, it was called Fagan's Christian College at the time. I worked so hard that I got ill at the end of it: I was studying until four in the morning. I was studying maths and I had only arithmetic before that, so with trigonometry and algebra and all those things plus Latin I had to start from scratch and I had only one year to do it. I had to do Latin, Maths, Geography, English and Maori studies in that one year to sit my Matriculation. I wanted to go on to university so I had to work very hard.

You were living with Pakeha nearly all the time in that period. How were you able to retain your Maoritanga?

That's another thing that I carried from my childhood wherever I went. Like the Gospel, like my belief in the Gospel. Also, for some reason or other, and I can't explain it, I never lost my Maori that I learnt at Te Hapua. I also continued studying it on my own. There were no courses in Maori language at university so I did correspondence with a teacher at St Stephen's College. He set the papers and marked them. But most of the time I studied myself and I seemed to migrate towards Maori elders and Maori hui and things like that and I sat and I listened. I listened to the speeches. I listened to the discussion and I listened to the format of speeches and so in that way I suppose I retained my Maori, what they now call Maoritanga.

You're both Yugoslavian and Maori. Was there a particular time or period of time when you decided as it were to emphasise your Maori side?

I think it came with me, as I was Maori in the village where I was living. I didn't think of myself as a Yugoslav except when the school children teased us. When they wanted to upset us they would call us 'ta-rar-ra', because that's how the Maori heard the Yugoslav. But, for me, that was just a teasing thing. It didn't worry me. So I was a Maori in that sense. I don't think I decided I wasn't a Yugoslav. I knew I was a Yugoslav but along the way I decided that the Maori people needed me more than the Yugoslavs. I could see the Yugoslavs were quite capable of taking care of their own. The Maori seemed to be the ones who were oppressed so that was the place where I would work. It's not a denial of my Yugoslav side, but a need to help, I think.

You went on to university, in fact at one time it was claimed you were the first Maori woman graduate.

The publicity was to that effect, but much later I heard that other Maori women had gone to other universities. One, I think, went to London to study but I don't know whether she graduated. There was a time in the history of our people when some Maori didn't accept being Maori. So it's neither here nor there at this stage of the game.

There was a time when Maori were encouraged to be educated in the Pakeha world, to 'assimilate'.

That's right.

Really to become Pakeha, I guess?

Yes. We went through that. It was a catch-cry emanating from the Young Maori Party led by Sir Apirana Ngata and Sir Peter Buck. 'Seek the knowledge of the Pakeha.' That went like wildfire through the Maori world and was one of the things that was taught to me. I suppose that was the basis of what we called assimilation. That's what we did. And I believed in it for a long, long time – and acted upon it, in fact.

What do you believe now?

We are going through a period of history now when we are trying to have the Treaty of Waitangi recognised and to be given the status of a partner as a result of that contract. The battle now is for that. It seems to me that the Maori people need recognition under the principles of the treaty; that they should retain their ranga-tiratanga. It seems the clause that contains tino rangatiratanga and the one that talks about sovereignty are seen as conflicting. For me the two words mean the same thing. My own interpretation is that because they are really two words used in two versions, the Maori and the English versions, they mean the same thing.

So I try to analyse in my own mind what my own people were thinking. It is my belief that the 'ceding' thing, the 'sovereignty' thing, was something that was in the minds of the missionaries and Hobson. But it wasn't totally what was in the minds of the chiefs because in the Maori version it said they retained their tino rangatiratanga.

The only way out of that difficulty is the concept of partnership. Partnership as equals and in equity. But how do we achieve that at this stage? It seems to me it must start at the very top where the changes took place. It was in the government where laws were passed that changed the situation of the Maori people land-wise, culture-wise and in all sorts of ways. It was there that it was changed. So the changes must begin there. Until that happens we as a people will always be the 'down under' partner, without equal mana, without our rangatiratanga.

Until that is done we would regard ourselves as a nation in ourselves, maybe having our own domestic sovereignty, unless you can come up with another word that makes us equal as a people. But in mana and in status this must happen within Parliament. Achieving that is going to be a very difficult process that will take hard work, painful work and painful understandings for some of us. Because the treaty was accepted by my people in good faith we ask for the same kind of grace from the other partner.

Some people try to speak of 'biculturalism'. I am not sure whether we are at that stage because my own understanding of biculturalism is from the individual's perspective. You are bicultural if you understand both cultures and you can speak both languages and not only understand but internalise a great deal of what is in those cultures. How that can happen is what people will have to work at together or separately.

The Maori people now are wanting to do their own thing because for a long time they have lived under a monocultural system. They want to move out of that and develop their own ways, Maori ways, in a freer situation. Whether that is the proper way to approach the situation I'm not absolutely sure. Maybe we need to re-learn things within our own culture, our own values and our own systems and practices before the two can really come together as a bicultural community or in a bicultural system.

This is the approach of Maori now. Let us do our thing our way first and you do your thing your way and then we come together at some point in time.

A major concern for you has been not only racism, but sexism. You have fought against discrimination and for the liberation of Maori women, both within Maoridom and the Pakeha world.

I became conscious of sexism when I was a social worker among my own people. I came across this kind of attitude towards women from our own men. And I recognised that on marae women were not allowed to speak. I tolerated that for a long, long time. I just sort of overlooked it but I couldn't accept the way they were treating women; for instance, when it was necessary for a family to have a home they needed to accumulate sufficient money for a deposit. But the men were very reluctant to part with some of their pay to allocate it towards a house. And the women, because they were the ones who seemed to be in greater need to be housed and to have a place for their children, sacrificed what they had, which was the benefit, in order to get a home. They suffered a great deal as a result of that. That really left strong feelings in my mind of the kind of suffering that the women were going through in so many different ways. I could go on but that is an example of it.

I understood the customs of the people and deliberately decided that I would not argue against women being denied rights on the marae until the reinstatement of the culture was ensured. I gave our people and our men over twenty years to do that. We had a resurgence of Maoritanga over the 1960s and I gave them that time. It was only after that period, in the 80s, that I made public statements about it because I felt that it was now time to recognise the individual rights of our women. So I worked towards that. I suppose I'm seen by our men as something that goes against the grain but that doesn't worry me any more. I feel that before I die I must speak out on these issues, even if it is with my last breath.

Lack of speaking rights on the marae for Maori women is a symbol for you, is it not?

Yes. It's a symbol of oppression. Even the marae itself is a symbol of oppression for me because it is there that I'm denied my very basic right of free speech. But it's not just the free speech. Women have been leaders lately in the political arena in all sorts of ways. You just have to look, open your eyes and see. It is the belief that women have their own wisdom to impart. The marae is the political arena of our people and therefore they should be given the right to express their understandings, their wisdom and their knowledge in those forums.

You haven't been particularly popular, have you, in Maoridom for speaking out in this way about the marae?

I don't think I have been particularly popular with some men. But I don't think I'm unpopular with the older generation. The older generation are secure in their understandings, and they're secure in themselves as far as their Maoritanga is concerned. I think it is the generation after theirs, the generation after mine, that resists. I suspect that some of that resistance is based on insecurity about their own position, and a desire perhaps to retain the last bastion of power that they have. I understand that, too. I understand that our men have lost their forums or their power in society and part of our trouble has been due to that. They're not in industry, they're not in politics, nowhere do they have power, our people. What do you do when you don't have power? You oppress those you can oppress.

I have been told, even this past week, that to allow women to speak on the marae would undermine Maori culture and would be its death-knell. I said that if that is what Maori culture is hinged on, then I for one wouldn't regret it dying. If that is all that is important in the Maori world then let it die. Because I don't believe it, you see. That's why I say this. I don't believe that giving women their rights as human beings is a destructive thing. I think it's a very positive thing and I believe that the liberation of every human person is part of the development of human society as a whole.

A good part of your life was given to the Maori Women's Welfare League. You were its first secretary and later you were president. What has the league given you and what do you feel you've given to the league?

I went into the league in a way by default. In the early stages when it was first established I had just returned from Hawaii where I had done a course in social science. But my ideas were regarded as American when I returned to New Zealand. Here's this woman coming back with American ideas. We have prejudices, strong prejudices, within the Maori people themselves and these have been exercised towards me quite a bit during my life. So I was not regarded as a suitable first secretary. Somebody else, a bit more Maori, not so well educated and without these American notions would be more suitable.

So they turned me down and appointed someone else but within a very short time she felt that it was not her place. She wanted very much to go back and work in the community so they had to look around for somebody to replace her. In the meantime they put a man in the job. After a while they seconded me to the job, having turned me down in the first place. I was not too sure whether I wanted to do the job, but I got into it. It was an exciting sort of exercise.

When it began, Rangi Royal was in control of the Maori Welfare and we became friends. He got to know me as a person without all those barriers and I got to know him so we worked very well together. He taught me a great deal in administration. Anything I know about administration came from that man. It was he who really established the Maori Women's Welfare League and I often say, 'You may not know it, but a man started this liberation movement!'

Mind you, a lot of our own women and people don't regard it as liberation. I do, because the league gave Maori women a voice, a public voice. They did not get it on the marae, the Maori forum, they got it through the league and it was through this man that we got that voice.

The league was the voice of Maoridom for ten solid years – exclusively the voice of Maoridom – and it was supported by Maori men everywhere. This is why I said before that it's a generation thing. In the early years of the league outstanding men like [Turi] Carroll and [Charles] Bennett came to league conferences, but they did not want to push themselves forward and the women to shut up. They sat around the conference walls and passed on their knowledge quietly. But they did not replace the women; they encouraged the women and they had no hang-ups about women speaking.

Ten years after the formation of the Maori Women's Welfare League came the formation of the New Zealand Maori Council. What difference did this make?

There began a division in leadership. Some of our women began to step back and allow the men the customary position. That began to change the forward move of our women. This is my interpretation of what happened. They could have continued as two partners. When I became president I tried to promote that. I worked closely with Sir Graham Latimer and the Maori Council and tried to do things together. We made submissions together and I did not feel there were any difficulties between us.

But before me, some of our women were attending the Maori Council and allowing it to take the lead and taking second place. That I didn't accept. I tried to say to them that once you come under the umbrella of another organisation then you are giving up your independence.

About three years ago you returned to the Far North to your home area. Before you did that you said, 'When I go back up north to the isolation I want to meditate. I want to know exactly who I am and how I link in with the world, with God, and with nature as an individual person.'

Yes, those were my aims for my retirement. I expressed the view that for all my life I thought as a group person and especially in association with the Maori Women's Welfare League I was, as it were, the collective mind. Whether there's such a thing as a collective mind I don't know but I felt that I always thought for our women, for our people, and very little about who I was as a person. Also, I reached the stage where I was mentally exhausted – I suppose the expression is, 'Stop the world, I want to get off!' I wanted to come back here to retire. Those were the thoughts I had then. I needed to know who I really was, who Mira was as an individual, because I didn't know. Maybe this is part of the human condition, that you don't really know yourself as well as you know others, perhaps, and others know you better than you do.

Anyway, that's what I was hoping to do. But unfortunately I lost my husband before coming back, and those plans had been for both of us. He would have come back here and done what he wanted to do. He wanted peace. He wanted to roam the beaches. He wanted to go fishing. He wanted to get away from the pressures of the city.

I wanted to meditate. I wanted to know, I suppose, where my soul was linked to. Maybe I had some mistaken idea that I would know if I came back here, in the isolation here. Anyway, that's the way it happened, so I came back without him. That obviously changed the situation considerably for me. Certainly, I came back here to peace, but the silence screamed at me. And there was a feeling of desolation. The whole scene changed, as if this whole area was an area where people were exiled to and I was being exiled in a sense through having to come back alone.

That was the feeling that was in me and it was very difficult to cope with when I first came back. But at the same time I became a bit more conscious of my surroundings, the trees and the wind around me. I would look out of my house here at the trees in the evening and they would be absolutely still and I used to say to myself, the trees are now praying because they're still. I became aware of the fantails around me because they were the only company – living company – I had and when I worked outside they would fly around me. Some people regard them as a bad omen but I didn't. I regarded them as company.

So I had that feeling of desolation and loneliness, and then people began to ask me to belong to this and that. The government was wanting me to join this committee and that committee and I decided that maybe I needed that. I needed to get away. I can stand the loneliness maybe two weeks at the most and then I must go away. So I began to say yes to these demands on my time again.

And that's where I am at the moment, except that I do read a lot. I read a lot about feminism, about theology. My friends were sending me books because I needed something to occupy my mind and the books seemed to be my company. But I have a timetable for myself. I woke up very early this morning, I was up about half past four. I was awake and couldn't sleep so when daybreak came I was up and working outside. That's my programme. I do physical work from seven o'clock in the morning until ten. I come in for my breakfast and then I do quite a bit of reading and answering letters and homework for all these committees. I spend my time doing that sort of thing until the afternoon and then I go out to work again.

I work very hard physically. It's very heavy work but I am still trying to sort things out. My mind is not getting much rest from all these things that I'm doing. I don't know. Maybe you can tell me, or somebody else can tell me, that separating yourself from other people is not what is intended for the human soul. Maybe you still need to relate to other people, otherwise you get ingrown or something. I don't know. Yet I was wanting to be outgoing, to reach out to other dimensions, to find out certain things for myself. I wonder if I'm judging myself now. I wonder, having read some books connected with cosmic justice, whether maybe I'm supposed to have this experience of isolation for some reason that's unknown to me. If so, I am accepting it. I am not in a sense unhappy. I might be lonely, but I'm not unhappy. Am I making myself understood?

It seems that there is quite a difference between being lonely and being alone.

Yes, there is. There is. I am alone, yet not alone. My surroundings comfort me and my beliefs also comfort me. Where my mind goes comforts me also. So that's where I am at the moment.

Do you feel you know who Mira Szaszy is now?

I can't say absolutely, because a lot of things passed through my mind when my husband died. A great many very personal things. Questions that need to be answered, so I'm not too sure. If only I knew something of him still exists, but I have no proof, not a single thing to tell me that there is. I would be much happier if I had an indication of that sort. Is it that all that's left of him is up there buried? That's for me a very sad thing to think about. If something still goes on, then I would be happy because that relates to myself, I guess.

Inside me I feel that there is something beyond, beyond what I am now. There must be. Maybe it's not thought. Maybe it's something that you know without being given, inside of you. You know that there is something else, another destination. Maybe it's that I've been indoctrinated, but I don't believe so. There are feelings that come up inside me of things that I believe belong to somewhere else, to long ago, in a sense. Maybe I existed in the long ago and still continue to exist now and maybe will continue on. I don't know. I don't know whether I know myself any better than when I first came back here.

So your search for meaning, in a sense, still goes on?

I think it will have to go on. I don't think that I will find what I'm searching for while I live, unless somebody proves it to me, makes it very clear to me. My search will go on.

This interview was first broadcast on National Radio on 11 January 1989.

POSTSCRIPT
Dame Mira is still heavily involved in the fight for women's rights and Maori issues in general. She feels the place of women in Maoridom has not improved to any great degree in the past six or seven years. The one thing that has changed is that she is now receiving more support from younger women, who are picking up the cause of improving the status of Maori women..

The demands of government and other groups are still heavy and Dame Mira continues to wrestle with the problem of finding enough personal time for herself and her family.

Dame Mira Szaszy

Eru Pomare

Eru Pomare

Eru Pomare was described as a man who comfortably bridged two cultures, Maori and Pakeha, when he died suddenly on a tramping trip early in 1995.

As Dean of the Wellington School of Medicine he was one of this country's most respected medical academics and health professionals and a foremost expert in Maori health.

His grandfather, Sir Maui Pomare, pioneered Maori health services, both as a doctor and as Minister of Health in the early 1900s. It was his widow, Lady Miria, who left Eru Pomare in no doubt about his vocation.

ERU POMARE: I never had any doubts about what I wanted to be, but she [Miria] reinforced that at every possible opportunity. When visitors came she'd say, 'Oh, here's Eru. He's going to be our doctor.' She had a big influence on my life.

You are following a family tradition in health, aren't you? Your grandfather, Sir Maui Pomare, was a doctor and a politician and your father worked in the health area too, I think?

Yes. My dad, Te Raka Herea, worked in the Health Department. He was a public health inspector and he used to run the course in public health for health inspectors at the National Health Institute. I also look to my grandfather as a very important role model.

He was the first Maori doctor?

Yes. He qualified in the United States – in Battle Creek, Michigan. The Dean of the Medical School over there was J. H. Kellogg. One of the treasures that I have at the moment is all Maui Pomare's medical books from those times and many of the textbooks were written by J. H. Kellogg. He was, of course, very much into health promotion and disease prevention and talked about all the bad things like smoking and drinking and wearing clothes that were too tight. You just have to read these old textbooks – they make very amusing reading. Many of the messages they had then are, of course, just as true today.

So yes, my grandfather was the first Maori doctor and I look up to him as someone who is a role model. The other person who was also important to me was Te Rangi Hiroa, Peter Buck, who was from the same small northern Taranaki tribe, Ngati Mutunga. I remember meeting Peter Buck as a child. He visited us at Hiwiroa out in Lower Hutt. It must have been not long before he died. He was interested in us as children and I can remember him sitting down and my grandmother saying to him, 'Well, here's the doctor, Peter, and you'd better be nice to him and tell him what it's all about.' I can remember him telling us stories. He was a very warm person and another whom I felt was a model. He had obviously achieved and I wanted to be like him and Granddad. So that's where I am now. I don't know if I've achieved half of what they have, but still, they're the sort of goals to aim for.

The home you grew up in as a child was steeped in Maori tradition, wasn't it?

Yes, it was. It was a very interesting home. When Maui Pomare and Miria were married they built this house on the Western Hutt hills and lived there. I think it was 1903 when the house was built, a big house. There were very few people who lived around the Hutt Valley at that time, but it was obviously a very busy house. There were people coming and going and staying there. I remember the old horse stables there. They had a horse and buggy and used to go up and down the valley.

Maui was very busy with his medical work initially and then, of course, when he went into Parliament that meant there were all sorts of dignitaries who were coming and going all the time. My mother and father carried on something of the same sort of tradition.

Hiwiroa was a place that people remembered very fondly for its hospitality – whether they were Maori or Pakeha, whether they were dignitaries or a swagger or someone who'd just come and wanted to stay overnight. I remember the house was always open. The doors and windows were always open.

The house itself was built around a meeting house and it had the most wonderful treasures, taonga, in the house – greenstone mere and all sorts of other treasures. It always made me wonder why someone hadn't walked in and stolen all those things, but it never happened. When I lived there nobody even tried to steal anything from that house.

It was a great place to live. We lived among these treasures, which had really interesting histories, and my father used to spend a lot of his time when people came talking about the various taonga, and they were obviously a delight to many people who came. In that sense our house had very deep Maori values to it. On the other hand, it was a house that Pakeha also felt comfortable and warm in. So it was an interesting childhood from that point of view.

You grew up in a very extended family, didn't you?

I did. As children we used to spend our weekends out at the pa at Hongoeka Bay, near Plimmerton. That was a great place. We used to go out there every Friday. We had a little bach out there and a bit of a woolshed. As soon as we got there we children would usually all disperse to the various families that lived out there. We would be off staying with Aunty Francie or Aunty Hazel, and my Aunty Ana and Uncle Mo lived there too. So we were in and out of the houses of relatives and there were lots of children of our own age so it was a very rich time. I think we learned there how to be children. We learned how to grow up. We learned about all sorts of things – about the sea, about gathering kai moana, about fishing. We dwelt on all the stories of the people that came and went.

I can remember vividly one of the chaps who had just come back from the Korean War, Jimmy Tuck we used to call him. He always used to go there. He liked fishing off a particular rock and I can remember following him down there onto this rock by the sea and sitting there for ages talking to him and asking, what was it like in Korea, and did he kill anybody, and what was it like shooting and all these other horrible things? We had all sorts of experiences. There were Te Atiawa and Ngati Toa relatives there.

My mother is from Mahia and she's from a very big family, the Ormonds from Mahia Peninsula. She had three sisters and ten brothers and many of the families were very big families. Just about every Christmas we would go up to Mahia Peninsula to the huge extended family. Summertime usually brings back memories of Mahia Peninsula. So yes, my extended family on both my mother's and father's side have been important to me and to my development, even to this day. Those people I grew up with as children, we still recognise and support each other and I feel very secure in that knowledge.

I understand that, although your childhood was steeped in Maori culture, your father never spoke Maori to you, is that right?

That's absolutely true. I can also remember from an early age my grandmother, who was a fluent speaker of Te Reo Maori, would often have kuia who would come and visit. They would be talking away in Maori and whenever we used to go round and listen we used to think it rather strange that they were talking in Maori and we could only speak in English. But she would wave a stick at us and tell us to go away and not to waste our time interfering or listening to what she was doing. In fact, she actively discouraged us as children from learning Maori. She would say that it would inhibit our progress and if we wanted to make any progress in the world we would need to be very conversant in English and everything that was associated with an English education. So we, as children, were never encouraged in any way to speak Maori.

I never ever heard my father speak Maori. I often wondered why he didn't but I don't suppose there were many occasions where I saw him in a position where I might have expected him to speak Maori. There was always someone else who spoke on his behalf. So anything I have learned has come in much more recent years.

I owe a lot of gratitude to one particular kaumatua of ours from Te Atiawa, Sonny Waru, who a good few years ago now, fifteen years ago at least, took several of us aside. I remember him saying to me, 'Look, Eru. One of these days you're going to find yourself in a position where, if you can't stand on your feet in terms of your Maori side, it's going to be embarrassing for you and it's not the sort of thing that we would expect from someone who's holding a prominent position within Te Atiawa.' I can remember going away at weekends up to Manu Ariki, which is up by Taumarunui, and going to the wananga up there and having lessons on how to conduct myself, and it's been absolutely invaluable to me. Before I became more conversant in some of the Maori protocol, I would have felt most uncomfortable about or would have deliberately tried to avoid a lot of situations for fear of putting myself in a position that made me feel uncomfortable. So I'm really grateful to Sonny Waru for doing that.

What I've learned has also come from Onslow College in Wellington back in the 1970s when my children were there. We'd go up there as a family and have Maori lessons. We also organised some family Maori lessons here. So that's me, in terms of Maori and whai korero and so forth. I know just enough to get away with it. It's probably a side of me that has developed in more recent times.

If I can put it this way, you were one of 'the chosen ones' in a sense. You were marked out for special training for leadership. This is one of the features of Maoridom, isn't it?

Yes. I remember when I went to university I won a Ngarimu Scholarship and later on I was sponsored by the Taranaki Maori Trust Board. They also put something into my training overseas. I'd always felt when I accepted these things that there's an obligation to pay something back or to do something in return. But I was never quite sure how on earth I was going to do that. I couldn't imagine what I could do. I used to think, well, surely just being a doctor isn't enough. Most of the people I treat would probably be Pakeha anyway, so there wasn't any sort of direct payback in that sense.

So it was interesting to me that someone like Sonny Waru just out of the blue wrote me this letter and said to me he believed it was time now, that there were some things that I needed to know and the sooner we got on with it the better. That was it. It just happened. That it happened on a particular day or a particular year to me was a totally unpredictable event, but it was one of those things that have been very important to me. It's been important in terms of my development and I suppose the sort of things that I can give back to those people who supported me when I was young and trying to find a career for myself. So payback time is now.

You went to a school that was fairly Pakeha – Wanganui Collegiate – didn't you? Was it an Anglican school?

Yes, it was an Anglican school. It was a very posh school, but those secondary school days were some of the most enjoyable days I've ever had. My parents and, I guess, my granddad and certainly my grandma were adamant that the way ahead was to be educated 'properly', as they would put it.

We lived in a house that in Maori terms would have appeared very luxurious because it was large. It was like an old homestead and we had a lot of land – eight acres of native bush. It was a beautiful place. But I always used to feel that in Pakeha terms it was a bit of an old broken-down old house. When I was a small boy I always felt a bit uncomfortable about asking friends, and they'd be Pakeha friends, to come to my home because we never had things like washing machines or any of the sort of mod cons that we were led to believe all Pakeha families had.

I had the same sort of feeling when I was at Collegiate in Wanganui in later years. I never asked anybody to come because I used to feel just a little bit uncomfortable that they would see this big old place as something that was slightly inferior. I was a bit sensitive about that.

But the school offered a very good education and I think I've always had a competitive edge to me. That might not be evident to people but it has been there. I've always wanted to achieve at a high level and I certainly got the opportunity for that at Wanganui Collegiate, where a great deal of emphasis was placed on discipline, on putting time into things. Also, people got rewarded when they did well. That was one thing I learned.

I remember after School Certificate it was the first year they'd issued Scholars' Ties at Collegiate and I felt very proud of actually winning one – and proud that I was a Maori person who was doing that. That was something that has driven me probably as much as anything. I have always wanted to achieve at a high level, at the highest possible level that anybody else could achieve, and for being Maori not to be a barrier to that.

There were very few Maori at that school. There was myself and my two brothers and two other brothers who followed on after that, and there were a couple of other Maori from Wanganui. They provided a sort of family for us and I used to go in the weekends to the home of Matthew Pine, the artist, and his mother. She was fantastic. Many weekends she would ring up and ask us out to her place and that was something which we really appreciated.

You were a boarder at school?

Yes. It was a big boarding school. Sport was another thing I enjoyed at that school. There was a very great competitive spirit and sport was always something that the Pakeha boys would look to us as being natural achievers at, and I think all of us were at various stages in the rowing eights or the cricket or rugby teams.

Someone asked me once whether I'd noticed racism there. In a sense there wasn't, but I think we were in such a minority that we were never a threat to anybody. We were amusing, I suppose, to some people. I can only remember once one boy saying something derogatory about my being a Maori. I just said, 'You do that to me again and I'll have you!' And he did and I think I beat him up and that was the finish of that.

Many people will be surprised to hear that. You're known very much as a gentle, moderate person, are you not?

Oh yes. I am very gentle and very moderate. But I think the other thing I have been aware of is that I have a white skin and don't look Maori, unlike my brothers. I've got one other fair brother, but my other brothers and my sister certainly have brown skin. It has meant that people who don't know me or anything about my background have often said very many hurtful things. Again, my daughters, who are also fair, would come home from school and say it was terrible, the racial things that happened at their school.

But at Collegiate in Wanganui I was never aware of a real problem in terms of racism, not to the level that my own children have said of local schools here in Wellington.

Can we explore a bit further for a moment this competitive part of you. To what extent is your competitiveness on behalf of, or because, you are Maori?

I think I've always felt it's because of being Maori. We've always been told that Maori don't achieve at the same level as Pakeha. You don't have to go far to read all sorts of statistics to back that up. But I've always believed that, given the opportunity, Maori would achieve at the highest possible levels. It's always been in the back of my mind, whenever there's been a challenge. It's been something that has spurred me along from within myself to prove that Maori can, in fact, achieve when given the opportunity. I think we were very lucky. I was lucky I had parents who believed strongly that education was important. I believed that and it's certainly something my grandmother and Maui Pomare believed in, that education was of absolute and paramount importance if we were as a people to have power to make choices about what we wanted to do in life. So I think there has been a very strong sort of twist to me that being Maori has made me doubly competitive. It may not seem so outwardly but inwardly there's a fierce competitiveness in terms of achieving.

You come from a stream, if I can put it this way, of Maori who have spoken very strongly about the necessity of getting the best of education in order to compete in the Pakeha world. But there's another stream, isn't there, that feels differently? It is very angry and believes in strong protest, in cutting down a tree on One Tree Hill, for instance. This is another way of dealing with race relations or the position of Maori in New Zealand, is it not?

Yes, certainly. Very clearly there's a balance between those things that might be seen as Pakeha and those that are seen as Maori. I always remember Apirana Ngata's words, which tell us we should take the best of both baskets, of both Pakeha and Maori worlds, if we're wanting to make our way in the world and I think that's true. I think my granddad, for instance, was probably perceived as someone who went overboard in pushing the Pakeha education side of things and I feel comfortable with that. I think that wherever we go we've got to push to the limits of one side or another. And today, whereas some of our, what might be termed Maori extremists, are pushing the treaty and treaty issues and tino rangatiratanga to the other limit, they also have a legitimate place. Because inevitably we'll probably compromise and settle somewhere in between.

We need to have those boundaries pushed. You've got to have the balance in between and we've got to find the right mix of these two extremes. There's the cultural side, which very much brings Maori cultural heritage to the fore. Our Maori heritage – my Maori heritage for me, as a person – is of paramount importance. It tells me who I am, where I belong. It's all about whanaungatanga, which is very much part of my childhood. That's the family, and still is. I mean, those are the sorts of things, the comforts, the support I get in whatever I'm doing. That's a very important part of me and that's part of my whakapapa, part of my genealogy.

Then there's the Pakeha side, which I see as being the education goal. Those are the sorts of tools that have allowed me to bring my work into reality. They've allowed me to give back to the Maori community something to repay that which has been given me in the past, in terms of support, in terms of career development and so forth. I mean, inevitably we need to find a balance or a mix of both the cultural and the sort of work ethic type of concept.

I wonder what part religion or spirituality has played in your life? You seem to have had a strong Anglican background.

Well, we were brought up as Anglicans. We went to an Anglican church school. But I would have to say that religion has probably not been a strong part of our family upbringing, unlike in many Maori families. Apart from going to church occasionally, or being part of a hui where spirituality and protocol do in fact bring in religion at times, I wouldn't say that they've had a very important or strong influence on our life at all.

My guess would be that there's a strong core, however – to give it a label, a 'humanistic' influence or attitude of caring for others in the community. That's strong, isn't it?

Oh, there's certainly that. If you're thinking of religion in those terms, in the humanistic side of things, oh, very much so. In my family we were taught as children how important it was to be hospitable to people, to always help people, to be honest with people, to trust people. All those elements were very important values that were instilled in us when we were small – an example from our parents themselves. Particularly my father. He was a fairly stern chap. If we stepped out of line he would beat us. Well, I certainly got more beatings than any of my other brothers for such things as being nasty to our sister, telling lies (or what he perceived to be telling lies) or stealing. We might have pinched our mother's cigarettes or something like that. We would get beaten, just like a good public school flogging. And that was something awful I can remember. It didn't endear me to my father all that much and I can remember my mother's anguish when my father used to thump us for things like that. But it certainly drummed home to us that we needed to be honest, to work hard and not to misbehave, and if we stepped out of line we paid for it.

The question of Maori health. I mean, everybody has to deal with health, but there is this label 'Maori health', isn't there? And you have a lot to do with this?

Sure, I guess that's something that has become really very important for me over the last fifteen to twenty years. Again, it's one of those things that has come upon me. I'd always thought, in some way or another, I would be able to contribute to the Maori community in the health sector.

When we talk about Maori health the only reason we think of it as being an issue separate from health in general is that our statistics tell us there's a disadvantage to Maori people, which highlights that there's a problem that needs to be addressed, and there are ways of doing that. So it's something I've been very much involved in, in quite a number of different ways, for several years and it's become more time-consuming, over and above my normal daily activities. Increasingly so.

It would seem that when we use the phrase Maori health we are really talking about Maori ill-health, aren't we?

Yes. We talk about ill-health a lot, but one of the very interesting things, and I think a very important thing, in talking about Maori health is that we have concentrated on the term health as opposed to ill health. So we find a lot of very positive things are being emphasised within the Maori community. Things that promote good health – exercise, healthy eating, and also spirituality, the importance of whanaungatanga and family support – as opposed to focusing on diseases such as renal failure or asthma or heart attacks.

So it's health, and concentration on health. I make no apology for that term because it points to an important direction that we are taking.

So what are the major reasons as you see it for Maori ill-health or lack of health, poorer health?

Well, there are just so many different factors and they all play a role. There's no doubt that Maori are disadvantaged, and many families terribly disadvantaged, in certain parts of the country and certain places where we find that poverty is a way of life. It's not too difficult to understand that these families will have a health disadvantage as well, so there's the whole socio-economic side of things.

One of the things we've found out in more recent times is that access to health care is much more of a problem for many Maori people, and for poor people in general, than we would want it to be. Think about the services we take for granted – that if you've got the flu you can just nip down to the doctor and throw your $30 or $40 on the counter and get some antibiotics and 'she'll be right'. Those are the sorts of things that many Maori families, many poorer families, are unable to even contemplate because of the cost. So many of these people will leave things be and hope they get over whatever is wrong, and maybe they will, but at some cost. They are prolonged costs, such as being less able to look after their often large families. It's just more difficult. So there are cost factors as well that are barriers to access for Maori people.

There are also cultural barriers, which vary in different parts of the country. Many Maori actually feel very shy about going to see the doctor. We call this whakama. They are very shy about going to see doctors or other health professionals. Geography is another thing in certain parts of the country. Isolation and, again, probably a cost factor relating to that as well. Access is really an important issue and it's much more important than I think many people realise.

I remember when we were doing our ministerial asthma inquiry, one of the aspects that was particularly relevant back in Manu korihi up in Waitara, back home, was the whole importance of history in relation to barriers to access. You might think, 'History! What on earth has history got to do with barriers to access?' But we had some of our people talk at quite some length about the history of land confiscations around Taranaki, especially around Parihaka. And those stories are actually just as real and as pertinent today as they were back in 1881, when people distrusted Pakeha institutions and what they could deliver.

So access is a big thing and, I think, the disadvantages of poverty, some of these lifestyle things, they're all inter-mingled with the bigger issues that affect the population as a whole, such as unemployment. Again, they fall on the most disadvantaged in the community and many of our Maori and Pacific Island families fall into that category. So it's a pretty complex issue and a solution to the problems won't come from any single answer. Obviously political issues are important. If you're talking about unemployment the solution is probably as much as anything a political realisation that a solution is important.

There is also individual responsibility for these things, but that requires being well informed, and many of the issues we take for granted are things that our Maori people have really never heard about, never been informed about. That makes it very difficult when you're trying to make informed choices about what you should do – whether you should go down to the local chemist and get a cheap remedy, or go to the doctor because you might actually have something serious wrong and this will save you money in the longer term. So information is power and the means of getting good information out to the community is all-important.

You're a Maori who, if I can put it this way, has made it in the Pakeha world. But you are very much Maori still, aren't you?

Yes I am. In my heart I've never ever thought of myself as being other than Maori. And that's not obvious immediately to many people who might look at me with my pale skin. If people don't know me they don't identify me as a Maori and, in a sense, I sometimes feel that's a disadvantage. But, on other occasions, if people don't think of me as Maori there may be things that I get away with that I might not have got away with if I had a brown skin. I really believe that probably is the case.

I feel very strong. I feel part of, just a very small part of, a continuum of people, such as my father and my granddad, but also part of a very strong continuum of Maori women. My grandmother was particularly important in that respect – my mother too. She's still alive and she's the most wonderful, warm, hospitable person, who looked after us and instilled in us those values of kindness, hospitality and generosity. There were grandmothers who were, and I can remember them, famous in their own right. Te Rau o te Rangi, or Kahe, as she was known, was one of the few women who signed the Treaty of Waitangi. She is famous also for the name that she gave to that stretch of water between Kapiti Island and the Paraparaumu coast. That stretch of water is called Te Rau o te Rangi. She once escaped and swam from Kapiti Island to the mainland with a baby on her back.

The other great-great-grandmother on my granny Miria's side was Maura Pani. My granny used to say she remembered her relating stories about when Captain Cook first arrived in Poverty Bay. My granny lived to the age of ninety-four. Her mother and grandmother each lived to over 100. These were long-living women, and so there are interesting tales from there.

On my mother's side I've got Rongomaiwahine, from Mahia Peninsula. Rongomaiwahine in Maoridom was a very famous woman indeed, so I've got a lot of wahine toa on my side. That's important to me because many of the Maori health advances in recent times, if we look critically at what's happened, have actually been driven by our Maori women. The men haven't been all that visible in these exercises. It's the women who have been driving these through, so I think of those strong women in terms of influences on my own life.

This interview was first broadcast on National Radio on 17 January 1995.

Margaret Mahy

Internationally acclaimed children's author Margaret Mahy has this to say in one of her stories: 'When people find the place that suits them best and poets find words and rhymes to tell about it, there's a good chance that everyone will live happily ever after.'

But life for Margaret Mahy is far more than a fairy story. She has a great interest in the deep philosophical questions about life and its meaning; questions such as, 'Who am I and why are we here?'

MARGARET MAHY: I am a female European New Zealander and, therefore, I've got the advantages and the disadvantages of a certain range of choices that I had nothing to do with, choices that were made on my behalf by my parents and by fate and all sorts of things. And I have to operate within those constraints. But, of course, within those constraints, like anybody else, I can get in touch with infinity. And the extent to which I do this is the extent to which I define myself as a person.

I think that like most people I operate within a range of perceptions that include myself as a being belonging to a certain sort of society, and as I see myself in my own head. As to why I am here, I don't have any neat answer to this. For anyone who studies anything to do with conception and birth there seems to be a wide sense of randomness about this. And yet, on the other hand, sometimes underlying apparent randomness you get quite a lot of determinism too, but none of that is anything I've consciously determined.

Putting it very simply in terms of why I am here, I suppose I am here to do the best I can, which sounds a small amount, but of course to do the best you can is asking a tremendous lot of anybody.

Do you have to be a good person?

Yes, I think I try to be a good person, but I certainly don't always succeed and there are a lot of things I have done, and probably will do, that I feel ashamed of or inadequate about. The other thing is, to say that you want to be a good person is nowadays a very suspect thing to say because it's got a lot of overtones of Victorian morality. The idea of actually trying to be good often suggests a certain sort of didacticism and a certain sort of piousness that is certainly very unfashionable at present and for which you have to apologise in some ways.

I don't know many people who, in day-to-day conversation, admit that they want to be good people, and yet I think a lot of people do, really. They are just nervous about the admission. It seems to align them with a system of moral judgment and that's become out of date to some extent. It is possibly the terminology that has become out of date or suspect rather than the actual idea of wanting to be good. But I do want to be good.

How should you, Margaret Mahy, be a good person?

Well, some people argue, I suppose, that to be good you are to be yourself in the purest and fullest way that you possibly can be. But you certainly have to be careful about that, because it seems to me that, again, getting back to our unpopular idea, quite a lot of goodness is built on some level of sacrifice, and this is a very unattractive idea in democratic times. Nobody wants to be the sacrifice and nobody wants a particular group to be the sacrifice. Nevertheless, it seems to me that, as an individual, if you really want to be good you do have to live with certain ideas of sacrifice. Having said that, I don't think I sacrifice myself a great deal.

Who says you should be a good person? Where does that come from?

There are several different contexts in which you need to define yourself. There's the context of your awareness of yourself as an individual, which says in order to be a good person I have to fulfil myself in a variety of ways. There's the social context, which says you also owe a duty to the people around you, perhaps immediately to your family, but also to the people in Ethiopia and so on. By sharing the human condition you are also responsible for other human beings.

And then, I suppose, there's the cosmological context, the context of the universe, which suggests that great movements and suffering of people are meaningful in ways that are at times in conflict with our social obligations. Your social obligation is probably to your immediate social group in a certain time.

You seem to have some belief that you have a sense of responsibility to fulfil yourself, to fulfil your potential, to use your gifts both for yourself and for others.

Yes, I think you do. But I think there sometimes comes to be a limit to which you do that. In other words, there is something very self-indulgent about me sitting here being a writer in a room of my own at a time when a lot of people in this country are without work and in need.

I am never quite sure whether, for example, if I chose to become a social worker and to work directly for others, I wouldn't be doing a better moral thing than sitting here and being as good a writer as I can be, which is, of course, very fulfilling for me as an individual. I am aware of the fact that I do spend so much time writing, which is probably the thing that I do best. I am also supported by a society that makes that possible and there are some societies where this is just impossible for individuals. There are probably a lot of mute and glorious Miltons spread around the world simply because their society doesn't enable them to get their thoughts into any kind of order or give any structure to their imaginative ideas.

There certainly have been times when, historically speaking, I would probably have been expected to go out and work at the age of twelve doing housework for somebody, and would have spent my life governed by those particular necessities. Now, as a writer, I am upheld by a certain social level and a certain degree of affluence, which doesn't mean that there haven't been times when it has been very financially difficult to be a writer. I am also upheld by a lot of people who are doing things like calling and collecting the rubbish in the house, or servicing the telephone. I have a friend and neighbour who comes in and does housework for me. All the work of those people, which is done from personal necessities of their own, actually in some ways upholds the work that I do, sitting alone in my room writing.

Writing somehow has an image of being intellectual and imaginative, which places it apart from and above those other jobs, but I don't think it is. It is a trade just like any other. But it happens to be the trade I feel I am good at and the thing I do best and therefore I feel some justification in doing it.

Do you think you chose to be a writer, or were you chosen in a sense?

I suppose I would have to say that I think I was chosen. I don't want to sound too pretentious about this, but I started writing stories down when I was seven. I am one of a group of writers who started from childhood. But before I could write I would tell stories by drawing pictures of what was going on in the story.

So, I suppose I had some instinct, if that's not misusing the word, to record and to structure ideas, to write them down, to present them and to preserve them in some way. I used to talk aloud a lot when I was a child and make up stories which I told aloud to the air, and, I suppose, to some part of my listening self since nobody else did.

I was about eight or nine when I first published something. I sent poems to the *Bay of Plenty Beacon*, which is a Whakatane paper. It came out about three times a week and it had a children's column. I'll never forget seeing my first story in print. It was about two kittens who caught a mouse and came back singing:

> *Our first mouse,*
> *Our best mouse.*
> *We'd find them better*
> *If we searched the house.*

I can remember standing in the drive of our house entranced at the sight of my name in print. It's easy to read things into situations when you look back at them. Seeing your story in print you know it's your story, but it also makes it seem as if it's not your story, as if the print has transformed it. Because I was brought up in a house full of books, it had somehow given my story a legitimacy that it didn't have when it was just mine. It had, in a sense, been given vindication by print.

Nowadays I don't think that's necessarily true, and I think a story that's told by a parent to a child has every bit as much legitimacy and vindication. But print exercises such a power in our lives for those of us who are brought up with print that it gives an illusion of added vindication.

I gather after your first publication there was a long gap until you were published again.

There was a long gap. Between the ages of about eleven and twenty-five I didn't have anything published but I kept on writing. I wrote very consistently, and although I was always told that I'd never make a living as a writer I never gave up the idea that I would be a writer some day.

What was happening in all those years when you were still writing but not being published? Was it something that drove you or led you to do this?

I think in my particular case writing and reading are very closely linked. Reading wonderful books filled me with some sort of wish to be part of that system, to submerge myself in a certain set of imaginative experiences that so entranced me that I couldn't bear to be separated from them.

Of course one of the things that has continued to occupy my mind has been the intrusion through imagination into reality, into what we call reality, and the way people structure reality according to certain sets of ideas that are really to do with their imagination, and to do with the question you asked me in the beginning, 'Who are we and why are we here?'

People structure their moral life according to certain sorts of social necessity, I suppose. That social necessity often feeds back and helps to create the religious system. I have always been very interested in the extent to which imagination helps to create our perception of reality.

There are also some realities that are pretty intransigent and no matter how powerful our imaginative impulses are they don't alter certain sorts of realities to any usable degree.

You have said previously, I think, that imagination transforms the world, that it's a force for change and enlightenment.

Yes. There have been times when my life has been financially difficult and subject to a lot of social strain. I was a solo parent and often without a great deal of money, and before I went to work, and even after I was working for some years, there was a great deal of struggle. Particularly as, when I began work in 1966, a working woman was, in effect, expected to act as if she didn't really have children, in terms of asking for time off when they got sick and everything like that. And I do think that is a genuine problem. I don't think it's vanished now.

But, you see, I think that quite a lot of the hard times I went through I was actually able to interpret as a sort of adventure, because of reading and because of imagination. That doesn't mean to say I always enjoyed them, or that I was light-hearted about them or anything like that. I was subject to the usual fits of depression and anxiety that people are subject to in those circumstances. But I did have some sort of imaginative context in which I could command the situation to quite a considerable extent and therefore I could come out of it relatively light-hearted.

Do you use imagination to escape the harshness of the world, or is it more positive?

I think it's a bit more positive than that, although I must say where the harshness of the world is concerned a certain degree of escapism isn't necessarily a bad thing. People always speak of escapism as if it is the same as cowardice but often it is quite sensible. It is a question of degree. You can't escape it, really. After a certain point, attempts to try to escape actually turn out to be very destructive. But up to a certain point – I think Tolkien says this in his essay – fairy stories exist for consolation, among other things. And he suggests that escape isn't necessarily a bad thing.

But I think it is more positive than escape. It is the extent that you are able to interpret your experiences one way or another. So that certain sorts of experience that have been chosen are a little bit different from circumstances that are imposed.

What do you want to happen – what do you hope will happen – when people read your books? Are they not to some extent escaping when they read your books into imagination and fantasy?

I hope they will have some of the same sorts of experiences that I have had reading other people's books, I suppose, which is a sense of a whole lot of connections being made with the world. Some of them are tangible connections in terms of, say, accounts of domestic life. Someone will read these accounts of domestic life and say, 'Yes, I know what that's like, that's what my life is like. I have not been singled out by fate to be inefficient and to spill tea when I am carrying it from one room to another, and I am not singled out to not cope terribly well with all the great varieties of demands on one's time first thing in the morning.'

Margaret Mahy

At the same time I hope they will be encouraged to make imaginative connections with the world – not identical to mine, but their own imaginative connections. While you are doing this you are looking out and thinking, 'There's the sunlight falling and it's had a long trip to get here. It's come from the sun, which is ninety-three million miles away. It is travelling at 186,000 miles per second. It is falling on those leaves, which are taking it in, photosynthesis is taking place, and we are living in a world of wonderful structures, amazing events. If I could see that tree properly, see what that tree is doing, it would not just be that familiar shape but it would be like a continual changing fountain of events. At the same time, I am being transformed myself.

My body is dispelling old cells, creating new ones. It is progressing in a certain direction. All these marvellous things are going on and I am standing in the middle of this room spilling tea and having to mop up the floor. Of course, at the moment you spill the tea and you have to mop up the floor, you think, this is the last straw. I'm going to be late for work and I can't go away and leave the tea soaking into the mat, or something like that.

But, at the same time, somewhere, some other part of your mind is still making these connections. I suppose I have to make an act of faith that that is quite a good thing for people to do, and to hope that the stories I write at certain levels and at certain points in the story help people to make these sorts of simultaneous connections both in terms of day-to-day actions and in terms of some sort of imaginative complexity.

You use laughter a great deal in your books and, I think, probably in your life as well, and you have in the past described laughter as a spiritual force.

Yes, it is often seen as being clownish, and rightfully too, because there is this great clownishness about a lot of laughter, but I do think that it is also a spiritual force. I think it offers release. I know that it has some very mysterious functions.

In one of Kurt Vonnegut's books somebody says something about maturity being a great disappointment unless laughter can be said to remedy anything, and I think, too, that laughter offers a lot of consolation sometimes. So it is not exactly always black humour. But confronted with a lot of situations in the world you have a choice between laughing and crying and I quite often choose to laugh.

In the end, I suppose, one is ultimately confronted with certain situations where one is forced to tears. But in quite a lot of situations that just precede that ultimate one I laugh and I feel some sort of release. I also feel that I have made a connection with the system that I am adding to and that is supporting me, a system of response in this case. I'm certainly not the only protagonist.

You see laughter as a spiritual force – why spiritual?

Probably because it's the closest word I can get that makes sense to other people. Although some people, if I talked about certain things like laughter as being spiritual, and talked about some of the things that I laugh at, would regard it as probably being the reverse of spiritual, which they would see as a serious thing. But what I'm saying is that laughter is also serious in certain circumstances. It's part of the serious way in which people respond to the world. But because it does pass, imperceptibly at times, into this clownish area it is sometimes seen as the definition of laughter, and there is light-hearted laughter, for goodness sake. That's one of the wonderful ways in which laughter operates.

I suppose I do find it harder to laugh in the ways I did when I was fifteen or sixteen when I would go to films and things like that and laugh so hard that I would be united with laughter's apparent opposite, that is crying. People say, 'I laughed till I cried.' It can work the other way, too. You can cry until you laugh. Your crying can sometimes become sufficiently grotesque for it to turn into laughter.

I find it harder and harder to laugh in that old light-hearted way that is just pure amusement, that makes you come away feeling really good. You feel at ease with the world and optimistic about things.

Are you less optimistic than you were about the world?

On some levels only. At some levels I think my optimism or pessimism doesn't make much difference. At other levels I am a bit more pessimistic than I was because I think sometimes the wish to be good can do a great deal of harm.

The whole process of colonisation, for example, which is a mixture of selfishness and the feeling that Europeans are the true men of the world, and therefore had the right to do what they liked to other and lesser men. And also the apparently genuine wish to improve the lot of the people who were being colonised by introducing them to aspects of the Christian religion or to get them to dress more modestly. All that sort of thing actually seems to have done harm. I'm really thinking about what some of the colonised people have to say about things nowadays.

You are not a Christian, are you?

No, I am not. I would have to say that I am not because I don't believe in salvation through Christ. I do believe I behave morally, fairly indistinguishably from Christians, because, I suppose, I try to behave towards other people as I would like to be behaved to myself. I believe that I am constrained by a morality every bit as arduous as Christian morality. But I would not count myself as a Christian because of my inability to believe in those sorts of mystical elements of Christianity such as salvation through Christ, or, for that matter, that God is universally beneficent in the social way that he is supposed to be – that he looks after those who love him and arranges things for good.

There are other views of God, such as that he does arrange things for good on the whole in a cosmological way, which sometimes can of course involve the extinction of whole populations and things like that. There I would have to think twice. The trouble is, the word God has become so strange in the mouths of some people in that it is very paternalistic and very limited, and 'Old Testamentish'. They believe in a spirit of reward and retribution. I don't actually believe in that. I believe in reward and retribution, but not according to any system quite as logical as parts of the Old Testament, at any rate, seem to indicate.

What about the supernatural?

I am not really a believer in the supernatural. People are often misled by the nature of invention in that, if people write realistic novels about having alcoholic parents or about great miseries about certain sorts of marriages, there is a great assumption that the writer must have gone through that themselves. Sometimes I am, of course, writing from knowledge, but only knowledge of the lives of friends or, in some cases, because I imagine what it would be like to be in that particular situation. There is a tendency for a lot of writers, I think, to use bits and pieces of their life and to re-assemble them. And, I think, they synthesise a great deal. But, by no means are all the experiences in a realistic novel necessarily the experiences of the author.

In rather the same way there are two assumptions about somebody who writes supernatural stories. One is that people think that everything they write is invented and that none of it has any reference to reality. The other is that it must all be true. People have sometimes said to me things like, 'You obviously know a great deal about witchcraft.' I don't. I invent it. I have a great deal of general knowledge about history, and I have a general knowledge about a whole variety of things.

But, no, I don't believe in the supernatural. I haven't had any supernatural experiences myself, and, although I have spoken to people who have said they have, I regard that in a lot of cases as non-proven. I believe that there are areas of life where things happen that can't be accounted for, but that, I think, is simply because we are still very ignorant and I suspect that quite a lot of those events that seem supernatural to us are still within nature in some way. We still have an infinite amount to find out. I suppose, in terms of our present knowledge, there are certain experiences that people are entitled to describe as supernatural, but I haven't had any such experience and I certainly don't write to promote belief in it.

But what I do do, partly because I enjoyed reading supernatural stories so much when I was a child, is to use the supernatural as a fairly ready metaphor for certain sorts of imaginative states.

The other thing is that I do think that we live in an absolutely astonishing world. If we were to look honestly at the world and to see what is truly going on, we would be struck absolutely still with astonishment. We wouldn't be able to get on with everyday life like mopping up the tea we have spilt on the floor. So, in a way, our physical systems are created at variance with our imaginative and intellectual systems. If we were to look at the world truly, even out of the window at this moment, we would see plants and sky and clouds and know that up beyond there are the stars; the whole universe is existing around us.

We get through each day by forgetting about that for nine-tenths of the time, and we get through our lives with our physical systems filtering out that astonishment. I find that supernatural stories in one way or another restore me at times to those moments of astonishment.

What connection do you make between your awareness and the vastness of the universe? Here you are, one unique individual.

I think there are necessary and ongoing connections the whole time. I don't think that a black hole or anywhere in the universe is any more important in essence than I am. We are all things that are going through continual physical modification, a transmission of energy. At this stage a certain variety of the elements have come together to have a degree of self-awareness and awareness of the universe, which has a mysterious and necessary function to play.

I don't know, in terms of the universe, that I am any more significant than the plants growing out there. I'm part of a range of significance and within that range I try to do the best I can.

You were, I think, a rather different child. In fact your difference, your uniqueness, was encouraged by your parents, is that right?

That's true in a way, but I think all children are different children. I am able to talk about my own particular difference, my own particular difference and self-absorption. We are all born in some ways to be self-absorbed because we are shut in a particular body with a particular nervous system and particular perceptions and experiences that start to be different even with identical twins. They start to differentiate us. I am sure that all the children in my class were different children, but I was certainly particularly aware of my own difference from the others around me.

You were unusual, if you like?

Well, yes, I now think I was eccentric, although I didn't at the time. I made imaginative assertions and tried inappropriately to bring them through into real life instead of realising that they could only exist as imaginative ideas, and a lot of them probably were to do with expressions of ego, too.

I remember that I was certain that I could speak the language of the animals, and yet I knew, in some ways, I couldn't do this. I still don't think it was a direct lie, although it might just as well have been. It was a way of inviting a whole lot of other people to play a game they didn't particularly want to play, or inviting other children to become involved in a speculation in which they weren't interested. I insisted on this and they rebelled against it.

I tried to show that I was a person who could speak the language of the animals by, over a fairly brief period in my life, eating leaves, drinking out of puddles, doing things that seemed to be animal things to show my oneness with the rest of creation. Of course I was subject to a lot of derision for this, and, even after I realised uneasily that I was separating myself off from my fellows to an extent that I didn't wish to be separated, I continued to maintain that I could do those things. If directly challenged, I ate leaves and berries and anything that anyone gave me, in effect. They would say, 'Eat this leaf!' and I would eat it and they would say, 'Ooh, ooh'.

I suppose I was lucky not to be poisoned. People said this at the time, and I said that I was proof against poison, that I couldn't be poisoned, and I never was, as far as I know. I did try and stand back from it a bit, but other people didn't forget and every now and then children would challenge me about this and I just kept on maintaining it until I was in Form One. By then, people had forgotten this sort of eccentricity, but if they remembered it, I was so normal in so many other ways, I suppose. I was turning up to school and not doing particularly well, on the whole.

In fact, you were seen as a bit dumb?

Yes. I was sort of puzzled by that, I must say, because I was a very good reader and I wrote well. But I was going to school at a time when a fairly high priority was placed on neatness and other sorts of areas that I wasn't particularly competent in. I wasn't very good at maths. I was always well behind in my maths book. My mother always used to comfort me by saying that girls aren't good at maths, they tend to be better at English, which was, and still is, one of the clichés that underlies our education system.

There seems to be an almost innate desire in all of us to find some sort of pattern or purpose, some simple formula, that things mean something.

Yes, this is, 'I now know what things mean and I am now in possession of it and I can order my life.' I think that in quite a lot of our life, both our physical and spiritual life (not that I think the two are necessarily disconnected in the ways that the more platonic and even Christian systems tend to suggest) there is a great contest between form and chaos, between form and some sort of anarchy.

I think that to practise as a librarian you are standing on the borderline between form and anarchy, because a lot of librarianship is concerned with form and making knowledge available, for example, passing on information. In order to do this you have to give it some sort of form.

Of course, the amount of information that is potentially available to us, our individual perceptions of the world, as well as acknowledging the validity of other people's individual perceptions, bring us close to more information than our systems can cope with. We are confronted by this sort of anarchy. I think that one is perfectly entitled to try to give form to this in order to make it usable.

I think personally, however, that it is a mistake for people to take the form they give things and then say, 'This is *the* true form and everyone else must conform to this in order to make me feel safe with my form.' We all seem to do this to some extent. We find that, if somebody else has imposed a different sort of form on this anarchy, we feel ourselves threatened by it and we want them to re-order it.

That, of course, underlies a lot of political and philosophical and religious conflict. We don't like the forms that other people give, and of course when I say 'we', I mean any system in the world, whether it is the Moslems or certain branches of Christianity or Buddhists. Not only do they set up that form for themselves but they have to give it legitimacy by imposing it on other people, or getting other people to agree, or, of course, at times imposing it by force. That's within history and in the present day.

Looking back on your life, do you see a sort of pattern? There have been certain turning points, perhaps coincidences. For instance, the time when you were writing for a school journal and it went on exhibition in the United States seems to me a tremendous leap forward and a turning point in your life. It started you on an international career. Your stories were recognised in an international way for the first time.

Yes, that's right. It was a great change for me – greater than I realised at the time. At the time I was absolutely overwhelmed with the glory of the moment. When I look back I can see that as a child I was very keen to write books, to have books published, because books were things that I had, unconsciously in the beginning, but increasingly consciously, chosen as things of great significance to me.

A book is a form of communication and it is communication of a very intimate form in a lot of cases. People confide their souls in books or they share astonishing information. Astonishment about a fact involves some spiritual shift, too, I think – sometimes small, sometimes enormous. The discovery that the earth was not the centre of the universe seems to have involved an enormous spiritual and imaginative shift.

I think that the idea of a book, the idea of not only being a receiver of communications but a communicator was a very seductive idea to me. And when in 1969 somebody offered in effect to publish a book, that was a wonderful moment for me. And I do look on it as a turning point.

Do you think you have found the place that suits you best?

Yes, I think I have.

And will you live happily ever after?

Well, it depends to a certain extent on whether people in the outside world also find the place that fits them best. We are all interconnected and it is all very well for me to be in the place that fits me best. But, as I was saying at the beginning, sitting in the place that fits you best can sometimes be a bit selfish if other people haven't got places that fit them reasonably comfortably too.

This interview was first broadcast on National Radio on 9 January 1990.

Sir Edmund Hillary

Sir Edmund Hillary is probably the closest person New Zealanders have to a 'folk hero'. His conquest of Everest was but one achievement among many. As explorer, adventurer, environmentalist and diplomat he has gained a place in New Zealand history that is probably unequalled by anybody else. Yet strangely, all his life he has had to overcome strong feelings of inferiority.

He grew up in the small South Auckland town of Tuakau. His parents held strong views about what they saw as injustices. They gave Sir Edmund his strong beliefs about the responsibility humans have for other human beings. Yet he and his father didn't always agree.

SIR EDMUND HILLARY: We had fierce arguments at quite an early stage. My father was a very firm gentleman, maybe a little bit harsh at times. If it was a matter of disagreement I used to end up in the woodshed being thumped by my father. I think it became a battle of wills between him and me. The main thing my father wanted was for me to admit that I had done something wrong, whereas I was absolutely determined, whether I'd done wrong or not, that I was not going to admit anything. Actually, I don't think I ever did admit the error of my ways, rightly or wrongly. I don't say this was a particularly worthy approach on my part. It shows that I had a stubborn will even in those days. I think I must have been a very uncomfortable child for my parents.

Your mother had been a school teacher and encouraged you as far as your education was concerned, didn't she?

Yes, my mother provided the more inspirational side of our family activity. She was very anxious that her children should be well educated, even though this meant a considerable drain on the family finances. All three children were very thankful for her determination, even though my father frequently said we simply couldn't afford to send us to such and such a school. He said it would be much better if we came home and worked and helped with the provision of food. My mother was much quieter but her will prevailed and all of us ended up getting a reasonable education.

You went to Auckland Grammar, I understand, and at quite an early age?

Yes, I was the sort of 'child genius' of Tuakau Primary School. Because my mother was a school teacher she pumped me full of, I thought, rather useless information. But I did have a lot of general information and the teachers at Tuakau Primary

School liked teaching me because I could absorb it relatively easily. So, instead of completing my primary education at Tuakau Primary at the average age of thirteen, I finished there at the age of eleven. My mother was very determined I was going to a good school in Auckland even though we lived in Tuakau, fourteen miles away.

I went to Auckland Grammar, where I was a very unhappy child. It really had nothing to do with Auckland Grammar; I think I would have been inevitably unhappy all through my secondary school period. One reason was that I was very much younger than the average. I felt I was small and rather helpless. Also, I came from a country school. I had learned nothing about things like French or any advanced sort of mathematics. I was thrust into this high-powered environment and, for a while, I really found it quite a struggle. When I look back on it now I think I really didn't do too badly at Auckland Grammar. I certainly wasn't one of the bright students, I was a very mediocre one, but I did end up getting my Matriculation and University Entrance, so I couldn't have been a 'no hoper', anyway.

You say you were very small, at that time. It seems hard to believe now.

Well, because I was very young I was much smaller than the average child in my class. But, when I was in the fourth or fifth form I suddenly started growing. I grew six inches in one year and five inches in the next. So towards the end of my time at Grammar I was definitely one of the larger boys there. This changed my attitude and I knew by that time that I was physically energetic and robust. Every spare moment away from school I was working with my father at home doing hard physical labour. By the end of the school period I was a physically strong person. Not particularly good athletically, but physically robust.

There was an incident, I think, with the gymnastics instructor when you started at Auckland Grammar. He didn't think highly of you physically?

No. This affected and still affects the whole of my attitude to life. It was when I first went to Grammar. We all had to go along to the gymnasium to be assessed for training by this gymnastics instructor, who I regard as one of the most unpleasant teachers I have had anything to do with. We stripped off and I can clearly remember him just looking at me with scorn and saying, 'What will they send me next?' He told me I had a bulging ribcage and my back wasn't very straight. He told me everything that was terrible about my physical set-up. I was absolutely mortified, of course, and this created in me an enormous sense of inferiority which, even though I developed into a somewhat larger and robust person later, I personally still retain. I still think I'm a rather strange-looking character, even though I know I'm reasonably normal – except rather large.

81

This was something that influenced your attitude not only to your body but also to yourself as a person?

Even though I was only eleven I became very determined to become competent physically in some form or another. For three and a half years I travelled by train every day from Tuakau to Auckland Grammar and back again and as this meant virtually four hours on the train I wasn't able to take part in much sport. As a consequence I had to entertain myself in a physical way so I did a tremendous amount of walking and rushing around over the fields and jumping over fences. I got reasonably fit and certainly active in that fashion. Towards my later days at high school and early days in university I also took lessons in ju-jitsu and boxing.

I remember one occasion I was in the gymnasium. It was when I was taking boxing lessons. The New Zealand welterweight professional champion, a very strong-looking gentleman, also trained in this particular place but I was by then larger than he was and with a great deal longer reach. The person who ran the gymnasium asked if some of us would like to do a bit of sparring with this professional boxer, just for the experience and practice and all the rest of it.

Well, I said, 'Yeah, why not!' He didn't look all that tough to me. So we went into the ring and we sparred around a bit. He was obviously infinitely stronger and much more adept than I was but he was a little bit careless and he dropped his guard. I had a rather good straight left and I whanged him good and properly on the nose. I discovered that it really isn't a good idea to hit a very tough professional boxer on the nose. He absolutely lost his temper and laid into me, finally delivering the most tremendous upper cut to my solar plexus. I doubled up and that was the end of that little episode. The instructor said to me, 'You silly boy, why did you punch him on the nose?' 'Well,' I said, 'I thought that was what I was meant to do.'

One of the lessons of life?

Yes, indeed.

In those days, right up to university, you were quite a loner, weren't you?

Yes. I didn't deliberately choose to be a loner but it was because of the life I was living and the fact that I didn't have much to do with the kids at school because of going back home to Tuakau all the time. I did build up a few friendships with other young people on the train who were also travelling distances. But I travelled further than everybody else and so I suppose in a way I didn't have the social relationships that people tend to build up at their secondary school level. I would say that I really left Auckland Grammar without a real friend in the world.

I want to turn for a moment to your religious upbringing. You were, I think, an Anglican originally? Did you go to church?

Yes. My parents were very supportive of the Church of England but were not deeply religious people. My father did get involved in the administration of the church in Tuakau – he was one of the lay representatives who used to go to meetings with the bishop in Auckland. My father was always a great organiser and a great enthusiast about principles. He was a strong person in that respect. So we children all went along to church regularly. I never felt tremendously motivated by it but it was more or less the thing to do.

I remember at one stage we passed through a series of courses by the local minister so we could be confirmed and the bishop was going to come. It happened that the local minister's daughter was to be confirmed on this occasion so it was going to be a big deal. This minister was a very great enthusiast for his religion but I think he got a little bit carried away. He absolutely convinced me that when I was confirmed in the church I would receive the Holy Ghost. I didn't quite know what the Holy Ghost was but obviously it was going to completely change my life.

So on the day of the confirmation I went along to church filled with anticipation of the change in the rather mediocre person I considered myself to be. I duly went through the confirmation ceremony, which was very nicely handled by the bishop. But when I came away from the church I suddenly realised that I wasn't any different. I wasn't nobler. I didn't have any greater powers. I really wasn't any different from what I'd been before.

That was when my beliefs about the whole system began to be eroded. I did pass through a phase in which I, in fact our whole family, became interested in a lot of alternative-type religions. I read many books about theosophy, which I thoroughly enjoyed. It was really like science fiction in many ways. And we took part in what was called 'Radiant Living', which was sort of a combination of health instruction, physical activity, psychology and spirituality.

I seem to remember that the leader of the movement was Herbert Sutcliffe, wasn't it?

Yes, Dr Herbert Sutcliffe. He was, I think, born in Britain but he lectured all over the world and was a very competent lecturer on these topics. I think all of us were seeking something but we didn't quite know what. At that time 'Radiant Living' seemed to give it to us.

After that I'm afraid I sort of drifted away. I would say that, although I'm still interested in philosophy and in many religions, I don't personally have any deep religious beliefs.

You don't believe in God?

I don't believe in God in the ordinary church sense of God. I have the vague feeling, and I've argued sometimes with my philosophical friends very energetically about this, that the world and the whole universe are so complex and so remarkable in many ways that there must be some sort of intelligence behind it all. But as to whether that intelligence is the slightest bit interested in a little person like me away down here on earth I have considerable doubts.

What do you think of the idea that you as an individual have some kind of connection with the rest of the cosmos, with nature, animals, the universe, as well as other people?

I have learned to have a great affection for the environment. I have learned to love the mountains. As for animals, I passed through a phase after the war when I went out deer stalking and used to shoot large numbers of deer and skin them and carry their pelts in to be sold.

But as time passed I lost my enthusiasm for killing animals of any sort really, apart maybe from fish. I still enjoy a bit of fishing. I have become much more environmentally conscious, much more aware of the importance and the beauty of trees and flowers and birds and animals. I think they make up one of the more desirable aspects of our life on earth.

In 1939 at the outbreak of World War II you made an application to become a pilot and then you changed your mind. Perhaps at that time you might have been described as a pacifist. You certainly seem to have had leanings towards pacifism.

I suppose that's true. I applied to join the air force. I thought it would be absolutely fantastic to become a fighter pilot. But then I discovered it was about a year at least before I could go into the air force. This was towards the end of the stage in my life when I was still trying to solve my religious problems and beliefs. So I decided it wasn't worth waiting around all that time for it and that maybe I wasn't all that keen on the basic philosophy of war anyway.

I didn't really have to make any decisions on this topic. My father, who was producing large amounts of honey at this stage, determined that I should stay on in the business, and as all agricultural people who were necessary were retained on their farms at that time I was too.

Later I got very restless with this and much later in the war I did go into the air force. I trained as a navigator and flew on Catalina flying-boats in the Pacific. It was towards the end of the war and it was certainly the best holiday I have ever had in my life. I thoroughly enjoyed it, but I really didn't do anything much of great consequence.

During this stage you seem to have changed your views to some degree about religion and your place in the world. You seem also to have become a much more independent person.

Yes, definitely. I don't know exactly when the change occurred. When I started mountaineering and I was climbing something difficult or in a situation that was dangerous – you might fall or be avalanched off – because of my background I sometimes had the feeling that maybe a little bit of an appeal to God might help me get through safely. But I very quickly built up the attitude that if I was in trouble that was my business. I had to get myself out of it. It was no use me getting down on my hands and knees praying to God to get me out of it. It wouldn't do me the slightest bit of good. I adopted that approach and certainly that has been my attitude ever since. I say the best of luck to people who are having problems and wish to pray in whatever way they want to gain help. Maybe it's a slightly arrogant approach that I've had. I've always felt, 'Ed, you're in this problem and you've got to get yourself out of it.'

In your travels you have come into contact with other religions a great deal. I wonder to what extent this has affected the way you view life?

Religion is a very strange business. There have probably been more terrible things carried out in the name of religion in the world than for any other reason. I've had the opportunity to be involved not only with Christianity, but with Hinduism, the Moslem religion and Buddhism, and I've enjoyed being absorbed into at least the outer fringes of those religions.

When we took jetboats up the Ganges River in 1987, according to the local people we were making a religious pilgrimage. The Ganges is the holy river of India and literally millions of people came down to see us as we passed through. They thought we were making a religious pilgrimage to the source of 'Mother Ganga', which had all been started by the gods aeons before. I'd always thought that the Hindu priests were very reluctant to let foreigners go into their temples, but in Benares, which is the most sacred city in India, we were welcomed warmly into the temples by the priests. They blessed us and our boats.

It was a fantastic experience, actually. For the whole expedition, as we travelled up 'Mother Ganga', we virtually became Hindus in our outlook and in our philosophy. Once we completed the expeditions we all became sinners again, I guess, but it was a remarkable experience. I could see how important their religion is to the hundreds of millions of Hindus who live in India.

I would never try to persuade any person who has strong religious beliefs to change their beliefs. The only thing I would, perhaps, recommend to them is that they observe the greater things in their beliefs, the love for other people, for example, or helping others whatever their beliefs may be. These things exist in all great religions but they are not always observed very carefully.

Buddhism as it is practised in the Himalayas rather appeals to me. The Sherpas are Mahayana Buddhists of Tibetan descent. They believe that everybody must choose their own path. They don't try to inflict their religion on you. They say it is for you to choose your own way, to go whichever way you wish and that you will be rewarded according to how you perform. It's entirely up to you. They will not try to influence you. As a consequence you're invited into their monasteries. You can attend all their religious ceremonies, even some of their most important religious ceremonies. If you went in there and you stood on your head and you screamed and yelled they wouldn't complain about it. They'd probably say, 'Oh, he's a bit stupid,' I suppose, but there's no resentment about you doing your particular thing. They mightn't invite you back again but that would be understandable.

I've enjoyed going to many religious functions in many of the great religions in the world. My wife once said to me, when I was invited to go along to a church service here in New Zealand and I said I didn't know that I really wanted to go to another wedding or another funeral, 'If it was a Buddhist service or wedding or funeral you'd go like a shot, so why won't you go to a Christian one?' I said, 'You're right,' and I went.

Is climbing mountains a spiritual experience for you?

No. I do know people who have regarded climbing mountains as quite an uplifting spiritual experience. As far as I am concerned, it's always been a very stimulating experience, and a very satisfying one. Being successful on a difficult mountain gave me a great feeling of achievement. Perhaps it goes back to my early days of having to overcome my miserable physique and the feeling of inferiority that had been very strong in my younger days. I enjoyed the challenge. I even enjoyed being frightened, as I was a great deal of the time, especially afterwards. I do think that fear is a very important part of challenge. I don't think it's just confined to being afraid of death on a mountain or something like that. I think it's the fear of anything. Many people are absolutely petrified of talking to a large audience but if they can overcome it and enable themselves to put on a good performance and influence a large group of people it's very satisfying.

There's a book called 'Feel the Fear and Do It Anyway'. That seems to be your philosophy as well. Fear provides a very important opportunity for you to meet a challenge and grow, doesn't it?

Yes it does. My first book was called *High Adventure*. The original title I had suggested to the publishers was *Battle Against Boredom*. In those days my life was all go go, rush rush, climb this, do that. Everything had to be done at top speed and the one thing above all else that I didn't want to put up with was boredom. I thought that *Battle Against Boredom* was a very good title for my book. However, the publisher said, 'If you put a negative title like that on it you'll never sell any copies.' So I used the title *High Adventure*. But, for me, the battle against boredom remained for many years and still is, I think, underneath, a great deal of the reason that I still keep very active and I'm rushing around the world all the time.

This restlessness, this battle against boredom, this need to meet and overcome difficulties, are you trying to prove something to yourself, maybe, or to others?

Not consciously, perhaps. I don't really think I'm trying to prove anything to anyone much at the moment. But I often feel almost under a sense of obligation. I don't know what the origins of it are but I do feel a sense of obligation to get on with it and do things that I become involved with. Certainly in all my activities in the Himalayas – the schools, the hospitals and medical clinics and so on and my relationship with the people up there, the Sherpa people – I do feel a very deep sense of responsibility. Even though it means constantly travelling around the world raising funds for it, which I sometimes find quite wearying, I don't think I'll stop until I almost can't walk. It's because I have this deep sense of obligation that I've just got to keep doing it. I think a lot of that does go back to the attitude of my parents, who had a similar sort of approach all those many years ago and I just sort of unconsciously absorbed it.

You have strong feelings about what you see as injustice, don't you, which drive you to do things, sometimes to say things?

My father was very strong on justice, very strong indeed. He was a real battler, there's no question about it. I'm certainly much less outspoken than he was. I realise also that what I may regard as injustice not everybody is going to regard as such. I've become a little bit more liberal, perhaps, in that way.

I think nowadays I am far less likely to make utterances on things because I realise that in some ways I have an unfair advantage. Whether I know anything about a topic or not, if I speak strongly on it I'm much more likely to be reported than someone else who may have much more understanding and knowledge of the topic.

There are many things I do feel strongly about, however. One is the rubbish left in the Himalayas by expeditions, by my fellow climbers. I speak all over the world about it and I am widely reported. I feel the same way about unemployment and the fact that there are so many people who are not able to live as well and comfortably as we would like. I feel strongly about conservation and the fact that even in a beautiful country like New Zealand, which has so much going for it, we seem to have so many stupid restrictions.

Of course I don't always have the answers to these questions by any means but I think all we human beings have a right, if we wish, to express our concerns about these matters, even if we have to leave it to our politicians to come up with the final solution.

You have got yourself into trouble in the past for speaking out for what you called a bit more 'honest to God morality' in politics. One prime minister didn't like that very much.

Actually, like many of these things, that was something of a misunderstanding. I was invited by the Auckland Rotary Club to speak. Each year they invited the head prefects of all the schools in Auckland and they used to get some well-known figure to come along and talk to them. So I told these young people the future of New Zealand would be in their hands. They were the ones who were going to have make all the decisions in the future. We'd made a pretty miserable mess of it, I thought (I still do, actually). I just recommended to them that when they had the power to influence things in New Zealand that one of the things they should try and do is to bring more 'honest to God morality' into politics.

It happened that this was the period of the Vietnam War and the President of the United States was constantly in the news saying one thing one day and the next day he'd say something completely the opposite. All over the world there were these conflicting views and obviously some people were just lying through their teeth all the time. It really was a very uncertain period in the history of the world.

I didn't even think of the New Zealand politicians – I was thinking of all the big wheelers and dealers overseas. I don't think anybody in New Zealand was very happy about their attitude and what was going on in Vietnam. However, the prime minister and the Cabinet took my comment and gave it far more importance than it really warranted and the prime minister took it personally.

It was Keith Holyoake, wasn't it? He wasn't very pleased with you?

No, he wasn't very pleased at all. One of the other ministers, a quite aggressive sort of character – I can't remember his name now – kept sending me telegrams saying, 'Retract! Retract!' Well, I'd never ever heard anything like this in my life and there was no way I was going to retract. What I said then I would say now and it was perfectly fair and innocuous. It was just being taken rather seriously by our political masters in Wellington. So that went on for quite a while.

Sir Edmund Hillary

Then I went down to Wellington. I was president of Volunteer Service Abroad. It was the annual general meeting and my plane was delayed so I arrived at the meeting while Mr Holyoake was speaking. I thought it could be a slightly tricky sort of thing. I came into the room where everybody was seated and my deputy chairman was conducting the meeting. I went over and held out my hand to shake hands with Mr Holyoake but he refused.

That's happened a few times. Mr Muldoon once refused to shake hands with me, too. I refuse to take it as a deep personal thing if one has these little disagreements with people. I can remember when Mr Muldoon and I disagreed, very inoffensively I would have thought, on the level of aid that New Zealand was giving to foreign countries. I had commented that I thought New Zealand should be trying very hard to raise its aid to one per cent of the gross national product, which as you know is the aim all over the world. Mr Muldoon commented, 'Sir Edmund Hillary knows as much about the finances of New Zealand as I know about mountaineering.' I thought he had really won that one. There was no question about it. However, I think he was wrong because I think I knew more about the finances of New Zealand than he knew about mountaineering.

We met at a garden party in Auckland and Mr Muldoon, as he was then, came into the gathering and he looked rather lonely. He was standing in the middle of quite a large area of grass with nobody talking to him and a great crowd all sort of gathered around. So I thought, 'Oh well, what the heck, we had a little bit of an argument, but after all I do know him.' So I wandered over and reached out my hand and said, 'Hello, Mr Muldoon.' He just turned his back on me.

I think I can say, if I've ever had a disagreement with anyone, it's always been very short-lived. I'm perfectly happy to shake hands and carry on in a friendly fashion afterwards. But those were two particular occasions that I remember well.

What do you feel about morality in politics now?

I think that politics in New Zealand at the moment are at a pretty low level and I think this would be the general reaction of New Zealanders on the whole. All we can do is hope that attitudes and conditions improve.

One of the turning points in your life undoubtedly was the climbing of Everest. I'm interested to know what this did to you as a person, if anything.

I would say the climbing of Everest had much less effect on me than it had on the media around the world and the world in general. Climbing Everest was, for me, a great experience, obviously. It was very satisfying. I suppose in many ways, once again it proved to me that I wasn't the 'loser' that fellow way back at Auckland

Grammar had suggested I might be. I realised that we had been successful in a very considerable challenge. But I had felt the public in general really wouldn't be all that interested in our climbing the mountain. I thought the mountaineering community would be very interested and say, 'Good effort, Ed, climbing Everest,' that sort of business. But it was an absolute surprise to me when we came down off the mountain and started getting all these telegrams and letters and stories in the newspapers. There was a tremendous build-up about our success and I admit I refused to take it seriously.

I have always known that I'm a person of limited ability and I have no intention of giving myself qualities that I simply do not possess. But the media painted Ed Hillary as a hero and Tensing Sherpa as a hero. We weren't heroes at all. We were just enthusiastic mountaineers who wanted to climb a peak. We were strong, we were energetic with good motivation. But we weren't the heroic figures that the world wanted to make us.

I do realise that if I really set my mind to something, I usually try to ensure that I carry it through. I think I'm a reasonably motivated sort of person in that sense but I'm no particularly great athlete. I was strong, I could carry good loads and rush around the countryside but compared to a really good, say, All Black or something, I have none of that ball sense and great speed that these people have. I just made do with what I had and did reasonably well as a consequence.

Symbols are very important, though, aren't they, and it was what it stood for in many ways: the climbing of Everest made you a hero and from then on you've had to cope with all this media attention?

I haven't had to cope with it at all. I've just carried on the same way. I've taken advantage of the publicity, I guess. And the fact that I have a title has certainly made it easier for me to get support for other expeditions and later on for the aid programmes which, as you know, have become a very important part of my life, and environmental matters too. I realise that these adventures and all this publicity about Everest and in the Antarctic and elsewhere has been helpful to me and enabled me to carry on and do other things.

There is one thing for which I do take a little bit of credit myself, however. I have known a lot of very good explorers who for years and years have built up and planned to achieve a certain objective and ultimately they have been successful in reaching their objective, but at the end it's a tremendous anti-climax. They've done what they tried to do for years and years. Now, they have nothing left to do. I mean what are they, what's their life going to be now? Now that has never occurred to me. Even when I climbed Everest, even when I stood on the summit, I looked across at another great mountain down below us that had never been climbed and mentally worked out a route for how it could be climbed. So Everest wasn't by any means the end of life as far as I was concerned. It was much more of a beginning for me. I kept on and on, and these days I still have plenty of ideas about new things I want to do.

It's the challenge that is the thing for you, is it? The actual process of meeting the challenge, or pitting yourself against difficulties, facing fears?

It's the challenge and the fear and the overlooking of the fear that is the really important factor. I'm less enthusiastic about being frightened to death now than I was a few years ago, to tell you the honest truth. But I have realised that there are many things that I do now that basically I still find frightening. Even doing an unusual lecture before an important audience. I have to work pretty hard on producing a good talk. That can put one under considerable tension, so going along to that big occasion and presenting that talk is a very considerable challenge. If you end up doing it reasonably well that's great. Fortunately, I seem to get through one way or the other, but I do feel almost as much satisfaction as in days gone by when I climbed a mountain.

Shortly after Everest you married your first wife, Louise. That was another turning point in your life, wasn't it?

When I climbed Everest I was thirty-three years old. Then I got married and the next twenty or thirty years were very happy years for me. I think getting married provided me with contentment, warmth in my life – even having children, although children can be a proper pain in the neck at times, as we all know. Still, there was a lot of fun in it and a lot of satisfaction.

Also, I was still going off and meeting challenges and having exciting moments. So they were great days for me. Then I started to become increasingly involved in building schools and medical clinics in Nepal and Louise was also very much involved in that activity. Even the children were very interested and made a number of trips to Nepal with me. So they were very good days indeed.

Then disaster struck in 1975 when we were building a hospital at Phaphlu. My wife, Louise, and younger daughter, Belinda, were flying in from Khatmandu to meet me but the plane crashed and they both died. The only way I felt I could overcome the shock of it all was by just driving myself to carry on with the work we'd all been doing together – to complete the hospital and then to carry on by doing, building other schools and other projects, the sort of work that we'd been doing together for a long time.

For a couple of years I felt that nothing would ever ease the pain of the loss of really the two people I loved most in life. People would say to me, 'Time is a great healer,' but I simply didn't believe them. But in actual fact I did find that time eased the pain as the years went by. I slowly became more interested again in adventurous activities and enjoyed them and slowly my life changed. My very good friends, the Mulgrews, had been friends with Louise and myself for many years. Peter had gone with me to the South Pole and then to the Himalayas. He died in the Erebus crash in the Antarctic. His wife June and I became more friendly and ultimately got married and this once again has been a very happy relationship. So I'm passing through another phase of life where there's a great deal of pleasure and companionship.

I wonder if you have any feelings about life after death?

No, I really don't, I'm afraid. When my family died I just accepted that that was it. There was no use me bemoaning the fact, no use me blaming God or the pilot or anything else. I mean, they were dead so what was the point in it? This unquestionably has remained my attitude. I just look back on the wonderful years that I had with them, and they were wonderful years for me. So I regard myself as having been extremely fortunate. They were with me in a period of my life when there was a tremendous amount of love and affection and joy. A lot of people never have that opportunity, but I was very fortunate indeed. So I appreciate that fact and the sadness that followed, well, it was just a burden that I had to put up with.

You, yourself, have faced the possibility of death through illness, haven't you? Do you ever think about what might happen to you when you die?

Oh, I don't worry too much, to be honest. I realise that I've been carrying out activities for many years now in which there is the potential for disaster. I take it for granted that when that time comes I will just duly depart this 'mortal coil'. What I have always tried to do is to ensure that if something should happen to me at least my family are well looked after, that they're not going to be in poverty and find life difficult on my departure. I think this is a very, very important thing. I think you can probably die with a fairly easy mind if you know that your family is not going to suffer financially as a consequence.

What do you feel about growing older? Because there came a time when you realised you couldn't climb mountains as you used to any more.

I think once again I am fortunate because I have found it quite easy to adjust to challenges according to my age and physical ability. Initially, I was one of the 'bombs' of the party. I wanted to rush off ahead and be fastest up here and get to the top there and all that sort of thing. It was very much a physical challenge type of thing.

Then, as I got a little bit older, I was very much involved in the planning and organising of expeditions and activities and the raising of funds. The mental side of it came into it much more. Then it developed into a very deep feeling for the welfare of people and that took up a great deal of my effort and my attention. I wasn't so worried about climbing any more. I was much more interested in doing things that would help people who needed a little bit more help than I did. Now I have finally reached the stage when I'm a good deal more ancient, but I still have the desire to carry on helping people, particularly in places where life isn't as it is here.

I've become very much more active and motivated about our world, about the environment and the need that all of us have to do something to protect this beautiful world, which, sadly, we are destroying rather quickly.

One of the things that matters a great deal to you, I think, is friendship. You spoke once about your life being a long line of friendships and said you couldn't have achieved what you'd done without them.

I've never really had vast numbers of friends. I've had a lot of casual and good friendships all over the place, but I wouldn't say I've had many deep friendships. The people with whom I have had deep friendships – we've done tremendous things together. I feel that I've benefited very deeply from those friendships and maybe they have too. We've achieved things together and we've laughed together a lot.

There's nothing that I've enjoyed more than sitting around a camp fire with a couple of really good friends, maybe reminiscing and laughing about things that have happened in the past, and planning things we're going to do in the future. With a bright sky above us with the stars shining and a crackling fire, and just dreaming, I guess.

Dreams have been important for you, haven't they – your boyhood dreams?

I've always been a dreamer. I still am a dreamer, of course, and I hope I never stop being a dreamer in one way or another. I think dreams are marvellous. As a child I found my pleasure essentially in dreams. I was a great reader of romantic books and I was always dreaming of myself with a sword slashing vigorously at villains and saving beautiful maidens from disaster. Later on I found that I was able to carry out some of those dreams, although perhaps in a slightly different way. I don't ever remember dashing off into the sunset with a beautiful maiden over the front of my horse or anything like that, but my dreams were really involved in overcoming challenges that had become of interest to me.

What about your dreams now? What's ahead for Sir Edmund Hillary?

Oh, I think I've got myself in something of a rut, although it's a rut that a lot of people would regard as very desirable. Last year I travelled round the world six times. This year I'm doing much the same. I go to many countries, I have many friends in lots of countries, but I'm working hard all the time. I don't really go anywhere much just for the pleasure of it. I'm doing fundraising talks or attending conferences, speaking at environmental gatherings and things of this nature.

I still find these things worthwhile and challenging and every year I go back to the Himalayas and talk to my Sherpa friends. We plan what we're going to do, what actions we're going to carry out, what building we're going to undertake in the forthcoming year. I find working with the people, listening to their views and doing what they want done is a very important part of my life. I don't want to just go in there and tell them what I think they should do, but responding to their desires and their wishes has always been very satisfying to me.

You are very much a New Zealander. You've always come back here to live. This seems to be your base, yet you could have lived anywhere in the world. How important is this country for you?

My roots are here. I was born in Auckland and my parents were born in Auckland and I feel that New Zealand is my home. I have had many wonderful times here. I enjoy people here. I've also been critical here at times and there are many things that we could do so much better, but I really do enjoy the feeling that I am a New Zealander and that this basically is my home. Which doesn't mean, of course, that I don't have very strong ties to other areas.

When I was High Commissioner in India for four and a half years one of the things that was very pleasant was that the Indian community would say to me, 'We know you are a New Zealander but you are also one of us.' They accepted me as part of their society and, as a consequence, June and I were invited to vast numbers of events and functions where we were the only foreigners. We were just accepted as part of the Indian community. We have a tremendous affection for India.

Speaking more generally, are you optimistic about the future?

I think I'm basically an optimistic person. Even with world environmental matters, which are pretty horrifying at times, I feel that we can't afford to be too negative about these things. We just have to get stuck in and do something about them. I think the more we can encourage people in general to accept this view the more likely it is that something will be done and both we and our environment will be improved.

We human beings are so incredibly clever at doing all sorts of things, technology and so on, and yet we're so hopeless at producing peace and happiness and freedom from hunger in this world of ours. We have a tremendous amount to learn. I'm one of those who believes that ultimately it comes down very much to the individual. If individuals are not prepared to accept that they have a responsibility, not only to themselves and their immediate family but to their country and to the world in general, then things will be pretty hopeless. I think it's up to individuals to accept the need to be positive and try to do something about it.

This interview was first broadcast on National Radio in two parts, on 3 and 10 November 1992.

POSTSCRIPT
Sir Edmund Hillary continues to roam the world, lecturing, writing and raising money for his Himalayan projects: schools, hospitals and medical clinics.

Jenny McLeod

Jenny McLeod shocked the music world in New Zealand in 1976 when she resigned as Professor of Music at Victoria University for a life of meditation and mysticism with a relatively obscure religious group, the Divine Light Mission.

Still only thirty-five, she had been hailed as a composer of near genius with such works as 'Earth and Sky' and 'Under the Sun'. But for Jenny McLeod something was missing.

JENNY McLEOD: I felt that I had got out of touch with my feelings in a way, because I'd got very intellectual in those days as the teaching thing went on. In the process I think I lost a bit of balance inside of myself. This is how it looks from here looking back. I wasn't quite aware of it then. But I felt I needed something that didn't seem to be there. In hindsight I realise that it was there all along; it was just that I had lost touch with it.

It was quite a profound point in my life where I suppose for the first time I began to take my life really seriously. But there was a gap. I'd had quite a lot of relationships that had failed to satisfy me. Various things had happened that I thought would give me satisfaction but they didn't. For instance, I bought a house and I thought, 'When I buy this house I'm going to feel fulfilled.' But it didn't happen at all. I'd write music and the pieces would be performed and while it was all happening it was very satisfying but afterwards it was all gone. I felt there was something not quite hooked up.

But outwardly you seemed to be very successful, didn't you?

Outwardly, yes. When you're younger you seem to have it all together. And I was pretty good at covering up my uncertainties. It would never do to show that one was in a bit of a mess. Teaching for me became quite a trial because I had to always appear to be completely in charge and know what I was talking about. When it comes to a subject like music, it's actually a very hard thing to talk about and only a fool can imagine that he or she has to know everything, because it's such an enormous subject.

Things that I thought I ought to be able to do I found I could not do and I had to spend a number of years subsequently finding out where the limits of things really are. There are things, of course, that we'll never able to talk about very successfully.

So at that time did you feel you had filled the gap in your life with the Divine Light Mission?

Well, it certainly gave me what I was looking for, mostly through quite a lot of unpleasant experiences, and I started to meditate. I took this very seriously but most of what I experienced in my mediations was a gradual realisation of what a twit I really was. One begins to see one's own shortcomings. Up until that point I don't think I'd ever really seriously examined myself. I had taken so much for granted and then I sort of sat down and meditated for eight or nine years.

Whenever I have gone into anything I've always gone into it boots and all – I just jump in and really go for it. It's a matter of extremes for me but I can't help it – that's the sort of person I am. And, of course, when you do that the lessons you learn are extremely painful but you learn them very well. So through that whole experience I kind of got my feet on the ground. It gave me something so solid that it's become completely part of me. I don't even think about it now. I mean I don't formally meditate. I haven't done that for years. But the whole experience of meditation just became part of me.

Could we describe it as an attitudinal thing? It's part of your attitude to life now, is it?

Well, I wouldn't even say that I have an attitude to life. My life and I are just one thing. I think, even to say that you have an attitude to life or have a philosophy is to make a division. It's got to be real. I mean, what you believe is not nearly as important as what you are.

What you are may start out as being a consequence of certain beliefs. But what I find with beliefs and attitudes is that they constantly change. You can take up one approach but as you approach the other side you see what was missing in it. In other words, there wasn't quite enough to it, so then you have to sort of examine all the other possibilities. Then maybe you find yourself doing a complete about-face and working your way through the opposite.

I mean, while I was still sort of thinking in terms of 'What do I believe in?' this happened to me over and over again. When you're, shall we say, spiritually young, like in kindergarten at first, it's all just wonderful because you're having a lot of positive things happen in your life. But when you begin to think you understand it, you see that all that is the trademark of every enthusiast – I won't go quite so far as to say fanatic. But the moment you do start to take your life seriously, powerful things certainly begin to happen to you.

I don't like talking about them because they're different for every person. But it's the effect of them that's important. Because it grounds you, it directs you, it makes you solid finally. Those experiences are very powerful but they also make you realise that there is a lot to learn.

Even what we're doing now is, to some extent, a meaningless exercise because we're trying to talk in words about experiences that are really impossible to put into words. We're sort of scratching around the surface. But to some extent you do begin to discover who you are. And this is something that goes on all your life, I presume?

Yes. For me, it all ended up with the questions going away and everything becoming focused back on music. Now I see I was always a musician but in the earlier days when I felt that the rewards of music weren't permanent it sort of changed for me. Now I have become completely focused on my work and I don't have any personal questions, really. I mean, I can't really talk about things like (I don't even like the word) 'God', because I find it a very unhelpful word. There comes a point when you realise you just can't – there's nothing you can really say about that. If you haven't got what you believe in your own soul what you talk about isn't going to help.

Once you have it then you can just get on with what you're really meant to be doing. I'm meant to be doing music. There's no doubt in my mind about that. So it's morning-to-night now. Every day I just get up and I work all day, and that's it – no questions. And the rewards are in the work. It's not as though you do something and expect later to have something back from it.

That something is dynamic and happening all the time?

That's what it has been like for me the last three years. It's been quite a long journey for me. It's only in the last three years that I've found a kind of steadiness. I've been through so many changes, ups and downs. It's quite alarming to go through those things if you haven't got something solid, but once you have found it, no questions. You can just get on.

I think everyone's got something in their life that is for them to do and once you've found that, then you can just forget about the questions, you can forget about the philosophy and you don't have to talk about God and all that because, with every breath, you're kind of connected up with your own life.

And you're on the right road. I mean it's something, as we said before, that is dynamic. It's something that continues day by day, moment by moment.

Absolutely. It's a different road for everyone. But I think it's probably the right road when you stop worrying about it and just get on with it. Often I'm stuck in my work. I get to points when I wonder if I've – I'm talking technically now – been attacking this musical problem the right way or has the way I've been approaching it been wasting my time. Maybe I'll try another way.

But, you see, all those problems that were formerly in my life are now just in my work. You might, in the past, think about your life: 'Have I been approaching things in the right way?' This is the way I questioned myself for years, but now, I can't really explain, it but it's all got turned into art. My whole life has moved into art. I don't mean it has just been turned into music, but my whole being is absorbed by art. Not just my art, not just music, but all kinds – painting and books.

Being creative?

Yes. That seems to me where the crunch really is because artists' work is spiritual, that's what we do. In a sense, we're sort of guardians of the spirit but artists create a new spirit, too. It's a fantastic responsibility, really wonderful.

Are artists sort of – we get this problem of God again and I realise that is a great difficulty – but are artists sort of co-creators in a sense? Artists are given gifts, aren't they, which it seems they have a responsibility to share, would you agree with that?

Oh yes, and they have a responsibility to themselves to make the most of whatever they've been given. That's good old biblical stuff, but you can't even lay down a law like that. I mean, when it's happening to you that's not the way you think about it.

I was interested yesterday watching Lawrence Olivier on television, talking about his growing up and the way the high Anglican Church featured so much in his younger days. He said that the passion with which people went about doing things in the church then was the same fervent kind of passion that went into his work. I really relate to that because it's the same sort of thing with me. I had to understand a lot of things about, shall we say, 'service'. To me the point of any religion must be to teach you that you must learn about serving. And then you've just got to get on with it. Everyone has different aptitudes so they'll all do it in different ways.

But until that's become part of you it's no good sitting around in church talking about service to God. It's no good just talking about these things. That's why churches are boring to me. There is life. Why sit around just talking about it all the time? You're only talking about it if something's actually missing.

There was a time, though, when church was important to you, wasn't there – when you were quite young?

I don't know if it was. You see, there was a nice pipe organ and I was the organist – well, I was one of the two organists for the church and I went for about three years. What I really liked about church was being able to play the organ – it had foot pedals and everything. I also liked the minister and his wife.

There was also a time, quite a long period in your life I think, when you described yourself as an atheist. Would you use that word now?

No. I mean an atheist is someone who doesn't believe in God. I just don't find these words even possible to use. God – what is God? And if you're going to say, 'I don't believe in God' what is this God? You have to define what you don't believe in. There is certainly a power beyond me but it is also working in me, through me. You can't be an atheist when you know that there's something there. But it's not a matter of believing. That's irrelevant.

As Jung said when asked if he believed in God, 'I don't have to believe. I know.' It has to be that way. If you're still wondering on the level of belief, well then, you've got some work to do, I think. That sounds incredibly arrogant, now that I reflect on it for a moment. Can one ever really know the full nature of his or her power? Of course not. I don't think so, not while we're still in the human body. I mean that's an enormous universe out there. I get quite angry when I hear these people in churches speaking as though they know what God is. (Which I've just done too, you see.)

I mean, one is just a tiny part of something that cannot be named by the human mind, that's what I really think, not to its full extent. You may have a wonderful experience of inner light and this and that. But how do you know what 'that' is?

I've had so many different kinds of inner light. The nature of spiritual experience is just as varied as the nature of physical experience and it's wrong, I think, to draw too many conclusions from specific experiences that you may have. If those sorts of things happen to you, then I think they're probably just to give you a kind of little boost along the way if you have been somewhat sagging, but what are they really? That's why I don't to talk about them in detail, because I don't think the specifics are important.

How would you describe the work you are doing now? You're writing a book, aren't you? Are you still composing?

Oh, I haven't composed anything for about two years. It will come back. I'm actually trying to draw together all of what seem to me to be the most important ways of thinking about music, technically, in the twentieth century and develop them. I'm really looking towards the future of music. There's been a lot of very obtuse thinking in music. It's not obtuse to the people who have thought it but it hasn't been very clear to the main body of musicians. So I am trying to understand that for myself and to kind of generalise as much as I can from it and explain it more simply for other people – other musicians, mainly other composers.

I suppose I'm really trying to make a new general theory of music that could carry us through for the next 1000 years, well, 400 years maybe – let's not be too ambitious!

Where do you think music is going? What directions?

It's going in every direction. The world of music is as big as the world of the human soul. There are the pop guys who can't read music at all and who work completely by instinct, but the material they're working with now was formulated technically hundreds of years ago by 'serious', if you like, musicians. So what the serious musicians are doing has its spin-offs over the centuries. Artists create archetypes, I believe.

Take the major triad, for instance. Now, anyone who plays a guitar, whether or not he can read music, knows what a major chord is. He doesn't know what it is, but he knows what it sounds like. He knows where he puts his fingers to get it. It just doesn't stop with the major triad. The serious people – by which I don't mean they're any better people – just happen to have the kinds of minds who need to formulate things clearly, theoretically. That has to keep developing. We can't just stop because these technical means wear out. The major triad is very hard to use now because it's just like certain words. They get overused to the point where they don't make an impact any more.

What is music for? I mean, basically it's sounds that arouse emotions and feelings, and you've described it also as a spiritual exercise. But what's it for?

It has a multitude of purposes. Different people will take it in different ways. Some people will take music as light relief. I can relax when I listen to some music. The heavy metal guys will get out there and rave and just go bananas and rebel against the establishment. For the middle-of-the-road rock musicians, music is for expressing the simple realities of one's life, of human relationships. For some people it's very sort of esoteric or more remote. It's not remote to me but it shapes something, it has a sort of spin-off, a kind of domino effect, similar to what is being done at the frontiers of medical thought, or mathematical, scientific and literary thought.

What is being done at these frontiers will ultimately affect our society. The sort of thing I'm doing now may seem to be a lesser human responsibility because I'm not relating to a wide public, only to the few people who can understand what I'm doing or are even interested in that. But for me, music is my life. There came a point where really only music, only art, could save me at moments of deep crisis. That's the point where I realised that the feelings I had thought of in the past as divine I had found in art. I had experienced them before but without knowing what they really were.

These are creative experiences in a sense, aren't they?

Well, you see, I think that just living is creative – just going out to make your breakfast is creative: you're making something. So what you do, how you have your house, the clothes you wear – I think this is all creative. I suppose there are degrees of creativity because people express themselves in so many ways. You open your mouth, that's creative. You're saying something and if it's real and if you're not just bullshitting or being a hypocrite or trying to put on an act then that's creative. Everything you do that is real is creative, I think.

So in one sense everybody is an artist?

I think so. It's just that we do it in different ways. I've got this certain kind of mind that loves to reflect on things, quite a mathematical mind. So in a way I'm back where I was years ago but I have kept in touch with my feelings this time. My life is much more in balance now than it was before.

You have always, it seems, been very open to all kinds of music. No one could call you élitist, could they?

No. I've really done the whole lot. I can't explain why it was that I was drawn to so many kinds of music, but I think probably now it was in order to have the widest sympathies I possibly could because now I need to have all those sympathies. You need to have those sympathies to keep yourself in balance, in a way. At least I do.

You're willing to listen to pop, rock, jazz, any kind of music, aren't you?

The only music I don't enjoy is bad music. There's about the same percentage of good music in every style. Perhaps, if you're lucky, five per cent of the music in any style is any good. You see, what you're looking for in art is the spark of something that's real, and that's something you feel, basically. It took me fifteen years to get to know popular music enough so that I knew what was good, because otherwise you're just swallowed up by the stereotypes. You've got to get to know the stereotypes before you can see where someone is very subtly doing something unexpected. Art is a matter of being familiar with certain kinds of language, too.

You had dreams, I think, quite a number of years ago about bringing the arts together, didn't you – visual, dance and movement, music?

I think I did, actually. But I haven't got that sort of juice any more.

Things like 'Earth and Sky' and 'Under the Sun'?

Yeah. Kind of great 'guzzump' concerts about all art work. But I haven't got great ambitions as a composer at all. I think my real work is this theoretical work, actually. I mean, I'm not a bad composer. At least, I'm a real composer, but I'm very minor as a composer. I'm not saying that with any sort of false modesty. You have to know where you stand in relation to the rest of them. But there is so much happening in my thinking now that it could probably take another ten years for it all to be thoroughly absorbed into my system. Because you can't really compose just straight off the top of your head from theory. It has to become part of you for you to be able to make real music with it. So this is a period of development and assimilation and I can't say what will happen. I may go mad again and try to create huge this and that. There are no guarantees. I never know, really, what's going to happen.

But you're happy where you are now? You like the road you're travelling?

Well, let's say that never in my life up until this period have I felt very happy every day when I wake up that I have work to do. And there's so much more of it to do. It's very lovely. There are no gaps, no holes in my life.

People may say, 'What about your friendships? What about people?' Well, I'm really a hermit now, but if people want to see me, they just come and we have a fine time when they come. I just stop working and we have a wee chat and we have cups of tea and laugh and it's fine. I haven't really got room or time for any more people than actually come to see me.

That's what I really feel. Other people realise their life through human relationships. There was a time when I really would have wished that I could do that too but eventually it became plain to me it's actually not what I'm meant to be doing. This is what I'm meant to be doing.

We haven't seen the last of Jenny McLeod the composer?

Oh, I don't know. Maybe you have, maybe you haven't. I just don't know.

This interview was first broadcast on National Radio on 20 August 1991.

POSTSCRIPT

JENNY McLEOD: In 1993 I did write a piece. You see, I have to feel like writing before I can write anything. I wrote it because it was for a situation completely other than the ordinary concert situation. It was for a choral festival at Ohakune and they wanted a piece that had a part for Maori singers in it. I thought it was an opportunity to put the local tangata whenua into the piece as well.

I also very much liked the fact that the Choral Federation was opening itself up in that direction, because I feel we have so very much to learn from Maori people. We have just got to get to know one another. I had a strong impulse that I wanted to do that piece. I also tried to learn enough Maori language in a very short time so I could write the words and make it a dialogue between Maori and Pakeha.

It brought a lot together for me, also a lot of my theoretical ideas. I had let them settle long enough so they could start to happen all by themselves. I would do things instinctively. Then I would analyse them and I'd think, 'Oh, my God, there's my idea!' It was a new way of doing something and my unconscious was doing it for me. It was quite wonderful. The unconscious for any composer or artist is a wonderful tool and partner. It's got to be a partner, though.

I finished the book. It's called *A New Guide to the Chromatic System*. It's off with the publisher but students are already using it. Now it all seems a long time ago. I'm not even thinking about the stuff that was in the book any more. What I retain of it is what is in my bones.

Jenny McLeod is at present mastering new music computer software and she's writing an orchestral version of her Ohakune choral piece. She's also doing some teaching and encouraging young New Zealand composers, who she thinks are streets ahead of those in Europe.

Is she happy? Jenny McLeod responds in this way:

I'm very happy. I couldn't be happier. But I don't really think that the purpose of life is to be happy. Happiness comes and goes. But I am never bored; I've always got something to do that I want to do. It might not be writing music but it will probably be something to do with that. I have a new friendship with Maori at Ohakune. It's wonderful. I go up there and I'm a member of the whanau now.

I like to have a balance. I try to have a balance, although I am totally obsessive about anything I'm involved in – I just get right into it. But it won't necessarily always be about music. Music is a part of life – it's a deep part of my life, but it's not everything.

Does your life have meaning now?

To me it does. If it doesn't I might as well go hang myself tomorrow. I couldn't see the point. I have to be doing something that I feel is worthwhile. Not just for me, but also helpful to other people in some way. You know, this idea that hopefully you are going to leave the world a slightly better place. That is the basic thing for me.

Jenny McLeod

Michael King

Michael King

Michael King is one of New Zealand's best-known authors, particularly in the biographical and historical field, and in seeking to interpret Maoridom to a wider audience. Books such as his biographies of Princess Te Puea and Dame Whina Cooper have won him wide acclaim.

He's very conscious of the gifts that have come to him from his relations with Maori. Michael King's own historical roots, however, have largely been influenced by Catholicism.

MICHAEL KING: I am a Catholic 100 per cent, not in the sense that I accept or feel comfortable with everything that the Catholic church as an institution represents, but in the sense that I was conditioned in my formative years by Catholicism. My view of life, my view of spirituality, my view of ethics, all sorts of other things like my love of literature, my love of music – I came to all these things through my Catholicism, and that makes me what I am. I've never considered being anything else; I've never wanted to be anything else. Certainly, there have been all kinds of other influences in the years since my childhood, but they've all been integrated into a framework that was initially set up and grew organically as a result of my being a Catholic in New Zealand.

How do you practise your Catholicism today?

I worship from time to time in Catholic churches, although I would have to say I also worship from time to time in other churches. I particularly became involved in worship through other denominations through my contact with Maori things. I spend quite a bit of time in the company of Catholics who share my values system. We talk about what we see as the problems of the world or problems of our community in terms that are conditioned by our Catholicism.

But I suppose more than anything else I practise my Catholicism by practising emphatically the values that Catholicism gave me; values such as the belief that it is in giving that one receives, the belief in the parable of the talents - that one is given certain gifts and has an obligation to use them, the belief that you do unto others as you would have them do unto you.

The things that regulate my behaviour, and I think should regulate the behaviour of others, have come to me through my religious upbringing, my reading of scripture, my reading of other people whose spirituality I respect, and the source of most of those things for me has been Catholicism.

To what extent do you see yourself as your brother's or sister's keeper, having responsibility for others, caring for others?

I think there is such a responsibility. There's a passage from St John that reads: 'He who sees his brother in need and closes his heart to him, how can the love of God abide in that man?' I believe that we have an obligation to be concerned about one another, and that to a very large extent we find God through practising and demonstrating our love for one another. I don't believe it means we should be always hanging over the back fence and watching what the neighbours are doing and wondering if we should be intervening, but I believe that where we see our brothers and sisters in difficulty we should be supportive and make it known that we are prepared to help if people want and need help.

I presume you believe in God in some form or another?

Yes, I do believe in God in some form. I don't believe in the kind of God that we were taught about at primary school: the God of the catechism who was that proverbial old man in the sky with a white beard. I was intrigued interviewing Whina Cooper some years ago to hear that she believed that she had died and gone to heaven but had been sent back again because God wasn't ready for her. The God she saw was a 'little Pakeha-looking chap', she said, 'with a long beard and flashing red eyes'. Well that's the kind of God of my childhood. The God I believe in now is the force in the universe for unity, for healing, for wholeness, the power that we see around us that enables life continually to resurrect and recreate itself. I believe there is such a power. I believe that life and our consciousness come as a consequence of that power and I respect it. I see us as all having an obligation to act on behalf of that power and not in opposition to it. Hence, in the very widest sense of the word, I feel an obligation to be pro-life and not anti-life. But whatever terms we use to describe God can only be metaphorical.

To what extent has your personal philosophy or religious outlook been affected by your contact with Maori? I presume it has.

Yes, I presume it has too, although it's rather hard to define how. One of the ways in which it's been affected is that from the time I first began to have intensive contact with Maori people and Maori situations, when I worked as a journalist for the *Waikato Times*, the thing that struck me most forcibly was that here were people in New Zealand who were intensely spiritual and who were not ashamed of being spiritual.

I suppose by the time of which I'm speaking, the late 1960s, many of the Christians I knew were becoming increasingly secular. They weren't as involved or as ostentatious in the practice of their faith as they had been previously, or as they had been when they were brought up. Yet here was a group of people in New Zealand who were highly spiritual, who began every meeting, event or undertaking with a prayer, who finished it with a prayer, who were conscious of spiritual values all the way through whatever processes they were involved in. That gave me pause for thought and impressed me, and it was a source of my admiration for those people.

I've also found a good deal that I can empathise with and share in Maori spiritual concepts. There are things like concepts of tapu and noa, sacred and profane, which, I suppose, are common to all religions. But there are also things like the Maori concept of mauri or life force: the belief that all things and places, including people, have an aura or ethos of their own, which seems to me to be a very interesting and useful concept, and one has to respect that. One must never cut across that. One must always take it into account in whatever one does that affects those people, places or things. I suppose that might be a finely focused articulation of something I've always believed, but encountering it in the Maori context has reinforced the validity of that kind of concept for me.

There are other things, too. One of the things I value most highly about Maoridom and the Maori language is the ritual that goes with encounters in Maoridom: the beauty of the language and the power of the oratory. New Zealand English tends to be rather restrained and constrained in its expression, particularly in expressions of emotion. Yet, alongside it in this country we have another language spoken, another culture practised, which is extravagant in its linguistic and emotional gestures. I rather like being part of that, too.

You would, no doubt, have empathy with the Maori love of nature and land and the importance that is given to them. This is something that is important for you, too, isn't it? It has been since you were a child.

Yes it is. I suppose, if I think analytically, I really acquired two kinds of cosmologies from my childhood. One was the more formal one of Catholicism. The other one was a very profound feeling of identification with nature, and that's there in Maoridom too. This, I suppose, is the feeling one gets that one is part of nature, that one belongs to it, that one does belong to *it* rather than it belonging to *you*. That has all sorts of consequences, including the fact that you respect the natural world and you have to be very careful that the human culture of which you are part does not interrupt natural processes, the capacity of nature to regenerate.

It seems to me that is the essence of the miracle of life: that although we as individual human beings die, other life arises out of the elements of which we are a part, and that applies to the land, the sea, the air and in fact the entire natural world.

What we are confronted with in the twentieth century for the first time is the possibility that human beings, through their insensitivity to this reality, can actually interrupt that process, actually stop it working, so that we have had through nuclear energy the capacity to destroy the earth. We also have the capacity to destroy life through things like perforation of the ozone layer and the trapping of greenhouse gases. Apart from taking the pragmatic view that one has to be cautious about these things simply to go on living, I think one should also come to the same conclusion through a religious view of life and through a religious view of nature.

Do you think everybody is religious?

I think there is a need to be religious in everybody. People don't always recognise it. People very often go out of their way not to be religious and in the process become religious. I can remember, for example, being taken along to a meeting at the Centrepoint Community by someone who was very emphatic and explicit about her rejection of Christianity and yet, when everybody assembled and bowed their heads and listened to a meditation from Bert Potter in an entirely secular way, what were they doing but taking part in a religious exercise? I think there is a need to be religious and I think that as people have ceased to practise their faith through Christian denominations there have been consequences. They've either had to seek other opportunities to fulfil the same needs or they've created immense problems in their own lives and the lives of their family through not recognising this spiritual dimension in their lives.

In your fortieth year – I think it was in 1984 or 1985 – you became ill and you had to take quite a lot of time out. It was a time of great reflection for you. What was going on at that time for you personally?

I became ill with a coxsakie virus and the problem was not just that I had it then, but that I kept getting it and never quite recovered. Several things happened. One was that I was reminded again what a great gift good health is, that it's the most fundamental thing we have to be grateful for because without it life becomes very difficult. I don't know that I'm a person who's been particularly ennobled by being incapacitated. I haven't liked it. I had to learn a lot more patience. I had to learn dependence on other people to a much greater extent than I ever had before and indeed, I feel that one of the reasons I survived through that period and bounced back very strongly is because of the total patience and supportiveness of Maria, my wife. I don't know that I would have done it on my own.

That whole experience has made me much more aware of my own limitations. It's made me far more tolerant of other people's weaknesses and illnesses. It has made me more sensitive about trying to help people in the circumstances that I was in. It was also a time for reflection. One of the things I did in that first year when I couldn't do anything else was to write a book called *Being Pakeha*. I wrote it because I was an author, my living was from books and I had to come up with something I could do while I was flat on my back without actually going out and researching it, so I wrote a highly autobiographical book.

In the process I got to think about some fundamental things about myself, about my family background, and the culture I came out of. That was a salutary experience for me because I'm one of those people who doesn't tend to reflect on things as they affect me, unless I'm literally knocked down, because the momentum of your normal life is that you're moving too fast to stop and think. So I found that a fruitful thing to do.

I'm intrigued by the fact that this autobiography was entitled 'Being Pakeha'. What was the reason for this?

First of all, I should say it's not really an autobiography, although it's autobiographical. If I do get to write an autobiography it will be about things that weren't in that book. *Being Pakeha* was what I called an ethnic autobiography. It was about things in my background that gave me a sense of identity. It was about the ways in which I felt I belonged or didn't belong to New Zealand, or belonged or didn't belong to my culture of origin. That was the focus of it.

I chose the title *Being Pakeha* because it seemed to me to be a suitable label for the book and for myself. But it was also representative of the conclusion I'd worked my way through because the questions I had asked myself were, 'What am I? Who am I? Where do I come from?' So I looked at my cultural antecedents, the fact that six of my eight great-grandparents were Irish, the fact that my Irish grandmother and my mother were so pervasively influential on my life. Because they felt they were Irish, did I feel Irish? What were some of the things that we colonial Irish inherited along with our Catholicism?

I also looked at the effect of the Scottish influence, the English influence, the circumstances that had caused my grandparents to emigrate to New Zealand and what had happened here. To cut a long story short, the label that I felt best described what I had become was Pakeha. Because, although Ireland is on the whole my culture of origin, I'm not Irish. I'm not English, I'm not British, I'm not even European. I'm a couple of generations removed from Europe. I've been back to the United Kingdom, I've been to Europe. I like being there. I feel a sense of affinity with that part of the world but at no stage have I felt I belonged there. I don't want to be described as European. I don't want to be described as Caucasian – that's an odd and offensive expression because it came to us and to our law via the racist legislation of the southern states of the United States.

In the process of thinking all this through I was also thinking about appropriate labels to describe what I am and I liked the word Pakeha because it's an indigenous New Zealand expression to describe my people, the people who were originally British and who were originally European but who, over several generations of being in New Zealand, have evolved a slightly different kind of culture. They've refined the European ingredients, they've been influenced by the land, they've been influenced by Maori and the only word I can use now that accurately describes what I am and differentiates me from other people in other parts of the world is this word Pakeha.

I also wanted to emphasise what I and other New Zealanders of my background had become and what we were becoming. I think this process of being Pakeha is a continuing one and we will continue to differentiate ourselves from other cultures outside New Zealand. We're not all going to become Maori. I don't think that's likely, nor are all Maori going to become Pakeha. But I think that for a very long time we're going to have these two cultural streams in New Zealand, of which Maori is one and Pakeha is the other. All immigrants coming to New Zealand, no matter what their culture of origin, whether it was Vietnamese or Dutch or Samoan or whatever, they too are going to, in a large part of their lives, become part of mainstream Pakeha culture.

You've had a rather rough ride in some ways in more recent years about writing about things Maori. What's your feeling now about the criticism you've received, from some Maori anyway?

I was never really hurt by that criticism because it never came from Maori people with whom I have worked. Any work that I did in the Maori world, whether it was the *Tangata Whenua* television series or books like *Te Puea* or the book on Whina Cooper, I had always done with the full consent and, indeed, the active encouragement of the Maori people who were the sources for that work. Those people were never in any way critical of either my right to do it or the way in which it had been done.

What was happening was that there was a Maori cultural renaissance going on throughout this period and gathering momentum at that time. I think it's possible that the very books that I was publishing were adding to that momentum because they were being widely used by Maori as well as by Pakeha who wanted to understand what was going in the Maori world. Part of that renaissance was a feeling that Maori people wanted to take control of their lives and take control of their culture. They felt they were the proprietors of their culture, and that Maoridom was better served if Maori culture and history was written about by Maori authors.

I could understand that feeling. As the jargon goes, 'I could hear where they were coming from.' I didn't entirely accept the argument, in the sense that I didn't believe that a Maori scholar doing what I was doing would have done it any differently from the way I did it, because I was using Maori sources, Maori evidence, Maori criteria for the writing of history. But I understood it as part of this feeling of Maori wanting to get back in control of Maori things and for that reason I did largely step aside from that work. I also felt that when a certain amount of time had passed and when more Maori had got into this field and were writing themselves that Maori would feel less threatened by Pakeha being involved too. And this is what has happened over very recent years.

There are more Pakeha people writing Maori history than ever before. People like Judith Binney, Angela Ballara, James Belich. Most of the Maori entries in the *Dictionary of New Zealand Biography* were written by Pakeha authors, and I have not heard any outcry about that. I think the predominant thing to be aware of is that this represents a great deal of interest and respect on the part of Pakeha scholars for Maori history and Maori culture and that is a much healthier thing than the previous neglect that Maoridom had to live with up till the 1970s.

What is your opinion about where race relations have got to in New Zealand now? There still seems to be a lot of stereotyping on the part of both Maori and Pakeha. Is this something you see as a difficulty or something that can be got through?

The stereotyping is still there but it's diminishing. It will dissolve as Maori and Pakeha people have more contact with one another. I have never been particularly worried about this cultural encounter process that we've been going through. If you look at it in purely demographic terms it was inevitable.

Up until World War II Maori and Pakeha people were effectively separated from each other. We didn't have a system of apartheid but, because of geographical and demographic considerations, most Maori lived in rural communities made up largely of Maori. Most Pakeha people lived in urban communities made up largely of Pakeha. And right through the 1940s and 1950s most Pakeha people grew up in New Zealand without ever encountering or talking to Maori people, let alone having them as friends or neighbours or workmates.

I was interested to hear Jeanine Graham talking recently about her project about pioneer childhood in New Zealand. She had a large number of interviews with people brought up in the early twentieth century and the most common denominator in those Pakeha interviews was that most Pakeha children never ever met Maori in their childhood. That was simply the way things were. You couldn't expect both peoples to have an intimate appreciation of and understanding of each other. Through the 1940s and 1950s the Maori movement to the cities gathered momentum. Maori moved into the suburbs and into jobs in the cities and the inevitable consequence was that the existing lack of understanding became visible.

It became apparent in things like acts of prejudice on the part of Pakeha people in not allowing Maori to rent accommodation, not allowing Maori to use private bars in hotels, not allowing Maori to be in certain parts of hospitals and so on. And yet, even while this was happening, an awareness of it was largely concealed from the population at large, because it was not widely talked about. It was only in the late 1960s and early 1970s when Maori protest groups began to make a noise about these things that the extent of racial and cultural intolerance in New Zealand became apparent. Since that time we've been through a process of bringing all these things out into the open and trying to do something about them and perhaps the most spectacular mechanism by which this has been done has been through the Waitangi Tribunal, because this has aired all kinds of land claims that are not news to Maori, who have been talking about them for over 100 years in some cases, but they are news to many Pakeha who didn't know these things were going on.

When I've heard over the last ten years Pakeha people talk about deteriorating race relations, when I've heard them say things are not what they were, I am conscious of the fact that the world they're talking about was an unreal world. They simply didn't know these problems existed. They always did exist, either actually or potentially, but it's only been in the last twenty years that we've actually begun to address them and we're still addressing them.

I think that's an entirely healthy process and although it's meant that we've been through a period where race relations have been rough and tough and difficult and where angry words have been said across the racial and cultural frontiers, I nonetheless think that this will ultimately lead to these things being dealt with, and the hurts of the past being healed. I'm already aware that this is starting to happen.

I know far more Pakeha who are aware of Maori aspirations and Maori needs and Maori grievances than was the case twenty years ago. I also detect among Maori friends a feeling now that they have some optimism about the ability of New Zealand to deal with these problems. They feel that progress has been made, whereas many of those same people did not believe or feel that ten years ago. They didn't even believe or feel it five years ago. In spite of the difficulties, in spite of the noise and in spite of the anger, I think we're moving in the right direction and I think we're going to be a healthier and a more harmonious society, a bicultural society that works, as a result of all these things.

Back in 1989 you were asked to review the 1980s for a newspaper and you said rampant materialism had fuelled greed on the part of the haves and dependency and envy on the part of the have-nots. I wonder what you feel now as we are coming into the 1990s? Do you feel the same way?

Yes. I would probably state that with even more conviction now. It's one of the things that has disappointed me very much about the direction in which New Zealand has moved in the last decade. We now seem to be being asked to measure ourselves much more in economic and materialist terms. There's no doubt about the fact that the gap between haves and have-nots is widening. On the one hand we have people in certain occupations earning incomes of quite extraordinary magnitude by previous New Zealand standards, and on the other hand, the number of people who are unemployed or are on benefits is growing at an equally alarming rate.

We have government ministers who want to measure human worth, it would seem, by people's productivity and capacity to generate income. It seems to me symptomatic of a society that has adopted a mindset that is foreign to the kind of values that I grew up with. It's been loosely called 'monetarist' or 'free-market' or 'new right'. I think it's dangerous. It's a viewpoint that measures people's value by their ability to perform in material terms; it's a 'devil take the hindmost' kind of attitude.

I'm reminded of something that Rex Fairburn said about the free market: 'The free market is the freedom of the fox to get into the chicken coop without anybody intervening or interfering.' That's the kind of society I feel we're moving towards and it bothers me. I've always been a great believer in the basic tenets of the welfare state. Everyone has a right to certain securities; they don't have to earn it. They have that right purely by being born a citizen of New Zealand, and that right includes the right to work. It includes the right to an education, and it includes the right to a free health service.

I don't believe that those who are working and are in employment cannot support this basic entitlement. We're told now that the country can't afford it and can't support it. If that is the case it's only because of the nature of our expenditure on other things which are not, to me, as crucial as those basic functions. So I feel very much at the moment out of harmony and out of sympathy with government priorities in these matters. And I don't like the social consequences of these policies.

What do you think can be done about them?

Well, I think it's important that people who feel that New Zealand values are being violated make it clear that they feel this, make it clear in their discussions with other community groups, make it clear through the media and make it clear in their communications with politicians because ultimately the only thing that changes political policies is the belief that people are going to lose office. That belief ought to be communicated very sharply to those who are currently in government.

You've been a journalist, a teacher and a writer. I wonder how your see your role and the extent to which you might be called a prophet? I don't mean in the sense of prophesying the future but rather someone speaking out about society and the things you feel strongly about. To what extent has this been your role as you see it?

Well, I think of myself as being a writer rather than any specific kind of writer and I think that writers do have a role that goes beyond simply earning a living. I've always felt that the role of writers, whether they be journalists or historians or even writers of fiction, is to shine a torch in society's dark corners and let people know what's going on in their own communities, to draw attention to things that are not as they should be, or, to change the metaphor, to hold up a mirror to society. People ought not to be surprised and horrified at what's going on; they ought to know what's going on in their own communities and it's the role of writers, whether they be journalists or historians, to carry out this function.

You believe, it seems, that writers and other artists have a moral responsibility as part of the fulfilment of their potential and their role in society?

Yes. They have a responsibility to put people in touch with one another, to see that communities and societies are being communicative, internally as well as with other communities and societies. They also have a responsibility where there are dark and slimy things crawling round under stones to pull those stones back and have a look and see what they are. There's a great danger, I think, that people can be left unaware of their problems and without the mechanisms to discuss them and deal with them. That's the whole *raison d'être* behind things like public relations officers employed by government or government departments. Their purpose is to enact and carry out policies as smoothly as possible with as few disruptions as possible. But the role of the writer is completely contrary to that. It is disclosure in the public interest. That's something I've always believed in and still believe in.

This interview was first broadcast on National Radio on 28 January 1992.

Charmaine Pountney

Charmaine Pountney is one of New Zealand's best-known educators. She has often been in the public eye, particularly during her 10 years as principal of Auckland Girls' Grammar School.

In 1992, after a period as principal and dean at Waikato University's School of Education, Charmaine Pountney resigned. Her major involvement is now working with her partner, Tanya, on their eleven hectares of land at Awhitu on the shores of the Manukau Harbour, where they've planted trees and a garden and raise poultry.

She continues to be involved in education issues, however. To many, her ideas are innovative and exciting. Others see them as controversial, even dangerous.

Charmaine Pountney's educational beliefs come out of a strong belief in the human potential and what it means to be a woman in today's society, and a deep sense of spirituality.

CHARMAINE POUNTNEY: Ever since I was a child I've had a strong sense of the cosmos as a huge and exciting place, a strong sense of purpose within the cosmos, and a strong sense of the creativity, love and power that drives the universe forward. It is a very optimistic kind of spirituality.

I can remember times that have been really precious to me. They've been my transcendent moments, certainly my moments of being aware of dimensions beyond the merely human. For me, that's what spirituality is. It's about being fully human, which is acknowledging being merely human as well.

The first time was when I was about eleven years old on my grandfather's farm in the Waikato, standing on a gate and watching the sunset and having this extremely strong sense of how beautiful the world is and how important it is to be in harmony with the beauty of the world and somehow keep the ugliness and the bad things at bay. Also to work, to work in a way that makes the world more beautiful rather than more ugly. It was a really powerful sense of religious mission, if you like, for an eleven-year-old. I guess that's the theme that's kind of carried through my life.

I remember another occasion. It was the first time I was really in love, deeply in love and my friend and I were on top of Mount St John. We'd been having lunch together and just looking at the city on a beautiful summer's afternoon. I felt totally in tune with her and just feeling this love that I felt for this person was a really important powerful force. This is what drives the universe towards good goals rather than bad. It's what made me want to treat her with respect and with utter concern and consideration.

What makes me want the whole world to be good? It's a feeling of such power that I want to share. I want to share it in all the activities that I engage in. So it is a real sense of love as the creative force of the universe. I know everyone who's in love for the first time thinks their love is the spiritual force of the universe. But I don't think that should be discounted. I think that awareness that human beings have of the spirit, of a 'we' feeling as Doris Lessing would call it, is of enormous importance to us in forming our whole relationship with the world, not just our relationship with individual loved ones.

I guess a couple of other really powerful experiences for me were connected with education, not surprisingly – special experiences at Auckland Girls' Grammar School. I'm talking only about the positive experiences at this stage because they are the ones that have shaped my positive vision of the world. One of them was the opening of the whare wananga at our school, Ki Mangawhau, the new marae that was developed at Auckland Girls' Grammar in the mid-1980s. At the opening ceremony the head girl and I were asked to be the first two to walk in the door of the carved house. We'd had a prefab, we'd had a centre, we'd had an old building, but it had all been changed and built into a really creative centre for tangata whenua, a beautiful carved house for the girls of the school. The moment of walking through the door into that revitalised building, into that new centre of power in the school, was a really profound spiritual experience. It was about partnership, it was about Maori and Pakeha working together to claim the best of both our cultures and to walk forward into a new kind of world. It was a really moving time.

I suppose the other one of a similar kind, again at Auckland Girls', was the opening of the Centennial Hall and how we were able to raise a million dollars and build a beautiful tiered auditorium in a girls' school, a multi-racial girls' school with predominantly working-class people, in the heart of the city. That was a miracle and the girls and staff and families and friends of the school made that miracle happen. It was a women's miracle – not that men didn't help; we had strong support from many men, but it was a miracle that was led by women and supported by women and happened in a very woman's way. The day we walked into that hall for the first time, into that beautiful auditorium, we knew that we'd created again a new paradigm really, for young urban women. It was something that gave them dignity and recognition and a place to be proud of themselves, of who they are and where they are. The ceremony with which we opened the hall was a spiritual ceremony. It started with a traditional Maori blessing, moving through a Christian service into an open feminist blessing. It was a truly inclusive ritual that we had developed ourselves, that didn't alienate anyone and that included all the people who felt proud to be there.

Those were very exciting experiences, moments of recognition that what you're doing is not just for here and now. It isn't just for work or for fun. This is for a cosmic purpose. It's for the spiritual direction of the people that you're working with. It's signalling that it's possible for human beings to continue to learn, move in new ways together and develop a new respect for each other, new kinds of relationships, new kinds of women. That's what my time at Auckland Girls' taught me.

But of course it goes back much earlier in my own life. I've mentioned the importance of women and of loving women and of working with women. I think that my spiritual development has been very much about recognising the importance of women and the absolutely vital importance for the future of this planet in having a proper relationship between man and woman. I don't mean 'proper' as distinct from 'improper', I mean 'proper' in the sense of the 'necessity', the term that Doris Lessing uses, that we must have a good and whole and respectful relationship where both men and women treat each other as fully human. Not as less than human, not as children, not as animals, not as monsters, but as truly human equal beings. Unfortunately that sense of women as truly human equal beings is really rare in our culture – in most cultures as I observe at the moment. It seems to me that it's almost as though it's a phase that we have to go through as a species, of claiming the full humanity of both the male and the female of our species, and putting the two rather fragmented parts together, putting the fractured parts together properly.

What I remember from right back in my childhood is strong women. My mother was undoubtedly the most profound influence in my spiritual and intellectual development. She was a woman of great courage, vigour, passion and energy. She devoted herself to bringing me up, really, and in some ways trying to enable me to do all the things that she'd been deprived of and hadn't been able to do herself. She was a woman who thought deeply about intellectual issues. We talked about issues like creation and evolution when I was a little girl. She tried to help me to understand things like Santa Claus and the tooth fairy as myth and metaphor at a young age, so that I didn't ever go through those times of shock, of feeling that the adult world had betrayed me because these things weren't true. She taught me about different kinds of truths. She taught me how important it was to read and to discuss, to talk, to think and to affirm people and to listen to people. All of those things came from her example, from her own actions and talking to me about them.

I had a grandmother, too, my father's mother, who was an amazing old lady, a quite unusual and somewhat wicked old lady in lots of ways, very genteel and very elegant and extraordinarily able with language. She had a memory of phenomenal proportions. She memorised a great long rhyming poem about all the kings and queens of England. She knew all the books of the Bible, she knew all the wonders of the world. She had a mind – it was what E. M. Forster once referred to as 'a mind full of mental luggage', suitcases full of it, mostly unrelated facts that she played with, really. But even that was a fascinating experience - to meet a woman whose whole world was lived through her mind. Her husband had been killed at the Battle of the Somme and she lived for a whole generation on her own. She taught me French and Latin before I started school. She taught me to enjoy words, and to enjoy playing with words. She told stories; she was a woman who taught me a passionate interest, a life-long interest in language, along with my mother.

My father was a really profound influence, too. He was a churchman. He loved church music. I rather think he liked church music more than religion, as such, but he was a passionate churchgoer and sang in choirs with great devotion. So I grew up with music and church liturgy and mathematics, because he also had a passion for numbers and numerology. He was an unusual man, very uncharacteristic of his age. He had played rugby when he was young but he certainly wasn't anything like the stereotype of the New Zealand male.

I spent a lot of time with the three of them as an only child and as a much-loved adopted child. I spent an enormous time being given love and language by these three people and growing up with a very strong sense, not that women ruled the world, but that women simply were the world and men were alongside them. But that was quite the wrong way round from the way the rest of the world saw it, as I discovered as I got older. I mean, most of the rest of the world in the 1940s and 50s thought that men were the world and women were kind of appendages. Quite early on in my teenage years I discovered that it wasn't particularly popular for young women to have ideas and want to debate them, or to want to have rational arguments – not to win but to have rational arguments and debates and to explore ideas. It was quite unfashionable for teenage girls in the 1950s.

My mother warned me. She said, 'Now, Charmaine, you must remember that men have fragile egos and you should never argue too much with boys because they won't like it and it will upset them. To be popular with boys you simply have to keep you mouth shut.' I didn't, of course.

She didn't either, and most of the women that I most admired and loved as I grew up through primary school, and particularly at secondary school, were women who spoke, women who talked, women who identified issues. They were women who were intelligent and questioning. So, of course, it was quite natural for me to grow up loving women and finding men a bit difficult to fathom really and a little unexpected in their primitive behaviour at times.

Are they still difficult to fathom?

I think I understand a lot more now, partly from watching the rest of the world, particularly the humankind within universities and government departments, but also looking at what happens on the farm. I think a great deal of male behaviour that we don't like – and I think a lot of men don't like it, either – is pretty natural animal behaviour. If we see it in that light and in that context, then the question isn't how do you punish people or how do you stop them being like that, it is how do you help people to grow up, to become more human? I think for me the challenge for both men and women is how do we learn to be more human?

Can I just take up this concept of being human? For you it seems that being fully human – female human and male human – is almost the same as being spiritual, is it?

Yes. I don't think I could feel fully human unless I was also aware of my place in the world as a whole. I'm fully aware of philosophical debates about issues of meaning and meaninglessness and post-structuralism and post-modernism and all that stuff. But the reality for most humans is that we need to feel that we're making a difference.

One of the key things about being human is that all of us, no matter what our education, culture or background, are capable of imagining what is not, as well as of knowing what is. We live in this paradox of always being aware that something else is possible, even if it's something as simple as knowing that if I'd thrown the ball differently I might have hit the wicket, if one happens to be a sporting type. Or, if I'd planted the seed a bit more deeply it might have come up a bit later, or something of that kind.

The ability to say 'if only', the ability to imagine what isn't, and then to make it happen lies right at the very heart of our being human and that, to me, is cosmic. It's about being a creator or a destroyer – a destroyer is only a creator working in the opposite direction. It's recognising that whatever spiritual presences there may be in the universe, we are spiritual presences too. We are part of the actual shaping of the universe, whether we like it or not. We therefore have choices to make.

Some people would say we have no choices. I simply affirm the opposite, and I know that's purely opinion. But I affirm the belief that every human being chooses whether to make the world a better place, to make it a worse place, or to try to keep it much the way it is. Consciously, at some times in our lives, and unconsciously a lot of the time, we try to take that creative role, try to shape the world in a particular way, whether it's cleaning the car, or trying to change the whole political system.

So you are daring to say that we, every one of us, play a part in the universe; that we all have our own unique contribution to make as creative beings?

We do. And we either choose to do it consciously and well, or we do it unconsciously well, or we do it consciously badly or unconsciously badly. Frankly, my preference is to try to do it consciously well and to try to encourage as many other human beings as possible to do it consciously well. I believe it's part of our spiritual and physical and emotional evolution as a species.

I think back to some of the theologians I read during my days in the Student Christian Movement at university. I read voraciously the then popular theologians – Bultmann and Tillich, Harvey Cox and Martin Buber and in particular Teilhard de Chardin. Teilhard de Chardin moved me very deeply because he talked about the evolutionary process. He talked about the planet, about the actual, inanimate form and then the Biosphere, the sphere of life circling the planet, then the growing together, the coalescing of a kind of film of living organic matter around the surface of the planet. Then emerging from that, creatures, matters of creation and creative as well. And then the really exciting development of what he calls the Noosphere, the sphere of consciousness, of consciousness and knowledge.

We live at a time when that is so conspicuously happening in front of us. I mean Internet is the planetary consciousness – so is Compuserve, no doubt. The planetary networks of electronic communication have put every human being potentially in touch with every other human being on the surface of this planet. Even the most ardent creationist would not say that technology was delivered in boxes from above – it has actually been fabricated by human hands and human brains on the surface of this planet.

That development, that network of consciousness, is the phase of evolution that we are involved with now. It's a phase of immense importance because if we use that network of human consciousness for co-operative purposes and for creative purposes, I believe we can move this whole planet into a new phase of its existence, indeed this part of the cosmos in a new direction. We can actually move it towards a cosmic good rather than heading in a most appalling fashion towards cosmic evil, towards the complete destruction of this planetary experiment.

Education has been very much part of your life. It is your life in many ways. How did you get into education?

From the moment of my birth, I dare say. I was born at Bethany and I have no doubt that my birth mother, in the half an hour a day that she was allowed to hold me, communicated with me whatever anguish of spirit she was going through and whatever love and passion she felt. But I have no doubt that the Salvation Army staff also talked as they fed the children and communicated their concern and their affection for babies.

Charmaine Pountney

Certainly from the moment that I was taken home at three weeks of age by my adoptive mother and father I was talked to and had knowledge shared with me and was loved and was communicated with all day, every day. So I received that immersion in the experience of being human, of being communicated with, of being talked to, of being cared for, which is at the heart of learning. In fact, if you wanted to sum up education, care and communication would be the two key terms. That's been at the heart of my experience right from the moment of birth and is of absolutely paramount importance.

My mother always said that she would have loved to be a teacher but she grew up during the Depression and it was not possible for her. But she was a teacher; she was a teacher every minute of the time she spent with me. It wasn't always positive. I mean, there were times when she got quite twitchy about my piano practice and thought I was doing unnecessarily badly and spoke quite sharply about it, and then I got more nervous and made more mistakes. She would never claim that she'd been the perfect teacher, but she was an amazing teacher for all that.

I've just had this privilege all my life of spending it with teachers and with learners. Of course, I did go to kindergarten and to school and I went to schools that of their kind at the time were good. Mind you, when I look back on some of what I learned, at Remuera Intermediate for instance, as a foundation pupil going from Cornwall Park Primary School, I realise I learned very quickly about class consciousness. Because one of the things inherent in that school at the beginning was a ranking order of the contributing schools. Remuera Primary was at the top, Victoria Avenue next, Meadowbank third and Cornwall Park fourth. I was an also-ran. We knew that hierarchy in the class we were put in.

I also learned how teachers can destroy lives. My best friend at school died tragically when she was very young. She was my best friend right through to about sixth form level, but her life was ruined by a teacher who systematically put her down. So I learned about savagery in education, just as I had at Cornwall Park when we had an infant school teacher who used to hit kids with a three-foot ruler and chase them round the room if they spilt vases accidentally. It was absolutely terrifying. I was never so frightened in my life as in her class.

So there was a negative side to schools but, on the whole, schooling for me was a very positive experience. I loved school and I did well, of course. With all those verbal skills I'd been privileged to be given it's not surprising that I did very well in the schooling system. I coped very well with the playground, too. I was quite dominant, naturally dominant - small and quite tubby but verbally very dominant - so I didn't have problems with being bullied or anything like that - not past the age of about four anyway.

So, for me, schooling was a very satisfying experience. Schools were exciting places and I used to play with a doll and a blackboard at home and hit the dolls when they didn't learn what I told them to and things like that. But the whole thing of being immersed in an educational environment and finding it satisfying is what led me to become a teacher.

Of course, when I was a teenager in the 1950s girls were teachers, librarians or typists or nurses and those were the only choices. As I couldn't stand blood and I was too noisy for a library, teaching was obviously the one. I didn't like university much because it wasn't exciting. It wasn't about learning. It was about memorising and being given dreary lectures by appallingly bad lecturers and it was much easier to sit in the cafe and read the books for yourself and enjoy the conversation. I didn't do terribly well at university, I must say. But I did enjoy the informal side. I enjoyed the Student Christian Movement and the reading and the talking.

You've been critical of many aspects of education. I know this is an impossible generalisation, but to what extent do you think modern education encourages young people to be creative?

In the best of our schools, particularly in really good primary schools, there are amazing and wonderful things happening. There are children creating stories and plays and videos and new kinds of thinking. They are coming through school developing enormous creativity and thinking skill and memory as well as good grammar and good spelling – really high levels of education by everyone's standards: basics, fundamentals, and the extras as well. That's what our best primary schools are doing. But at worst, schools are appalling places of oppression, particularly for people from other than the dominant culture, very narrowly directed towards social control rather than education. In between that, of course, we've got everything, and most schools are a mixture.

Secondary schools, on the whole, are worse than primary schools. They're actually much more like primary schools in the 1920s and 1930s because they're bound by the social structures. It's not because secondary school teachers are somehow inferior to primary, they're not. Many of them are superb people. But the secondary school has thrust upon it by society a social filtering role and a social rationing role that used to be thrust on primary schools when most people left at the end of Form Two. And that is still being thrust on secondary schools, even though it's now ridiculous for people to be thinking of leaving education at the end of secondary school.

Our secondary system is stuck in a time-warp and I blame politicians over the last twenty years for that – up until, I have to say, Lockwood Smith. I'm sure Lockwood would be surprised to hear me speaking with such warmth about him, but he has at least listened to what many educators have been saying for more than twenty years about the national examination structure – that you cannot afford to have an examination system based on an obsolete belief that only some people are capable of learning. Our whole secondary system has been based on that and before that, the primary school system was as well. There are still primary schools that assume this.

The belief is that human intelligence falls into a normal distribution curve – that a few people are very bright, a few people are really thick and the majority are kind of average, clumped around the middle. Now, that curve of distribution is a curve of random distribution. It's what happens when chance factors operate. That's the curve that is the distribution of height to, say, the population, or of weight or hair length or all sorts of factors. It's the distribution you get if you throw packs of cards down stairwells. But that shouldn't be the distribution you get from a consciously planned social activity. You intervene to create planned outcomes, not random outcomes.

I had this brilliant flash of revelation once in my office at Auckland Girls'. I was sitting there thinking about the School Certificate examination and I thought, there's something wrong with what we're doing. We've got this wonderful scaling system to make sure that bright students get good marks in all their subjects and dumb students get bad marks and average students get average marks, provided they perform reasonably equally across the areas. And it suddenly hit me! Why? Who says these people are bright, average or dumb? *We* do. We're actually constructing the system that makes them that way. We are perpetuating in our system an outmoded belief about people because the reality is that the human mind does not have to be subject to chance. We can change the way human minds function and we can plan for a population where all people achieve excellent educational outcomes.

A lot of the debate about education is not actually about learning or about knowledge. It's about rationing. It's about what can we afford in society. What we can pay for. What we can't pay for. How we set up standards so that only the bright people get through them or over them. How we put up a hurdle so that only the right number of people go on to the next jump. And debate gets very confused because a lot of the time people think they're talking about educational standards when they're really talking about where to put the hurdles and how high they should be. At other times people are talking about educational outcomes when they really mean social-control outcomes.

Unless we spend time on these issues and really unravel them and talk about them in an uncluttered and unemotional way, then we tend to get hooked into very simplistic, polarised thinking, such as external exams versus internal assessment, equity versus excellence, gender issues and social engineering versus 'back to basics'.

None of those should be in opposition to each other. People say 'competition versus co-operation', but it shouldn't be one thing versus the other.

The questions we should be asking are, 'How do we combine the best of these issues? How do we actually make sure all these things are important?' So that, for example, we have a national system of evaluation that uses external tests where those are appropriate, school-based assessment where that is appropriate, practical or written examinations where they are appropriate.

It's much like issues of cultural diversity. Instead of saying Maori versus Pakeha, we have to develop a kind of society that says Maori *and* Pakeha. Let's look at the best of Maori and Pakeha cultural practice, support Maori and Pakeha people to do their own thing in the most creative way, so that our society is enriched by both cultures. Not trying to make people pick and choose between them or saying one's better than the other. Finding out the best of both. It's a major issue in all our thinking, obviously, but in education we're particularly prone to dumping polarities into the argument and then thinking we've said something when we haven't at all.

You're saying that everybody can learn. Can they learn all of their lives?

Yes. I'm saying that everyone can learn far more than we're learning at present, far more effectively and for far longer. And that the majority of children who go into our education system should come out at the end with the high level of skills and knowledge and personal behaviour and emotional stability that the best of our students come out with now. We actually know how to produce that outcome. We have all the knowledge that would enable us in New Zealand to have a system of education – and notice I'm not just talking about schools, but a system of education, a planned series of opportunities for learning - that would enable every young person to emerge from that system at age sixteen or seventeen, as a really exciting, well-balanced, sensitive, interesting, knowledgeable, talented and skilled young person. That's what the best of our young people are now. Quite amazing young people.

Why doesn't it happen?

Because we're not applying the knowledge that we have. It's the story of our lives, isn't it? That human beings have all this knowledge and don't apply it. So much of our education is actually about teaching people to control other people or be controlled by them rather than to understand them. We also know about things like the way structures impede learning. The way racism and sexism embedded in the structures of our society exclude people. We know, for example, that if you want to teach mathematics just to girls or to Maori students you don't teach them a different mathematics. You don't teach them some watered-down version. But you do relate the mathematics to their experience. You encourage the students to bring with them their knowledge and experience in order to build upon it and extend it. We know how to do those things. There are tomes written about it. There are films made. There are libraries full of books on how to teach effectively and how to construct groups and institutions that organise for effective learning.

Why doesn't it happen? Well, that is a more complex question. It has a lot to do with people's fear of change. It has a lot to do with people who have power being reluctant to share it because somehow they feel that if they share it they'll lose something, whereas in fact the reverse is true. For instance my own example: by giving up a position of authority so-called, a position of power so-called in the school and in the university, I've given myself a whole new dimension of real power to do things that I didn't have when I was in charge. This is the kind of message for people in positions of power.

Have you dropped out now?

Well, no. I'd say I've dropped right in it, frankly. The whole thing about being in a position of so-called power over others is that you can do nothing creative at all from that position. You cannot make change of a creative kind happen from the top down, and that's what's wrong with the old pictures of God on high on a cloud firing thunderbolts and making people do things. It never worked. Otherwise we'd all be perfect by now, wouldn't we? We'd be terrified into it. Or we'd have learned the commandments off by heart.

The reality is that people can only learn to be good, they cannot be compelled to be good. They can only learn to create. They cannot be compelled to create. So that the higher, the nearer you are to the top of the hierarchy, the less you can do to make people creative. The one power you do have in those positions is that you can push obstacles out of the way, and you can certainly enthuse and inspire, but you cannot make anyone do anything good. It always comes from the flax roots and the grassroots upwards. That's where the plant grows from. It doesn't grow from the sky down.

I know about plants these days. I'm not just speaking figuratively, because my partner, Tanya, has planted more than 2000 trees in the last two years and that is a reality – that things grow from the soil upwards, not from the sky downwards. So one of the things about being in the position of power is that the most important thing you can do is get out of it. While you're in it, use it to get obstacles out of the way and resources to the people who are creative and to the people who are doing good things. You can shove the resources around and you can shove away the obstacles, but you will never make anyone better. Once you get out of a position of

125

power, you can become creative yourself again. You can actually learn to do things differently and you can shape new structures yourself.

What has your dropping in, as you call it, given to you personally? This change to your life?

Well, in a very real way, I wake every day 'surprised by joy', to use C. S. Lewis's term. I wake with such a sense of might and privilege and such a sense of being, spiritually as well as intellectually and physically, of being involved in doing what is precious to me and helpful to others. I wake with Tanya, and that's a source of great joy to me. I am here with a woman I love and someone I can spend the rest of my life with. We are proud of our loving relationship and the equality in it, and I'm moved by that. I wake up and I look out the window and there are rainbows almost every morning, and in the afternoon, when I look out the other side of the house, there are rainbows over the ocean. In the course of the day I do things that are healing to the land and helpful to people, in a much more real sense, I think, than I've done for years.

I'd like to think that what I've done in educational institutions has been, on the whole, positive and creative and supportive of people, and kind and loving. I know that's true because that's what people have taught me and that's what I share with them. I know that in the years at Auckland Girls' Grammar there was a real sense of love pervading the whole school, a sense of love at the heart of the human spirit, and a sense of the power of the human spirit to rise above all kinds of pain and anguish and terrible experiences. We saw the way in which a good community of that kind, of loving women, can take young women who have been battered beyond belief by the evils of this world and help them to become whole again. We saw that happening and we were able to contribute to it, so I know that a lot of what we did was of value.

But being now in a rural community and working on the land, there's a sense in which we're even closer to putting into practice the things that for an educator are often more theoretical than practical. The further up the hierarchies you get and the more meetings you go to, the more theoretical it becomes and the less you're doing it.

Tanya and I together see the importance of the relationship with tangata whenua, for instance. Not as some theoretical issue of biculturalism but as a practical challenge to us every day as to how can we most usefully form a decent working relationship with the people whose land this was and who have had it taken from them and who are now struggling to survive. How can we best work decently and respectfully with these people? How can we help our neighbours whose lives have been full of trauma and chaos? How can we help them to heal and to grow strong in themselves again? How can we help to heal feuds in the neighbourhood? How can we contribute to healing the land?

That is of vital importance to us. Because if we can't heal the land we live on and the relationships with people we live with, we might as well blow the planet up now and be done with it, mightn't we? So we are here planting trees, trying to avoid using chemical poisons, trying to balance the realistic limits of energy and time against the challenges of spreading asparagus weed and multiplying gorse. Where do you draw the line? How do you try with each choice to contribute to the healing and the betterment of the planet, rather than to its degradation and further destruction?

Those are real questions for us every moment of every day, and certainly they're real in every educational institution. But it's much easier in an institution to forget them for a while and just look at the timetable and the budget and get sidetracked into the maintenance of the institution as an end in itself. If you're a dean or a principal it's your obligation to spend a lot of your energy on that. Now, I have the greatest respect for people who do that well, because I know how hard it is from the inside, but I don't want to put my energies into that now and neither does Tanya. She's done the same thing in Social Welfare. We want to work again at that really important level where people live their everyday lives, ordinary people doing farming and working in factories and unemployed people. They're the ones outside the institutions.

Not many people spend all their lives in institutions – only long-term criminals and long-term teachers, basically, and some doctors and judges perhaps. Most people live their real lives in paddocks and garages and houses and factories, so working with people at that level is of vital importance to us. Because if we can't get it right at that level what use is all this education? And what use is all this spirituality and theology? So we are involved in putting it into practice. That's what spirituality is about for us at the moment, from day to day, but also keeping in mind the planet as a whole and the wider cosmos within which our planet revolves.

There have been darker parts of your life that were growth-making experiences.

Yes. There is no growth without pain. When I've been feeling pain in the most anguished way, for instance at the death of a relationship or the physical death of someone that's dear to me, I keep remembering the dead leaves falling off the trees in winter and the new buds and keep thinking how painful it must be for that bud to push out of the stem and the branch. Certainly, for me, there have been times of great anguish. Like my father's illness and death. He had been a good man all his life, devoted to the church, but to watch how church members fell away and did nothing to support him or to support us during a really sad and difficult time, his last three months, that was what put me off churches for a long time. I still am fairly off churches on the whole, although not off religion.

Other times, in the schools I've worked in, there have been times when the lives of children have been very full of pain, particularly at Auckland Girls' Grammar. I think of what happened to us in the 1980s. We had some particularly outstanding women in the guidance area and in the deans' network and so on. The girls trusted those women and began to talk to them about what was really happening in their lives. Long before the whole issue of sexual abuse came to the surface we were trying to deal with these appalling situations that were real for the young women in our care. We were trying to help them develop ways of taking their own power and dealing with the situations themselves, trying to challenge them, trying to help them to deal with drunkenness and physical abuse and sexual violence of the most unspeakable kind.

I can remember a young woman who was sent to us – it was the fourteenth school she had been to within a year – because she was so violent and so disruptive. It was eventually found out that she had been physically and sexually abused by both her parents and all their friends from the time she was born till the time she was fourteen. She was damaged beyond belief.

I can also remember situations where young people and their families were abused by institutions. There was an occasion when our deputy head girl, a wonderful young woman, had three brothers who were absolutely outside the law and doing unspeakable things. One of her brothers died in jail of a heroin overdose. Another brother was in jail on remand, not even found guilty of anything at that stage. He wasn't allowed out for the tangi and the school staff came back from the funeral absolutely ropeable because this young man, who was allowed to be a pallbearer at his brother's funeral, had remained handcuffed to a detective as they carried the coffin up the aisle of the church.

Unbelievably cruel things like that happened day after day to the girls in our school and the women on the staff. Many of them, too, had tragedies. So we had to share that pain in order to support each other. You can't teach children if they're suffering. You can't expect young women to sit down and do spelling lists if they've been abused by a drunken father the night before and have come to school without food. You have to deal with the needs of the people. You have to make them whole before they can learn something new. Before they even want to learn anything.

So we had to find ways of dealing with that pain and that anguish and, of course, it was dealing with that pain that enabled us to focus on the political structures that perpetuate those problems – on the profits that the liquor industry makes from cynically encouraging drinking in particular sectors of society, by continuing to have advertisements associated with pictures of male violence and then putting a few dollars a year into alcohol support programmes and anti-abuse programmes. We had to analyse the structure. We had to name the evils and the systems in order to help young women cope with them and to take charge of their lives.

In my own life dealing with relationships has been really painful for me. I've always found it really hard to cope with being left by someone, with change in relationships. I've been through times of enormous pain, quite irrational and neurotic pain really, and I've had to seek a lot of help to deal with that, to learn to heal in myself the grieving and the causes of that grieving that have caused my reactions to be out of proportion and inappropriate. I've had issues with alcohol myself and had to deal with those issues. In the process of dealing with those issues I have learned to identify with alcoholics, drug abusers, addicts of all kinds and to identify addictive patterns in my own behaviour.

All of us have those challenges of different kinds and, to me, the sad thing is that so many people go through their whole lives caught in problems of that kind, unable to get out of them, trapped in those problems because there is no one to help them do the learning that would set them free. Because there is no doubt that one can learn to be free. One can learn not to be addicted to alcohol. One can learn not to be possessive in relationships. One can learn positively to rejoice in one's health and one's freedom. They are learned skills, they're not something magical that happens from outside.

Becoming principal at Auckland Girls' Grammar was one of the major turning points in your life, wasn't it?

Oh, absolutely. I entered a new world. Up until then I'd taught only in co-educational schools and worked in co-educational institutions. Suddenly I found myself having to face the reality of women's lives, the reality of the pain of so many women's lives, the utter anguish that so many women experience through abusive behaviour around them, through violence and physical and sexual abuse, through exclusion from areas where they want to be involved, through being treated as children and treated as animals and just treated as things that don't matter. If you go to Auckland Girls' Grammar you walk along Karangahape Road and see women's bodies displayed on billboards like slices of cheese. Our society is a very demeaning and degrading environment for women, even in dairies, with *Penthouse* magazines on display.

Women are treated like things, but in a girls' school that is not so. Women are people. So you have the opportunity to see the contrast between the real world and what is an artificial community but a much healthier one. I mean, people often say single-sex schools are unhealthy. That may be true of boys' schools. But girls' schools, far from being unhealthy, are much healthier for young women than the society we live in at present. If we lived in a healthy society maybe that would be a different story. But, at the moment girls are safer, they're happier and they're much stronger in girls' schools on the whole than they can be easily in co-ed schools. In the best of co-educational schools staff try to create a climate where that's true, too, but it's much harder when you have a lot of adolescents cooped up together, with the macho and female images they bring with them and the pressures of the society around them.

What changed for you personally when you went to Auckland Girls' Grammar?

Well, first of all, my perceptions of what was true. I really thought, until I went there, that women could do anything they liked and I found out in the cruellest ways that women can't do anything they like. Many women are totally constrained by their circumstances. The circumstances have to be changed and the structures have to be changed, so it was my political awakening as much as anything. And, of course, it coincided with the women's movement in New Zealand, or at least the second wave of feminism. I started at Auckland Girls' in September 1978. In the Easter of 1979 I went to the United Women's Convention, where I was supposed to be co-ordinating a workshop on education. Three things happened for me there. One was that the people who came to the workshop all knew a great deal more about the limits of education and the political parameters of education than I did. They were far further ahead in their thinking, so I was quite seriously challenged at that workshop.

On a much broader level, however, I was absolutely stunned by the challenges that were thrown to the 5000 women present on the issues of racism, sexism and homophobia. We were challenged by Maori women, particularly Ripeka Evans and Donna Awatere and a group with them, to recognise the fact that the conference itself was a profoundly racist experience. In fact, structurally, it was for middle-class white women. There was nothing in it that welcomed Maori women or involved them, or even acknowledged their existence in any serious way. That was the first time I'd heard that challenge or the term 'structural racism'. The issues of sexism were, of course, widely debated at the conference and straight away, as soon as the challenge of racism was made in that setting, we had to see the links. We had to see that we were dealing with parallel forms of oppression.

The third thing at that conference was the presence of a large number of visible lesbian women and a speaker challenged heterosexual women to look at the ways in which they oppressed lesbian women; at the ways in which society used the label 'sexual deviant' to try to destroy women's strength, women's independence and women's solidarity; and the way the label 'lesbian' used by a critic meant something deviant and nasty, and was actually an excuse for avoiding the way in which strong and loving women could challenge the patriarchy.

One of the reasons the label 'lesbian' is often used so ferociously is because the people using it see very clearly that strong, independent and loving women are a threat to patriarchal society. They're a threat to the very way our society is organised. We are a threat because the way our present society is organised is sexually hostile to women, to children, to people of colour. It's a profoundly unpleasant society and it ought to be changed. When lesbian women challenge it they are behaving in ways that are perceived as unpleasant by those who like the status quo, but they're doing an essential social service by challenging those structures.

'Radical feminist' is a label that's thrown around a lot. Would you consider yourself to be a radical feminist?

Well, I would like to be, but I'm not at all sure that I really qualify. 'Radical' in the sense of wanting to go to the heart of things, to understand the roots of oppression and the origins and causes of oppression and to change those things, yes, I would like to become radical. I'm certainly a feminist in the sense that I believe passionately in the need to enhance the lives of women and to give recognition to the full humanity of women. So yes, I would be proud to be called a radical feminist. I think there are many who are much more radical, and certainly many much more active feminists than I've ever been. My energies have gone mainly into the education system and into changing schools and institutions, which inevitably has meant a lot of my energy has gone into men and into a broader range of issues, if you like. There's nothing broader than women's issues. But the point is that I have not put into the women's movement the kind of energy and focus that a lot of women have. So I don't actually feel entitled to use the label 'radical feminist' in that sense.

One of the things about being a woman who loves women, a lesbian, I guess, is that you give away motherhood, which is supposed to be every woman's fulfilment. What do you feel about that? Do you miss out on something in this way?

Well, of course many lesbian women are mothers and many lesbian women become mothers from choice, whether with the use of modern birth technology or because they have a male partner who they choose to make a baby with. But, on the other hand, many lesbian women do remain single and childless. For me, it's never been an issue. I've never felt a profound need to be a mother. I suppose it's partly because my work has involved so much mothering that, in a very real sense, that nurturing side which all or most women are brought up to have in our society, and which may have biological origins, has been fulfilled very much through work. A lot of the time in school you have to mother lots of students. Teenagers need lots of mothering and so do the staff, often, too. I guess, for me, that nurturing role has been fulfilled through teaching and I think that's true for a lot of lesbian women. There are many ways to lead a fulfilling life besides being a wife and mother, or a husband and father.

Women don't have to be 'just mothers' either, do they?

Exactly. That's right. Many women can find satisfaction in totally centring themselves in family care and that's fine. If women find that a really satisfying life, well, good on them. Some other women find it totally unsatisfying and don't want to have a bar of it and find total satisfaction in being an aeronautics engineer. Many other women are in between and like a mixture of nurturing and family life and professional or work life. In all of this what we all have in common is the need to have our skills and our contributions valued. All of us live with the reality that women's skills and values and knowledge are less valued in our society than men's. And that's an imbalance that needs correcting.

I look forward to the day, for example, where instead of people losing seniority by taking parenting leave, it becomes one of the criteria for promotion, that you have to take a period of time for caring services, whether it be for children or old people or ill people or whatever. A period out working in the community in a caring capacity would be seen as an advantage for promotional purposes. It would be seen as adding to and enriching your experience, because it does.

There's no question about it. You only have to look at the calibre of women who come into any occupation, and the calibre of men too, who come into any occupation from a background in family or caring experience, which is becoming more and more common. You realise that you're dealing with a far richer variety of human being than ones who've been just one thing or another.

One of the things you mentioned to me earlier was a quotation I made once about using our 'head, heart and hands'. It's very real to me now that you cannot be human unless you exercise all three of those capacities: the capacity for practical action, and for feeling and nurturing and caring for others, and for intellect, an intellectual striving and aspiration. Unless you have all of those in balance, at least for some of your life, then it's really hard to be a whole person. Obviously you can't keep them all in balance all of the time, or at least it would be difficult. Even balance has to be balanced, I sometimes think. But you do need all of these aspects to develop fully.

You've been closely identified with the fight against racism. Why is that?

Partly because through working at Auckland Girls' Grammar I saw at first hand the pain that racism causes. Also, because I've been challenged so many times to look at the waste that's caused by racism. Any society that has structures that operate to disempower or exclude significant proportions of its population is crazy. It's obscenely wasteful. And I look at a whole generation of young Maori people who have been excluded from the opportunity to earn a living because of the total racism of our society's economic and educational system. Because it's the economic structures and the educational structures together that have excluded such a high proportion of young Maori people, far higher than the proportion of young Pakeha people excluded.

I've seen how it happens and why. We had a wonderful young Indian woman go down to an interview for a job in a chemist shop in Queen Street and she was told that the job had been filled. A young Pakeha woman from the same school walked in 20 minutes later and was welcomed with open arms. I mean, racism is alive and well on every level in our society. There is personal discrimination of a vicious kind through to structural exclusion of a vicious kind and until we face that reality we won't deal with it. You can't heal a sickness until you acknowledge that you've got it. Well, we've got it in a bad way but we are beginning to face it and we are beginning to deal with it. It's like other human rules – we are capable of learning to grow out of it.

What are your priorities now?

We've moved onto an area of land and we are involved in communication and partnership. Those are our priorities. Healing the land and healing people. That's what we are committed to long term and that involves healing, creating and developing. This is where I become speechless and tongue-tied, because we can't make any grandiose claims for what we're doing. We're just trying to put what we believe into practice, so putting theory into practice is perhaps the best way of describing it.

This interview was first broadcast on National Radio in two parts, on 5 and 12 July 1994.

Ian Cross

*Broadcaster, journalist, novelist and former bureaucrat Ian Cross gained his
early education in small country schools (he was the only pupil in Forms One
and Two). He then went to Wanganui Technical College where, he says, the
only thing he was good at was English.*

*With no formal educational qualifications Ian Cross ended up as a copy boy
on Wellington's 'Dominion' newspaper.*

IAN CROSS: For the next few years I lived and worked in Wellington, until at the
age of about twenty-one or twenty-two I made my first journey overseas, to Panama.
I was heading for Brazil but never got there.

*I understand you hit the newspaper headlines as a gun-runner in Panama! How true was
that?*

Not really true at all. I was working with another young New Zealander on a banana
plantation on the border of Panama and Costa Rica. New Zealander Edward Scott,
a columnist on the *Panama American*, a Spanish/English newspaper in Panama City,
told us there were jobs on the newspaper. So we both resumed our journalistic
careers.

This was at a time of great revolutionary upheaval in Panama. A presidential
campaign was being run in a typically Latin American way. There was a lot of
chicanery going on, and the newspaper was the centre of one wing or faction of the
presidential campaign. It was owned by the Arias, a very influential family in Panama,
and it was subjected to a great deal of harassment. We spent a few nights in the
office (I'll never forget this, really) with a Czechoslovakian who, I believe, had been
a member of the Afrika Corps. We were armed and our job was to defend the
newspaper.

In the revolution, or the minor revolutionary coup, some guns were brought
into Panama and it is true we had a little bit to do with bringing them in and ensuring
that they were in the right place. But we did this in complete innocence. Naive as
we were, we were infuriated that our newspaper was being subjected to this kind of
treatment. So we just looked upon it as a sort of partisan act on our part to defend
our newspaper.

It ended up pretty disastrously. I left Panama on a cattle-boat with a couple of
Americans and my New Zealand friend went to Costa Rica and ended up briefly in
custody there until he was smuggled out to the coast and up to North America. We

simply got caught up in the turmoil of Latin American politics. This was in the middle of '48 or '49 and we just did our best to keep afloat and do what had to be done to survive.

You didn't fire a shot in anger?

Oh no, not at all. I'd have fled from a shot in anger. If that building had been attacked I hate to think what might have happened. That would have been another change of direction in my life because who knows what disaster would have occurred.

Did this experience contribute to the way you look at things?

It did indeed. Thereafter I became a convinced defender of western democracy, having seen the abuses of power, and what can happen to a people under the threat of terror. I remember coming across the body of a man in the street, not far from our newspaper. He had been shot by armed police and his body was in the gutter. Nobody touched the body until nightfall because they were afraid that if they did they would be identified as being his friends or supporters.

It was that kind of experience – the experience, I suppose, of lawlessness, the lack of order, the lack of discipline in society, the lack of tolerance – that convinced me of the worth of New Zealand's form of democracy. I recognised the value of its relaxed view, the way in which it is open to differing views, and this has remained with me all my life. I suppose some people would say it has made me a conservative, because when I came back to New Zealand many of my friends were embracing not so much communism as the idea of the Soviet Union as a model state. But I detested the idea of dictatorships. I detested anything that wasn't democratic, that wasn't open, that didn't allow the free expression of opinion without some action by the state or partisan action by people who opposed your views.

I've always been in favour of the openness of viewpoints and the expression of those viewpoints tolerantly and emphatically without any counter by another faction in society. So, although I despised communism, I never objected to the expression of communist beliefs. This meant that for many years I was seen as being out of touch with many of my intellectual contemporaries. I was sometimes seen as a reactionary, which I wasn't. Well, I suppose I was, in a way. I was reacting against something that I saw as a threat to our way of life.

I guess being a journalist is another way of keeping the channels of communication open, isn't it? Is this one of your drives?

Yes. I've always believed that possession of facts (not opinions), and a knowledge of the nature of the society around you, the workings of that society and the contemporary outcome of those workings, is essential to being a citizen of a democracy.

Journalism is the channel for the free flow of good information, and I was almost religious about it for many years. It seemed to me to be the most important factor in the health of society, at least equal to the intellectual and spiritual channels of communication within that society. I suppose most of my life I've believed that and I've always been distressed by what I've seen as the impure form of journalism. By that I mean journalism that gives people an incomplete view of the facts or inaccurate facts or a skewed or distorted account of what is occurring in their society. I think good journalists should be always be aware of the danger of that form of use of the journalistic channel of communication. The good journalist must regard himself or herself as the guardian of the integrity of their trade or profession because without that integrity, without that dedication to truth, facts, things known to be true, the whole business can fall not only lower in public estimation but occasionally into disrepute.

I suppose over the years that's made me a critic of journalism, whereas really I've seen myself as an evangelical guardian of the fundamental basis for the existence of journalism in a western society.

One journalist I've interviewed described journalism as 'God's work'. Would you go that far?

Well, I can actually remember – and note that I had a Catholic boyhood – when I was only nineteen or twenty sitting in a tram in Wellington and suddenly feeling that I was fulfilling almost a religious vocation in society and feeling elated about it. I didn't regard myself as a religious person. By then I had drifted away from institutional religion, but I must confess religiosity has been an element in my character. Perhaps it's frustrated religiosity, I don't know.

You grew up as a Catholic, didn't you?

Yes. I was taught by nuns, simple women I suppose by today's standards, but they taught me the difference between good or evil, or the fact that good and evil existed. I suppose a permanent inheritance for me from those very early years has been a complete acceptance of the doctrine of original sin. I still believe it's the only doctrine that accounts for, or makes it possible for you to live with the conflicting elements of human beings – the element of baseness as against the element of virtue, I suppose; the capacity for good and the capacity for evil that exists in us all. The nuns taught me that life had to be, in part, a continual struggle against what is bad in man's nature and an attempt always to fulfil the good. I suppose that might explain the

Ian Cross

religiosity in me. But I've always remembered that teaching with great affection and it's stayed with me all my life.

Do you have a doctrine of salvation as well? Is it possible to be saved from the sin that we may have had originally?

I don't believe in final salvation. I believe in temporary salvation, that if you hold the balance right and commit yourself to the good side of your nature that is a kind of temporary salvation. But I don't think there's any final salvation. I think the capacity for evil, to use that word, is always there and sometimes there are circumstances that can bring it to the surface. I suppose we see that in the behaviour of various people and various nations and different ethnic groupings. Some circumstances can bring out what those dear nuns would call the devil in us.

You have said, I think, that you have some reservations about the church as an institution, or institutional Christianity.

Well, I think maybe it comes to some extent from my personal background. I had a solitary boyhood in many ways and, because of that and the fact that I am largely self-educated, I have a mind of my own. To some extent I find it difficult to be part of a group or to be told what I should believe and the form in which that belief should be expressed. That takes me outside the church. And it took me outside when I was quite young, when I was starting to feel impulses to go in directions that weren't preordained.

I've always remembered the opening section of a book by D. H. Lawrence. It hit with me a considerable force and seemed for four or five years at least to be almost my credo. I can still remember the words: '… comes over one an absolute desire to move and, what is more, to move in some particular direction. A double necessity, then, to get on the move and to know whither.' I think that, in part, explains why I left the church, although I value religion in society. I also value the existence of denominations in society.

I value the belief in God, although my explanation of God is that vast complex of forces that bear down upon the individual that he or she can't hope to understand in thousands of years. In other words, a huge mystery of life itself. I accept that. I surrender to it and call it God. So I value the spiritual life of the community and I value the existence of its institutional framework, but I'm not part of it. I have a more personal and, perhaps some would say, isolated view of spiritual expression.

You have, I think, a desire to serve, to work for others. I think there's a 'do-gooder' in you. I know this word is often used in a derogatory way and I don't mean it in that way. There is a desire in you to 'do good', which stems to some extent from your early religious attitude. Would you agree with that?

Yes, I would agree with that. I don't claim any personal value for wanting to express that desire. It's something you must do or feel you must do, and in doing it you gain a sense of satisfaction that you don't otherwise achieve. In some ways in turning to write fiction I've detected in myself, I suppose, something of the same desire to explain, or to put into some sort of order or give an explanation for the seeming chaos and disorder of life around us, not just for myself but for other people. You know, to try to give it a meaning, and to that extent I suppose I'm only partly a fiction writer; I'm more a striver after an explanation.

I seem to remember reading that when you went from being a public relations man for Feltex to editor of the 'Listener' one of the temptations or things that attracted you to that job was the fact that you might be able to do some good. This was at some personal cost to you, which sounds either Catholic or puritanical.

Yes, I think it was. First of all, the main attraction was to get back to journalism and, what's more, to get back to journalism in a capacity that would allow me to express my own view of what journalism could achieve in New Zealand.

What was the cost, then?

The cost, which actually rather pleased me, was that I dropped maybe four or five thousand dollars in salary. I was pleased in the sense that it had no effect on me. It didn't influence me at all. You know, you make these tiny little discoveries about yourself, and sometimes they are discoveries that displease you but other discoveries please you, and this one did.

When I was considering taking the job there was a premature publication of the fact that I was on the short-list. A senior executive of Feltex wrote down and pushed across the table what I'd lose in my company superannuation and it was a very substantial figure. But I didn't care! I was genuinely pleased that I didn't care.

I don't think these are rational or deliberate reactions. They just simply happen to you: both the good and the bad in your reactions. They come from a source that is not deliberate or calculated.

It's part of the discovery of who you really are, isn't it? Or rediscovery, perhaps?

It is. I was very happy at the *Listener*. Perhaps I should have stayed there. I had certainly made the right decision in going there.

Later on a different form of that same reaction overtook me when I was asked to become chairman of the Broadcasting Corporation. It was both radio and television in those days. I was reluctant to leave the *Listener*, but given what I felt about the value of communication, and my belief in the creative contribution of communication within a democracy, I thought I could do some good. I'm not sure that I did, frankly. I tried. I suppose that's something. But it was the one battle I was constantly losing.

There were forces far greater than my personal position – not calculated forces, but almost natural forces. Economic, structural, political, the whole tide was moving against public broadcasting, against what I believe was the role of public broadcasting. In other words it was the advent of commercialism. To some extent I tried to ride it. I tried to go with it and control it. But I failed. In retrospect I can see that instead of trying to go with it and control it, keep it in harness and direct it towards the proper role of broadcasting, perhaps I should have drawn a line and said, 'Look, to hell with this. It's not going to happen! There will be no co-operation from me,' and tried to convince the board and executives to fight the good fight. I don't think it would have worked but I've often wondered what would have happened if I'd adopted that line.

Was there some conservatism in you, perhaps, that made you take a more moderate line?

No. You remember I had worked with a large company, Feltex, and had been trained by the Harvard School of Management. I did recognise the economic imperatives. I did recognise certain inefficiencies within the corporate structure. I did recognise that, unless there was an inflow of money into the system the system itself would decline.

The government had no intention of doing this. The Prime Minister, Robert Muldoon, made it painfully clear that the licence fee was not to be increased, so the only revenue we had access to was advertising revenue. Over ten years we had to rely more and more on that revenue.

Inevitably, especially on the television side, the executives became – I don't suppose the word 'enamoured' would be too great a way to describe it – with the power of advertising to give them resources and revenue, to make programmes. And therefore, I suppose, they largely became converted to the idea of commercial television. It enabled them to do what they wanted to do, which was to make programmes. And if those programmes had to be commercial and had to follow the line of the kind of market, the kind of audience that commercial television drove them to, they were quite happy to go.

It was wholly understandable, but the result was that with the change in legislation, broadcasting was taken to the point where it was told that it should think of itself largely in financial and profit-seeking terms.

Becoming a state-owned enterprise with the aim of making a profit?

Exactly, yes. And I was glad to go at that point. I knew that my idea of broadcasting had had its day.

Of course the war's still going on, isn't it? Questions of public and commercial television and radio.

The war is still going on. I've done my bit from the sidelines and I think the war will finally be won but it might take another five or ten years. It distresses me that such a major influence on children and the adolescent mind should be couched largely in semi-literate terms. In other words, we are not holding up to the new generation higher standards of expression, the wider range of creative exploration of their minds, and the stimulation that the best minds of our generation can bring to them through both radio and television.

Without that stimulation, without that stretching that, perhaps, books were for my generation, we will become a lesser people, lesser intellectually and lesser in spiritual terms. In other words we will become rather zombie-like non-thinkers, almost a sort of dull proletariat following overseas fashion and fads of the most ephemeral and trivial kinds, the kind that makes someone like Madonna a modern icon, or Michael Jackson an almost saintly figure in popular culture. It's that kind of debasement that worries me because I grew up in a society in which books were of overwhelming importance because of the richness that was available to you in them, in reading, even though you didn't always take advantage of it. If we don't find that richness, if it's not available to young minds in radio and television, we will be a poorer nation.

You have, I think, described the invasion of overseas values and standards through television and radio, particularly television, as a kind of 're-colonisation'. Is 'colonial' a dirty word for you?

In my younger days, in the journalistic and literary circle in which I moved, we saw New Zealand as a country that was evolving a distinct character of its own, one that drew upon the resources of its people, the consciousness of its people and the way they looked at life, as well as a realisation of our geographic position and the influence of Maori culture. There was the great hope that we would become a fully inde-pendent, self-realised people. That hope has slowly vanished. I was violently – verbally violent – against what I saw as the colonising influence of modern technology. Frankly, I've now become resigned to it.

New Zealand will always be a colonial country, in the sense that it is and will be largely dominated by overseas decisions and ideas. Not that I used to reject overseas ideas. They were very much part of me, especially in literature. But I feel now that we are essentially followers. We create very little of our own. Our economic thinking is international. It comes from over the horizon. All of our follies and fashions come from that same place. The impact on our thinking, the sources of our thinking, are invariably from across the sea, mainly from the northern hemisphere – Europe and the United States. There is no possibility of New Zealand evolving a character of its own. We are a provincial variation of the western world. I used to resent that a great deal. I had the ridiculous conceit – I suppose it must have seemed that to some people at the time – that somehow we would be creators of something different, the makers of a new small world.

I can see now that was a conceit and we should accept our situation as a cultural and, I suppose, economical and political part of the greater western world. I suppose our original contribution to that world will be through the talents and occasional flashes of genius that are produced among our people, but that talent and genius will be absorbed and be part of the wider world. Anything different in us will be more in the nature of inner explorations. We may stumble across, or an individual may stumble across, a life experience or a variation of that experience that is different.

I admire Maori greatly for their cultural renaissance, for their assertion of their identity, but that is essentially a minor tributary of the world's culture. It's valuable to them but I think inevitably it will be submerged and is being submerged by the same forces that overwhelm the Pakeha world. Nevertheless, I think the Maori does give the twenty-first century a definition of the New Zealander, just a faint outline of difference, and I think we should value that difference, but not fight against the inevitable position of being a provincial variation of western society and very much part of it.

Back in an interview in 1970 you said something like, 'There exists within me a commitment or belief that I want to express, but I know I have to wait my time if I'm to express it in a novel and a certain price has to be paid for it.' Have you been able to express this commitment or belief? Is this in the forthcoming book, perhaps?

Yes, I suppose *The Family Man* does contain a great deal in fictional terms of what I was talking about. Although I'm telling the story of a man and his wife and the difficulties and final failure of their marriage, as a subtext I have tried to have his character and responses reflect what was happening to New Zealand and, spanning his life from the early 1960s to the present day, give a reflection of what has happened to New Zealand. But it is only a reflection, and because you have to be true to the character that you're writing about, that you have created, you can only reflect it in his terms and his terms are sometimes a distortion, a refraction of reality if you like, and sometimes a reflection that I don't personally agree with. You have to be true to the character, so in doing that I've tried to portray a New Zealand male with his sense of time and place. Perhaps, finally, there's an element of disillusionment – a disillusionment I share, but I found it in the character.

Although this is not an autobiography, obviously there are parts of you in it, is that so?

Oh yes. I mean I've made him a journalist. It is a truism of writing that you write about places and people and experiences you understand or come close to understanding and want to explore. If I knew more about the insurance business or the banking business the character could have been a banker or an insurance executive. No, you write close to experience, observed experience and personal experience. You explore the nature of that experience through the characters you create. I dedicated *The Family Man* to Theodore Morrison, an American who conducted a course in English and fiction at Harvard University. He was a saint-like man in many ways. He always saw fiction as a means of explaining, in as near to truthful terms as you could express, a meaning of life around you – not necessarily the entire meaning but just a meaning you could give it. So I dedicated the book to Theodore Morrison.

You've said before that writing books isn't easy for you, that in fact it's some of the toughest work you've ever done. It also involves taking risks, doesn't it?

Oh, it does. I've always admired so-called serious writers, because you have to tap your subconscious. You have to go into unexplored areas of yourself and find out what's there and allow it to bubble up to the surface. Sure, you control it; sure, you give it order, but it can be a very painful and difficult thing to do. I've done hard manual work, I've done stressful executive work, but writing to me has been the hardest task of all. I've always had a great admiration for writers. I might dislike their writing or make personal judgments on other facets of their character, but I believe that they are essential in any society. We are lucky in New Zealand that we almost have an abundance of literary expression and I think that's one of the great signs of the health of modern New Zealand society, that desire to create and to express in literary terms, to record the written word. That is a great reassurance to me.

There's one person in your life we haven't mentioned yet. You mentioned your subconscious. I understand you have a person called 'Jeeves' who is a symbol for you of your subconscious, your intuition?

Yes. That's a rather facetious name, but I was a great lover of P. G. Wodehouse in my boyhood. One or two academics have been rather scornful of my praise of Wodehouse but I have been delighted in later life to discover that Evelyn Waugh and Graham Greene also held P. G. Wodehouse in high regard as a literary model. He's a beautifully simple writer in the things he could express and the world he could create.

Why 'Jeeves?'

Jeeves was the servant of Bertie Wooster, who could guide him at all times with the best advice and arrange his life, sometimes unbeknown to Wooster, in a way that produced the best outcome for him. I found that my thinking mind, my deliberately thinking mind, my conscious thinking, was adequate but often second-rate in retrospect, inadequate for what it was supposed to be producing for me. But I found that my intuitive mind, the mind that I could tap for my writing, had a high degree of accuracy. It was highly reliable. Perhaps that was in part an inheritance of an introverted youth. But, even when occupying a top job, I would always tap into my intuitive mind and listen to it and I always thought of it as Jeeves.

I'm not alone in that. I think many people, in fact anybody who has any sense at all, listens to the instinctive voice that is in them, and they should encourage it and nurture it. I've always done that and I always will. Once or twice it's made mistakes, but not often.

In a way it's trusting yourself at quite a deep level, isn't it?

It is, and I think everybody should do that. If you don't trust yourself or your inner self or your deeper self who or what can you trust? And if that inner trust is untrustworthy you're in trouble. But I've also cultivated what some people have found innocent in me – if you like, the child in me. I think every adult should nurture the child in them because in the child is so much of the truth about yourself. And, if you can keep that child fresh and responsive, I think you get a great deal more out of life and a great deal more enjoyment, even if it expresses itself naively or very innocently on occasions. You know it's naive or innocent but you forgive it because that's the child in yourself.

This interview was first broadcast on National Radio on 13 July 1993.

Irihapeti Ramsden

Irihapeti Ramsden finds it difficult to find a label that adequately describes the work she does these days. Perhaps the most appropriate is 'an agent of change'. She has been described as a 'Maori activist' and 'the Maori feminist who plies her beliefs through charm and humour'.

A busy conference speaker to both Maori and Pakeha audiences, and a consultant in the health and education fields, she is probably best known these days as the principal architect of the 'cultural safety' programme in nursing education.

A major turning point for Irihapeti Ramsden came at the age of forty-three when she realised that she had surpassed the ages reached by both her Maori mother and grandmother.

IRIHAPETI RAMSDEN: It was a symbolic thing. The whole story of colonisation for me was embodied in their lives. Both of them died far too early of tuberculosis, a disease that was brought here by other people. They lived long enough to produce their own families, but long before they could see the fulfilment of their lives they died.

For me, these were women who were caught up and died in the holocaust of disease that affected our people. But I had survived. I was now older than them, and for me that was a profoundly important thing. I felt that I had, in a sense, survived the holocaust. Now, there was some kind of work that I must continue on for their sakes, for the fulfilment of my life and that of my daughter, who will probably live longer than me.

In some way I was living out their lives. I will see the mokopuna. I will see the grandchildren they will never see. Because we are our people, we are our grandparents, we are our tipuna, I'm going to have the privilege of living to see things that they were never able to see because their story deprived them of that.

How does that affect the way in which you live your life now?

Well, I'm a city Maori. I'm urbanised. I'm the first generation of Maori born in town. But I go home constantly, back to the land. I'm deeply involved in the management of our land. I express my Maoriness through those rural things and through the things that they did. But I find myself in another time and place.

Nevertheless, I am absolutely committed as a Maori to the things that were important to them. I believe they are with us all the time; that there is never a time when we cannot appeal to them in some way or simply consult, check or tick off things in our lives with the spiritual accompaniment of our ancestors, of our tipuna. They are not able to be seen but we are them and they are us. The whole integration of their lives, their world, is just part of us. This applies to the land as well. Whatever little bit of land we have left in my family has to be protected. It has to be guarded, for their story and for the story of the people who come after us.

Can we explore a little more what they've passed on to you and the way in which they are present to you now? Are they, to some extent, a kind of support system for you?

Oh yes. Though it's arrogant to assume that they will always be supporting one particular mokopuna. They've got many people to think about. When I talk about them like this it's important that it isn't thought that we worship our ancestors. There's nothing of that. It's more part of the continuum. It's more part of being them and them being us. It's just knowing who you are and where you have come from. In my family we can easily go back thirty generations. We know who those people are. We know what they did and we can take our examples from them.

I can choose a tipuna in a particular situation and say, 'What did that tipuna do? How did he or she cope with what I'm facing now?' Because all human situations are essentially the same – whether they happened 1000 years ago or in 1990 is not relevant. So I can take examples from the tipuna and say, 'Oh yes, he is a clever man. I might just follow his example.' But it isn't ancestor worship. It's a togetherness, a completeness and a wholeness that is a joyful thing to be part of and my aroha goes to those who do not have those names and those stories. Those are the people that I care about because I am a lucky Maori. The holocaust has not taken the names away from me.

Being 'a lucky Maori', to use your words, also gives you special responsibilities, doesn't it?

There is a responsibility if you accept it and most Maori do. If you have certain information you are bound, you are responsible, to use that information to create change that will make the world a safer place for the mokopuna, for the people who are coming later and for those who are already here.

In my case I've been fortunate. Some of it's been hard work, some of it's been through the support of other people. Because of the support of other people I have been given access to information. Now, that information is required for change in this country and I feel bound to use it. Because in some ways our history has been dreadful in my family. We've been seriously affected by colonisation. But there have been powerful threads throughout that have kept us going as Ngai Tahu and Rangitane. If I've been fortunate to have those threads left as intact as they have been, then I believe I have an obligation to move that information on to create change so that other Maori can emerge healthily through this holocaust.

When I asked you what you did for your job, you had some difficulty in describing it. You said you were an 'agent of change'. So what are you changing from and to? Or how are you involved in that?

We've had a hell of a time over the last 150 or so years. We had a society that was perfectly workable, perfectly intact, doing it's own thing unromantically in its own way, and had been for over 1000 years in this country and 5000 years in the Pacific. Then along comes another group of people whom we will call the Victorians, who bring with them a very primitive set of behaviours and ideas and ways of doing things. They have two major assets. One is technology in the form of muskets and guns, the other is bacteria – viruses and disease.

The combination of those two things, backed up by the new legal system that was brought here by the Victorians, resulted in the most frightful damage to the old culture. Now, I find that an unacceptable and unfair state of being for the old culture. So, I see it as part of my work, as I do have some information, to bring about change through telling the people from the new culture what has actually happened.

One of the things that backs up the new culture is the education system, which omits a whole series of important things from its teaching, from its curriculum, from its syllabus. The Treaty of Waitangi, for instance, is denied. Attempts at positive change are called social engineering. In fact the whole system itself has been socially engineered from the outset to deprive New Zealanders, including Maori, of information about what happened in the last 150 years.

I think that's where my responsibility lies – to try to do something about those systems. To change the information so that New Zealanders can make reasonable judgments about what's happened here, not judgments based on ignorance and stereotyping.

You've said before that you believe the spiritual energy of Maori has been dissipated. What did you mean by that?

Not so much dissipated as relocated. I think it's been relocated in the practice of introduced religions. I have a lot of difficulty with religion because of its structure, its hierarchy, and how it is manifested by human beings.

Maori are a people who work all the time with spiritual energy, with wairua. Every day, in every occupation, everything we do is intrinsically bound up with wairua – working in the garden, cooking, where you put your hat, how you relate to people, whether it's raining or dry. Everything relates to wairua. So when you have a people who are so bound into that whole 'wairua-ness', 'wairua-tanga', I guess it is not difficult for them to look for other forms of expression of wairua.

When the missionaries came our people didn't convert for a long time. We were perfectly content with the way we expressed ourselves. It was not really until the diseases and social destruction got under way that we began to convert. Perhaps we began to lose faith in the old practices and wonder if the new ones had something to offer.

For many Maori the practice of Christianity and many of its branches has been a satisfactory and useful thing. But I think with the younger people now there's been a polarisation, a rethinking: what was wrong with our own religious practice? We've done what all post-colonised people have done. We've tested it and checked it out. Some have picked up Christianity and found it useful, others are moving back to the old practices, to the old way of looking at the world, and seeing that it really did have something rich to offer.

Did you, yourself, have a Christian upbringing?

Yes, well and truly. We were a city people. Ngati Poneke was where my life really started off, in the Maori community here. I was born into Ngati Poneke, which was very Christian-based. A lot of my early memories are of being at church at Ngati Poneke and hymn singing and very crowded church services. A lot of the early Maori missionaries came there, Roman Catholic and Church of England and so on. They brought Bishop Bennett in to baptise us as children, and our religious education was very much Christian-based at that time.

I was brought up by my father, a Pakeha, here in Wellington and he ensured that we went to church. We started with Sunday School and then graduated to Bible Class. We attended church regularly and I was confirmed into the Church of England at a younger age than usual because they thought I could understand. So I went in with the older girls when my sister was confirmed. I knew what they were talking about, but I didn't really believe it.

Have you abandoned Christianity altogether?

Yes. I don't know really where it came from but throughout my life I had learned about the old gods. Perhaps because I used to spend half my life at home on the Banks Peninsula, Rapaki and places like that. I must have got information from there. But also, when we were children our house in Wellington was filled with older Maori people. There were not many safe houses for Maori people in Wellington then.

What do you mean by 'safe houses'?'

Houses where Maori people could gather and be Maori. Our house was one of them. There was a lot of discrimination against letting flats or houses to Maori people; one or more Maori was considered to be a very poor proposition to have on your property. This applied also to visiting Maori, who came in to negotiate with the powers that be in Wellington. So they often stayed with us.

Sir Apirana Ngata used to stay at the Midland Hotel on Lambton Quay and we used to go and see him there. Sometimes we'd go and stay with him up at Waio-matatini. I can remember riding around on his horse with him looking at the land schemes.

Te Puea Herangi, Peter Buck, Hone Heke Rankin from the north, they would come and stay. We children were exposed to what they were saying and this included the wairua things as well, karakia and so on. My grandfather, Henare Manawatu, lived with us a lot and everybody coming through from the South Island used to stay with us.

Was your movement away from Christianity gradual?

Yes it was, although I don't believe I was ever a really committed Christian. I think it's an excellent philosophy if carried out properly but it's very difficult to carry out. I think I had always had these old influences, which came from my Maoriness, that denied the idea of monotheism. I find the idea of a bearded pink Sky Father very hard to accept when our nourishment comes from the Earth Mother.

By the time I went to secondary school I was quite confirmed in my own thinking. I very much believed that Papatuanuku is our mother and that she is our source of nourishment and that all things are related to all other things. So even then I had difficulty with the idea that human beings were in any way superior to other living forms on earth. As a Maori my belief is that we are only as beads on a necklace, neither more nor less important, but ourselves as well.

So these concepts were in conflict with the Christian ones. It didn't cause me great daily agony or anything. I just simply moved quietly over to the ones that I preferred and thought were more workable and I stayed with those. As I've become more politicised, got more information and begun to work in the area of change, I've become much more consolidated in the repudiation of Christianity.

My continued politicisation has identified Christianity as one of the tools of destruction of our people. Not every Maori is going to agree with that. Many Maori will probably say, 'Oh, there is a radical talking.' But, for me, that is the analysis that I use. I prefer to work with Papatuanuku. I don't mind being teina to the birds and the insects and the trees. That suits me fine.

Some Maori seem to use the Christian faith and hierarchy as a political tool.

Absolutely. We will go where our skills and information take us to create change. And the church, the church hierarchy, is still quite powerful in the community. Especially if it is united. So of course Maori people will work through the church. And many Maori are committed Christians as well.

You've been described in a magazine as 'the Maori feminist who plies her beliefs through charm and humour'. I don't know whether you've heard this or not. I wonder how accurate you feel it is?

I don't know where that came from. I think there is more than one way to skin a cat. I believe that confrontation was really important in the 1970s because we had a very complacent little country here about race relations. It was important to wake that taniwha up. And there were some very brave people in the 70s in this country who did that. Part of the reason was the progression of young Maori through the education system who emerged with formal educational tools and with the commitment and the wairua of Maori. Those people were labelled and treated dreadfully by the community but they did the early consciousness-raising. I guess then people like myself moved in, in the late 70s, and began to pick up the shards they left behind, to try and work through change, by giving the same message and giving the same information, but delivering it in a style that the shell-shocked were able to assimilate.

I'm quite capable of doing it the other way as well. But I think, perhaps, bees like honey and it's quite useful for bringing them in and once you've got them in and they're comfortable you get to the nitty-gritty. If it creates useful and lasting change then it's a style of delivery that I don't mind adopting. If they have been made too comfortable by the charm and humour I would have been most unsuccessful.

I guess there are times when you feel angry?

I feel very deeply and constantly angry. That's the thing that motivates me – anger and grief. Grief for the loss of our land, our mother. Grief for the loss of all the men and women who are part of that land. Grief for the theft of our story and grief for the loss of our sovereignty. It manifests itself in a different kind of working style I guess, but my motivation is certainly anger and grief.

You seem very successful at keeping that anger controlled. Does it ever get out of control?

Very rarely. If it gets out of control I'm no longer effective as a change agent. Part of working with people, particularly Pakeha people, in giving this information is to give it in a logical and credible way and this means control. I must field their questions.

I must be in a position to think clearly and to give answers that make sense to them, but still preserve the reality of our people. We have to be quiet in our thinking but there's chaos underneath.

Sometimes I've had to sit and listen to what is really terrific abuse of our people. I could allow myself to sink into anger. But that would make me ill. I think by nature I'm an optimist. So it's really a combination of my own optimism, my own self-control and my personal hope for the future that prevents the anger from controlling me. I have recently become a severe asthmatic. There is a cost for workers at the interface of cross-cultural issues.

Where do you see we've got to in New Zealand, particularly in Maori/Pakeha relationships?

Probably the only significant thing I can say is that we're not where we were ten years ago. Interestingly, one of the prime movers for change has been the church, and that has to be acknowledged. The Roman Catholic Church, the Church of England and the other churches – particularly, I think, Methodists – are doing a lot of work.

The government, of course, is always a difficult taniwha to grab hold of because, depending on the proximity to election time, the government is responsive to the wish and whim of the people and the wish and whim of the people is often guided by spur-of-the-moment, ignorant or ill-informed decisions. I know there are individuals in government who are trying to create change and there certainly were in the last Labour government, although I think some of the things they did were a mistake, or made without realising the implications – for instance, setting up the Waitangi Tribunal. There have been useful outcomes and we have to look at those. So that's all I can really say. We're in another stage of transition now and I don't quite know where that's going to lead us. These are new times in our history.

The important thing is that Maori are in a state of change, that we're part of this enormous international movement of indigenous people. We are never going to let anything like the colonial experience happen again. There are more of us and we're healthier. We're also coming through with formal education tools and adapting them to our own use and I think that is where the change will come from. It will come from that group of people who now have the energy and strength and courage to keep creating change in our country as part of this whole international movement of skill and information-sharing and local application.

Although I'm an optimist I think we've got hard times ahead – very rocky, very bumpy – and there will be more anger and more grief. There will be, I think, a retrenchment, a polarisation inside our country. But Maori are not going to let what happened to us before ever happen again. We're still in survival mode. But some of us have moved to a point where we have the luxury of reflection, which we've never had time for before. We have just had to get on and live. Now some of us are beginning to look at strategy for change and you'll find people appearing all over the country, many inside the government, some outside the government.

Do you see educating Pakeha as a major role for you? Because you move freely from one world to the other, don't you?

Yes, it seems to have gone that way. That's because of the kind of upbringing I've had. I've developed a lot of Pakeha skills, so it's just evolved that way. Now I do a lot of work with Pakeha. But I also work with our own people, working on decolonisation, alerting them to their story. Our people have consistently been the victims of the education system and we don't know a lot of the names. We don't know a lot of the story. I believe that those who can name the names control the meaning. The sooner we reclaim our own names and share them the better. There's nothing wrong with one lot calling the mountain Egmont and the other lot calling the mountain Taranaki. Personally I believe it should always be called Taranaki, but that lies in the future and the movement is going that way. There's no reason why things can't have multiple meanings in this country, for the health of all the people in the country.

Health is a particular interest and area of work for you, isn't it – mental, physical and spiritual health?

Yes. I trained as a nurse in the early 1960s and, as you said, some people work through the church system; I've worked through the health system. The expression of my wish for change comes through the health service because that's where I have some background. I learnt quite early as a student in the 60s that the health service was actually killing Maori people. It was not healing Maori people and part of that was the denial of Maori spirituality, the denial of any kind of Maoriness and the requirement by the health service that everybody be treated the same. There was this frightful thing called cultural democracy: people were to be treated the same regardless of race, culture, creed, politics and everything else. The very essence of their humanity was being denied by the health service. That's the area, I believe, where I can create some change. I hope so.

You used the word 'decolonisation'. How do you do the work of decolonisation?

This, again, is part of an international movement. What you have to do with people who've been through the process of colonisation and have been much altered from their original state, say 100 or 200 years before, is alert them to what has actually happened. What happens to many of our people is that, try as they may to come

151

through the system appearing like Pakeha, dressing like Pakeha, aspiring to do things like the Pakeha, they find they just cannot ever achieve it. The Pakeha people continue to identify them as Maori and so often our people come to a point where they think, 'What is Maori? What am I? I can't be like them. They won't permit me to do that. The other kids at school call me a "smelly brown Maori".' This has happened to my daughter and happened to me and no doubt happened to my mother and her mother in the education system.

We are continually being defined by the other group as not the same as them, even though we're being told we're all one people. So what's the story? The job of change agents and people working with our own people is to tell the story so that in the end people can choose their Maoriness as their route to strength. There are many, many Maori who are strong and content in their Maoriness. But there is a large group of young people now who don't know who they are or where they've come from. I think it's eighty per cent of our people who now live in towns, and of those eighty per cent, it has been estimated that about twenty-five per cent now no longer know their tribal name, their iwi names. Now, that's not because they've deliberately tried to forget them. It's because there has been a social process in hand that has denied those names to them.

What people working in decolonisation do is tell them the story of the denial of those names. They don't say, 'You have to be Maori or you have to express yourself in a certain kind of way,' but just say to them, 'This is the story. This is why you're the people of poverty in this country. This is why we came from being a sovereign people to now being people who are thirty-nine per cent of the unemployed in this country. This has been the process.'

The important thing is not to blame individuals – or Pakeha individuals – for it, but to help our people identify and analyse the processes, to be useful to our people in that kind of way. Once our people have got hold of what's going on they realise that it's not inevitable or a self-fulfilling prophecy.

I still hear people say, 'Oh, I'm just a dumb Maori.' We're not dumb. We are an amazingly adjusted, competent group of people who have been told from the outside for some reason that we're dumb because the education system that's been recently set up here and not designed for us (it's been designed for the colonists' children) has failed us. We're being told that we fail because there's something wrong with us and the prophecy becomes self-fulfilling. The ultimate outcome happens when the colonised believe what the colonists say about them. The mind and spirit then become totally colonised.

Decolonisation teaches Maori how education was set up, for whom it was set up and its impact on people who have another kind of education system. That's how it

Irihapeti Ramsden

works. It's not a rigorous process of saying, 'You must be Maori in this or that kind of way.' People make their own choices from there.

This interview was first broadcast on National Radio on 22 January 1991.

POSTSCRIPT
As the main architect of the 'cultural safety' element in nursing education, Irihapeti Ramsden describes it as giving the person who receives the service the right to comment on the service and say whether or not they actually feel 'safe'. She says this is a subjective judgment on the part of the person concerned and that is what some people don't like about it.

IRIHAPETI RAMSDEN: Safety, in this context, is about whether a person feels they can approach the service and have access to it and whether they feel they can communicate with the people giving the service. Safety isn't about clinical or technical skills, but if a person doesn't feel safe to approach the service they're not going to get the clinical or technical skills anyway. We use this subjective term 'safety' to give power to the consumer.

The term 'cultural' we use because it came out of the Maori experience of awful deficits in health service delivery. The 'cultural safety' process was identified and designed by Maori people in an effort to close that gap. But 'cultural' not only refers to people who are ethnically different from the person giving the service, but also cultures within cultures, such as people who have HIV Aids who currently come mainly from the homosexual community. If a nurse is homophobic there are going to be real problems for members of the homosexual community in terms of access. And they are certainly not going to feel 'safe'. They will feel at risk, unhappy and uncomfortable, and the communication and access problems will be major.

There are also the cultures of age and youth, rich and poor. Nurses are now taught a great deal about understanding themselves before they dream of working with anybody else.

Since the original interview Irihapeti Ramsden says she remains optimistic in the long term about race relations in New Zealand. In the short term, however, she feels we will have to go through some 'tough' moments. She thinks the government is beginning to realise that it has to deal with a large group of feisty indigenous people and that Maori are becoming politicised much more rapidly.

Irihapeti Ramsden believes there is probably going to be some retrenchment by the government and conservative elements are going to make things tough for a while:

We are healthier and stronger. There are more of us. We have a clearer political analysis. We are thinking more critically and insisting on change and overall this is a healthier thing.

The maturing of this country, our growing up together, is going to be like any teenager. It's going to have its really tough moments. If we are going to reach any kind of maturity, which I believe we will, it will be due to a process of 'tough love'. But for the first time since colonisation began there is some hope of real change so that the children who are Maori are going to get a fair go at the resources of this country. It might not be in my time, but it's coming. It is totally unavoidable and inevitable.

Whatever the strategies for change may be, it must be understood that we are in new times, that we are finding new ways of communication and power and resource re-distribution. These mutual activities need to be seen as healthy and creative. Denying, resisting or obstructing good communication can only prolong the inevitable work which must happen as we move towards reshaping the future of this country.

It will be reshaped. We have a better chance than most. A small population, interacting on a range of levels, and contained as we are on these islands of ours, we cannot avoid each other. We have only one treaty and a reservoir of notions of justice, not so much from the older generations but from the young.

Change is exciting and inevitable. Unlike my mother and grandmother, I want to see our mokopuna taking their part in it.

Jack Shallcrass

Jack Shallcrass is a well-known advocate of liberal opinion. Now retired after more than forty years as a teacher and lecturer in education, he still leads a very busy life. He's much in demand as a conference speaker and is involved in projects to give skills to unemployed people, civil liberties, educational and environmental groups. He is also educational adviser to the multimillion-dollar Telecom Education Foundation.

It was a very different Jack Shallcrass, however, who joined the merchant navy at seventeen after the outbreak of World War II.

JACK SHALLCRASS: I was a very 'trad' middle-class Kiwi fellow, who wanted to do all the right things and was expected by my family to do the right things. The right things were doing reasonably well at school, playing every game in sight, particularly getting into the first fifteen, but also playing cricket, boxing, running, swimming – the lot – and being praised for these achievements and reinforced in doing these things. This was only what was expected of people of my age in the middle and late 1930s. That was how most of the people, at least the boys I knew, behaved. Looking back, it was rather different for girls.

I had fairly traditional views. They were about our relationship with what my mother referred to as 'Home', which was England, though she had been born in Australia and had had no direct connections with England for goodness knows how long. At school we regularly sang 'Land of Hope and Glory' and other songs about the Empire.

We were fed a diet of imperial history, of the royal family, of loyalty to the Crown. This was taken for granted; this was what we breathed. We were also taught to be kind to animals and knew our social duties. We owed things to society, although how general that was, I don't know. Then came the war and suddenly the world was a very different place.

One of the powerful influences for me was being on a merchant ship sailing from Liverpool down to southern Africa, around the African coast and back up again, so you had a long time at sea. There was a very sharp-minded radio operator on the ship and he and I gradually got into the habit of talking. He was older than I was by some years but he probed me about what I believed in. I'd say goofy things, looking back, like 'Oh, to be back in England in the spring.' I had a girlfriend there, which partly explained it. But he looked at me one day and he said, 'Do you know what you're talking about?' And then he proceeded to let me have it. He said, 'You want to get back there. You think it's a great place. It's the most snobbish, class-ridden society the world has ever seen. It's full of gross injustice.' And he told me all about it. This was a total revelation. Suddenly I was seeing the world through somebody else's eyes. I don't know whether he was a Marxist; he was certainly a radical thinker. I imagine he had been influenced by the left-wing book club kind of thinking of the pre-war days, which had helped people to see their own country and themselves in a different light. Then he laid it on me. And after that I progressively saw things in a different light.

As the war went on I had increasing doubts about war as a way of settling international problems, particularly when it got right to the end and the steam had gone out of it. I can remember being in the Red Sea one night talking with a friend and there was a plane, I suspect an Italian spotter plane, buzzing around a way up there somewhere in the dark, and a friend of mine said, 'What the hell's he think he's doing?' After a while he said, 'I wonder what he's thinking about?' Suddenly it was a person there. And here we were; he might have been going to drop something on us, who knows, but here we were, human beings, strangers, thrust into a situation where we were going to do each other harm, and what for? That doubt kept on niggling and niggling until when I came home I really had made my mind up pretty well that I wouldn't have anything to do with any other wars at all. But I didn't know whether I would have the guts to stand out against it if it came to a point.

Then I joined a theatre group, Unity Theatre in Wellington, and it had a number of people who had been conscientious objectors during the war and we used to talk. I became very friendly with one of them in particular and we used to talk about the war and he said, 'Well, after what I've gone through, if there's another one, I think I might have a look at it.' But I said, 'Nat, I'm quite the reverse.' It's not a question for me now, of course, at my age, but it bothered me for years.

So how did I come back? I really was no longer a fan of the royal family or the imperial tradition. I thought of myself unequivocally as a New Zealander. If anyone had referred to England as 'Home' I would have snorted at them. I was just part of a whole generation of New Zealanders who 100 years later fully accepted themselves without qualification as New Zealanders. This was our place. This was our turanga-waewae, and we were it, for better or worse. The kind of traditional religious beliefs I'd grown up with and practised seriously, they'd been blown away just like dust. They just didn't seem to be relevant to me any longer.

What were those traditional beliefs?

I was brought up as an Anglican and sang in the choir, taught Sunday School, was confirmed, and I practised it very seriously. I can remember at my confirmation concentrating my mind totally on this experience. But even then, I think in retrospect I was wondering why it wasn't a more illuminating experience, why I didn't feel joyful or transported by it. I think, looking back again, one of the reasons I went on doing it, and all my friends, male and female, did also, was that that's what you did at that time. You just all did it together. It was part of the tradition. I don't know if that's the tradition with young people now. I suspect not nearly so much. Khandallah was a village then, and all of us who were Anglicans went off and did things together. We went to dances together and so forth. And religion was part of it, a kind of a background to it.

But when I came back I had to examine it very seriously and I just found that it really didn't offer me anything any longer. Of course, being in the services, with a fairly fundamental and raucous attitudes to all sorts of things around you, you learn about the very strong and healthy scepticism of men about war and about everything. So being very young with older people around you, you are influenced by this. I think that helps you to look at things afresh and decide where you stand.

I came back, I suppose, a humanist and certainly that's what I am now. I just have no doubt that everything that happens here individually, and perhaps in the universe, is our responsibility. There's nobody else to carry the can and whether people choose to believe in something outside of that, as a kind of lode star, well that's fine, I'm very happy for them. I don't and I can't be persuaded that there is anything else there.

One of the great influences on my life was reading Teilhard de Chardin, the great Jesuit philosopher, who argued that the basic force in the universe is an evolutionary one, that everything is in the process of change and that through that force, life appeared and developed and produced us. And, he says, by some accident we have a central nervous system that allows us to be introspective, to be able to observe ourselves and everything else. And this places on us the responsibility to see that future evolution, future change, is guided by some moral or ethical basis. And the only source of that is us. That is our burden.

I remember reading a lot of French philosophy at one stage when the French were arguing furiously about this and all saying the same thing – that one of the tragedies of modern man is the loss of the medieval church and medieval faith because that explained everything. Since then we've been wrestling with how we can accept the responsibility that was formerly carried by the church. Whatever happens is on us. The world is a reflection of us and everything in it. And there's no cop-out. The buck really does stop here.

What does your humanism have to say about the survival of the fittest?

I'm sure there is a great deal in this, but it is not an absolute. This is one of the things people wrongly attribute to Darwinian philosophy, that the only way in which we survived was by tooth and claw, by competition, and only the toughest survived. In fact, biology no longer believes this. That we survive and creatures other than humans survive is at least as much by our capacity to co-operate as by our capacity to compete. My inclination is that the capacity to co-operate is greater than the capacity to compete. If you accept yourself as a humanist there is a responsibility on you to recognise that what happens in the world is at least partly to do with you, that it is your responsibility and that you should have a go at trying to change it. I mean, if we're tearing the world apart because we're failing to recognise the environmental imperatives, we ought to try to do something about it ourselves in our own lives. It isn't necessary to go into the street and wave banners. It isn't necessary to take petitions to Parliament or to join societies. What is necessary is to do something about it in your own life. You don't throw bottles away or paper away. You recycle. You try not to foul the environment. If you smoke you try to stop smoking because that's an environmental hazard that's harming other people. If you go on and become an activist in your society so much the better. That's what a humanist would say. Now, all that requires co-operation – not just acceptance of responsibility but the acceptance of the need to co-operate with other people.

To what end or purpose?

To whatever end there seems to be general agreement upon. For example, with the environmental movement, at the very least to see that when you die you haven't made the environment in which we live a worse place, that you haven't altered it adversely. If you can do a little better than that, that's a plus. And the sum total of this, taken over the planet, may mean that we give ourselves and the planet a chance to survive. At the moment its chances of survival are probably less than fifty-fifty, so that's the starting point. You say, 'How can we share with other people?' One of the ways we share is to try to alter other people's opinions and behaviour, and that's why we join groups and try to get other people to join groups. This is by mutual persuasion and I am greatly heartened about this.

In the postwar world New Zealand has come to a non-nuclear position. And that's not happened through any sort of political or social leadership. It's happened because little groups of people such as the Quakers, the Campaign for Nuclear Disarmament and latterly women's groups, in tens and hundreds of thousands, have simply talked to each other and said, 'Look this is silly. There must be another way of doing it.' The politicians only came in right at the fag-end of it. That was when the polls started to tell them that seventy per cent of New Zealanders felt this way.

158

Now, there hadn't been any overt leadership for that to happen. It happened simply because people observed the dangers of the world and deep inside them something said, 'No!' And a lot of them organised and a lot of others were persuaded and that's something that no political party can overlook in this country. It's a kind of recognition that you see a problem and you ask yourself what can be done about it. I think human beings do this more readily than we care to recognise. Our leaders tend to treat us like sheep, but sheep are not stupid creatures. Sheep are really quite intelligent creatures, but because of the way we treat sheep, they behave stupidly. So do we, when we are treated stupidly. I think we should have considerably more faith in people's good sense in what they are doing and the judgments they make. The anti-nuclear issue is one case in point. I think the environmental one is also going much the same way.

At the present time New Zealand seems to be operating as a market-oriented economy or society. Where does co-operation come in there?

Oh, co-operation comes into it very powerfully at the social level. In the market economy I think at present we're operating at a fairly crude level in the way we are organising for competition. Sooner or later there's going to have to be some social intervention to safeguard against the worst effects of that, so we don't get ripped off. Inevitably, if private competition is allowed to run free, people get ripped off so that even in the home of private enterprise, the United States of America, there are very stringent social controls on what private enterprise may and may not do, how far they may be able to develop in eating up the other competition, for instance. So they accept this. But in the way in which private enterprise actually works, the evidence indicates that in the big corporations in the United States and in little industries too, the ones that are successful are those that co-operate with their employees.

There was a huge study done over three years on behalf of the United States Chamber of Commerce. Some 300 corporations that were succeeding were matched with 300 corporations that were failing and likely to go out of business. The one common factor that differentiated the successful from the unsuccessful was the degree to which employees believed they could influence policy, the degree to which their employers took them seriously.

The Japanese management style takes the workers seriously. They do not set them in a different world. They all share the same cafeteria. They all share the same conditions of work. They are consulted. What they suggest is taken seriously and they can see that it's often implemented. They are part of the enterprise, a co-operative enterprise.

The other management style is really 'tooth and claw': that crude primitive social arrangement that treats people as though they're not people. But even within a competitive economy, the most successful parts of it – that is successful economically, financially, socially and personally, and successful in the satisfaction they give to consumers – are the parts that adopt co-operative leadership.

Now, this isn't a dilemma; this isn't a contradiction. It simply means that you cannot make competition an absolute. We're a mixture of competition and co-operation. As human beings, sometimes we are one and sometimes the other. We use our central nervous systems to try to observe what is happening and then to make the best contribution that we can to it for ourselves – that's the selfish part, the competitive part – but also for the good of society because we need a healthy, functioning society. Interdependence is one of the most powerful and least understood imperatives of life.

One of the things that is very important to you, I think, is the value of what we might call 'ordinary people'. And that influences your philosophy on education too – the teacher is also a learner.

Oh yes. Very much. And here again there was a big influence in my life and this was the great Brazilian educator Paulo Freire. His position is that all human beings are capable of learning, even people who are apparently so seriously disadvantaged neurologically or physically that they have to be institutionalised. They are still capable of learning. That means capable of changing their behaviour, because that's what learning is. I became convinced fairly early on as a teacher, and this has grown over the years, that given the right conditions and the right sort of learning environment, the right motivation, the right help and the right amount of time necessary – all of these things – that most, if not all, human beings are capable of learning anything that they are required to learn or that they want to learn.

Even in the academic world there's evidence of this. If you create the right conditions for people – you don't have one-shot measuring systems, a final examination and pass or fail – if you say our job is to learn this amount of material and to understand these principles, then everybody sitting in your classroom, a group or community, a social group or whatever it is, is capable of achieving that at the highest possible level.

Some will take longer than others. The reason that so many people behave dumb in our society and believe themselves to be academically inept – stupid, if you like – is because we have made them so. The education system has been used for so long as a selection device, to select the best people to do certain things. This has meant that the others were rejected and got little to reinforce them, or give them feelings of satisfaction to help their own self-image, or give them something to aim at. And we applauded ourselves because we thought we were so smart. We were finding bright people who were able to leave this little country and go overseas and do wonderful things and say to the world, 'What a lot of smarties we are. What a great little country this is.'

Those people were probably going to do it anyway. What we didn't do is ask, 'What have we done to all the rest?' We are face to face with this, right now. We live in a world where there is no place for the unskilled or the people who believe they are stupid because the world requires different skills, more skills, the capacity to change skills, the capacity to adapt, to meet new conditions – this is the nature of the world. Even digging ditches is now taken over by people who can operate machinery.

So what we have to look for is a way in which we can help people to achieve universal competence. Everybody should be competent in the basic things – in learning, in knowledge – and, even more important, able to take progressive responsibility for their own learning. I don't mean their learning just in the academic sense of getting certificates and doing formal learning within formal institutions, because all through their lives they are learning. Every day we all learn something. The evidence to support the belief that this is possible is overwhelming. All we have to overcome is the notion in our heads that schools and educational institutions are places where you sort the sheep from the goats. If you took long enough for everybody to pass, that is to become competent in what they're doing, academics in particular would go screaming mad because they would say you're lowering standards. This is absolute nonsense. They are caught up in a bit of medieval superstition. They don't recognise what human beings are capable of doing. It's the conditions in which we put them that make them behave otherwise.

Some lovely work has been done on this by a man called Alan Tough from Canada. Alan came out to New Zealand a few years back and had a look at some work here. He got his researchers to go around talking to ordinary people, knocking on doors, going to the shop floor in the factory, stopping people in supermarkets, talking to people behind the counters, and he said, 'We're going to find out what they've been learning.' Being slightly goofy in these matters when they're dealing with ordinary people, the research students, the graduate students, went to people, knocked on their doors and said, 'We're engaged in research study. Can you tell me how many learning projects you've been engaged in lately?' And of course they said, 'What?'

Alan said we were asking the questions the wrong way. Go back, he said, and ask them if they've learned anything lately. Of course they'd learned things lately. What sort of things had they learned? They had learned to make jam, learned how to deal with the baby's colic, learned how to put up a fence, learned how to bleach clothes, learned how to preserve food, learned how to do a valve grind on the car and so on.

These are the important things. They are about living. 'I'm learning how to start dealing with my husband's alcoholism.' 'I'm learning how to deal with my wife's sharp temper.' People are learning to change, to adapt their behaviour. These are the critical things. People who learn those things can learn anything. And we all learn these things. We may not learn them completely, but we all at least have a go at them and manage one way or another. People are capable of doing it.

Alan discovered that, of all the things that people declared they had learned, less than five per cent had been learned in institutions. We really do learn in our daily lives. But the education system has captured the term 'learning' so it has become something that you do out of books and in classrooms. And that's only part of it.

I now strongly believe that what institutions of learning ought to be doing is making use of knowledge to help people refine and understand their daily lives. If they don't do that, they're really just adding another layer that doesn't make much contact with the rest of life. Regrettably, when a lot of people go to learning institutions it's something they have to do in order to get on with their daily lives. They can make more money if they get a degree and lots of people go through and get very good qualifications without any observable impact on their behaviour. Institutions, especially tertiary institutions, ought to be places where you are able to reflect and refine and see what other people have experienced. That's what knowledge is. To see what other people have experienced and discovered in order to help illuminate your own life. To see the life of your society and your place in it. We haven't got to that. Some individual people do, but I don't see the institutions doing it. We've commercialised them to such an extent that they're really just another form of commercial exploitation for production. I think we've got to progressively get away from that and I'm hopeful that we will, as the modern holistic societies begin to take a greater hold upon our consciousness and perceptions.

What do you mean by holistic in this context?

Holistic is where people see life as a whole and everything as interrelated. We've grown up in an industrial age for a couple of hundred years or more in which we've been very successful in fragmenting life in all sorts of ways and by producing, getting down to smaller units for production, for distribution, for control and so forth. And this has had a huge impact upon our own habits of learning, the way in which we perceive reality, so that we tend to put things into pigeon-holes. I mean, we think of 'pre-schoolers' and we think of 'the aged' and if you're ill you go to hospital and until recently your family was only able to come and see you three times a week. If your children were in hospital they preferred you not to go at all because it upset the children. We wrench a creature out of his or her environment in which they feel comfortable and make sense of life and plonk them somewhere else. Then we deal with one aspect of their lives, a particular illness, or a particular condition, and we wrench them out of reality and put them into something else that is numbing, frightening, all sorts of things so that *we* can deal with it. It's that kind of fragmentation that is our modern mindset.

We need to be more holistic. If you have to take a child to hospital, for goodness sake have at least one of the parents there all of the time. In a sense the children's hospitals have led this renaissance in medicine and are quite superb about it. I've had experience of it and I have the utmost admiration for them but I'm trying to illustrate a general tendency. What children's hospitals have done stands out. They're ahead of the field. You try to understand things in their relationships. We're learning a lot about this from environmentalists, from the whole ecological movement.

You're beginning to find in some of the tertiary institutions people breaking down the old intellectual and academic barriers and saying, 'Look, you can't understand "this" unless you really understand "this and this".' So inter-disciplinary courses are beginning to emerge. You're getting universities like Sussex, which is set up on a total inter-disciplinary basis, trying to break these old fragmented habits of mind.

I think people are beginning to understand this when they look at the ways in which politicians are trying to solve the economic problems by dealing only with economics, in many cases dealing only with a particular aspect of economics instead of seeing it as something that is embedded totally in the way in which society ticks. We've yet to find a political party – apart from the first of the Green parties that emerged in the early 1970s – that has produced a holistic plan for the country; that has actually thought of the way in which 'this' is dependent upon what happened 'here' and what happened 'there'.

When we're faced with real difficulties, as we are right now, the old fragmented habits assert themselves, so you have people trying to solve all sorts of problems by concentrating on only one aspect of the thing and then wondering why it all falls apart. We wonder why people are cynical and why people refuse to believe and why they laugh hollowly, spitefully, in all sorts of ways, at the efforts of the politicians to deal with problems. Even if we don't understand that they're using outmoded means to deal with modern problems we have a strong feeling inside ourselves that they haven't got a hope. They're baying at the moon. And they're using an old dog to do it.

In the last year or two I've worked closely with politicians and observed them and I think that's unjust to them. Because if they were to come out and say, 'Look, we've got to start thinking holistically about this and this is what I propose and how I'd like to see us do it,' they would be laughed at by their colleagues. They just wouldn't be there after the next election, so to this extent politicians are reflecting us, and the worst sides of us.

My hope is that just as New Zealanders came to a non-nuclear position through word of mouth, through being convinced by discussion around dinner tables, in families, in churches, among friends, that we will come to an understanding of the ecology of living, the holistic way of seeing things, understanding the relationships and interdependence and seeing that whatever you do is going to require some sort of trade-off here or down the line. The hope is that we will come to that ourselves and then, just as political parties came to a non-nuclear policy, they'll come to ecological policies as well.

Do you actually see this happening?

A little bit, yes. Some of them are really talking and thinking environmentally, or at least if they're not thinking environmentally they are learning to use the words and phrases. I'm not sure it's progressed very far. It's hard to tell at the moment because the sort of 'New Right' thinking of Treasury is so dominant in the minds of politicians, simply because of the pressing nature of the economic problems.

You give the example of the anti-nuclear policy of New Zealand as a sort of a grassroots populist uprising of opinion and attitudes and values. It seems fairly obvious to say that if we worked co-operatively in New Zealand we could solve our economic problems and social problems. Do you see any evidence of this in New Zealand today?

No. Not yet. What I find is people talking about the issues themselves but feeling helpless when confronted with dealing with the very specific ones like unemployment, for instance. I think it will come, and it has to come unless we are going to go into a sort of 'laager' mentality of the privileged protecting themselves against the un-privileged. That would be very destructive because the cost of obtaining the privilege eventually becomes prohibitive, so we will have to find ways of working this out. I think eventually it's a value thing. It's what people are prepared to accept and that's going to be decided, at least to some extent, by people working out co-operative ways of doing things, working out ways in which they share the planning, however it may be carried out, and learning how to negotiate and to agree on things. It means being prepared to accept the positive and the possible; being able to hold to the ideal but do what is possible on a daily basis.

All of these things are necessary but I think eventually it is going to reside in this ecological cast of mind that sees everything as being related. You don't solve unemployment simply by subsidising jobs. You've really got to see this as part of a social process that is governed by a sense of fairness and justice.

We're very strong on 'band-aid' solutions, but not on thinking ones, not on value ones. You could almost say it's about religion, if you take Lloyd Geering's definition of religion as 'a concern for ultimate values'. That's what we're on about. When I said to you at the beginning I forsook my religion, that's only if you think of religion as being something belonging to the churches. I wouldn't say that a humanist was a religious person unless you accept – this is a contradiction in terms in a way – Geering's definition of religion and then I think that all human beings are religious in that sense. Now that requires no divine intervention or divine guidance or anything outside of us. You can be a total materialist and still have, and be guided by, some sense of value – if not ultimate value, at least values that for the time being are pre-eminent to you. That may mean being on shifting sand because values shift, but then, if we're honest, so have all the religious or Christian values and institutional values. They have shifted like crazy. We are all in this. We are constantly required to examine and edit and reform, re-interpret, to re-understand. This is what I imagine is the way towards eventually solving our social and our economic problems. Of course, as we solve them there will be more. That's the other thing that's hard to accept. I don't ever want to be around when we reach the perfect, because that means we're dead. That is a form of death. Struggle is an assidual part of life, an assidual part of being human. But that doesn't mean you don't have a goal, you don't have your eye fixed on it, whatever it may be.

The concept of heaven is seen as the goal, what you're going for. But it's a very peculiar one the churches present us with because it's not one we are required to strive for except to behave ourselves in the eyes of some external authority.

There's also the oddly unreligious concept of hell, which always seemed to me to be a strange for a God of love. It's as if you have to have that as a goad, otherwise people are not going to behave themselves. That seems to me to be really a denial of love.

But the concept of heaven, that's not human to me. The human thing is that you are, you have become part of the struggle that produces the kind of vision you have. I think that's essentially the humanist view. And it's back to Teilhard de Chardin – a Jesuit, for goodness sake – saying exactly the same thing, making sense to all and sundry except to his Jesuit colleagues, who couldn't tolerate it. And he was asked by the Pope, 'Please don't publish this stuff until you are dead.' And being a good servant of the church he didn't. But what he was saying makes sense, I think, more universally than the particular dogma of particular sects, because it's very universal. This is an all-encompassing view. This is an ecological view. This sees life, sees humans, as part of all life, part of the universe, part of what they are engaged in making. He blew my mind when I first read him I thought he was wonderful. I still do.

The belief of the interrelatedness of all things on this earth – or the universe for that matter – gives equal value, does it not, to nature, the environment, to people? It's about equality.

Oh yes. It is about equality but I think that's an offshoot. I think it is really about dependence. It's about accepting the truth that, as John Donne says, 'No man is an island.' If a piece of the promontory should fall away we are all the lesser. 'Ask not for whom the bell tolls. It tolls for thee.' It tolls for all of us so that when anything happens anywhere, if it is destructive, we are all lessened. We may not be immediately lessened or diminished but eventually we are.

And if you hear it, I hear it.

That's right. And until we recognise that, all we are doing is shutting our eyes to something that is inevitable. We may not know the price, our children may not, but their children will. As a species we are still stuck with this notion of superiority versus inferiority, of competition, of 'I don't want to have to give up something so that they can do better.' Until we can overcome that, how on earth are we going to solve the problems of hunger, over-population, of illiteracy in the world? How can we proceed towards any sort of justice, no matter how constrained, when one country – the United States of America – consumes over half of all the manufactured goods, minerals and commodities of the world? And when in that country there are tens of thousands of beggars in the street? You want injustice? I'll show you injustice. I can show it to you in the middle of the richest country in the world. But that country itself sits in the midst of outright, rank, disgusting poverty.

These things are only solved when human beings think of themselves as being part of all other parts of life, be it vegetable or animal. How do you save the rainforests? Because if we don't save the rainforests we don't save the atmosphere. The rainforests are the engine of the atmosphere and people around the world in their millions are saying, 'We've got to save the rainforests.' But we have no technique of management, no authority, no political mechanism to handle it. Alongside this most of the problems pale into insignificance. But they are all part of each other because unless we find ways of producing a sustainable environment and sustainable economies then we are going to go on being destructive and eventually we will all suffer.

In this world with all its problems, this country with all its problems, do you have hope?

Oh yes, of course. That's another great human quality, that even people who declare themselves to be pessimists keep going. They must believe that something is likely to happen or might happen. So you keep on doing what is possible – never as much as you feel you should do, I hasten to add – but you feel that it's possible and you feel that it's worth bringing children into the world and that your grandchildren are going to have a chance. And there's sufficient evidence, you have sufficient little victories, to make you believe that it's possible.

I learned something very important from Michael Fowler after his first term in office as Mayor of Wellington. He was writing a chapter in a book for me and I'd gone to talk to him about it and I said to him, 'Michael, what have you learned?' 'Oh,' he said, 'two things. One: I've learned the limits of power.' He had wanted to get the motorway through Aro Street but the local people had stopped it in its tracks. He said, 'I've also learned that if you get it right half the time, you're doing well.' It seems to me that's not a bad set of guiding principles for people exercising political power. You're only going to get it right half the time. What he was recognising, and what we must recognise and accept, is that we're always proceeding on the basis of imperfect knowledge.

In my view the dream, the ideal, the goal, therefore, becomes doubly important. Because that shows you when you've got it wrong. It also gives you an idea of how to get it right so you keep on adjusting and adjusting, but no way can you adjust sensibly, rationally, appropriately, unless you have some vision of what it's in aid of. Do you hope? Of course you do. So long as there are ideals of any kind there is hope. That's really what gets people out of bed in the morning and off to work, or about their business for the day. That's what keeps international politics going, often against all the inclinations. It's the vision of getting it right occasionally.

So what is your vision, your ideal world?

My ideal world is one where there is a widespread sharing of the hope that it can be better, and a shared vision of how we may do it. Because only when that happens will it be possible to start overcoming the sectional and regional and national jealousies and privileges. I don't see an end. I don't even want to think about the end. I think that would be foolish. Because in this world you must be absolutely, acutely conscious that we are in possession of only some of the facts at any given moment and that even as we talk, people are discovering things that could make nonsense of much of what we previously believed with regard to the facts. It proceeds so fast that it's all the more important that we have these enlarging goals as a basis for measuring the new things as they come along. I suppose my vision would be primarily the hope of a growing awareness of interdependence, of mutual responsibility, and secondly, the hope of a progressively broader, more international acceptance of that and then finding ways of doing something about it.

This interview was first broadcast on 13 August 1991.

POSTSCRIPT
Jack Shallcrass continues to lead a very busy life as a conference speaker, educational consultant and advocate for civil liberties, the environment and giving skills to those who are unemployed. He also continues to believe that the most important question to be faced by New Zealand and the rest of the world is, 'How do we produce a sustainable society within which the quality of life is enhanced?'

Jack Shallcrass

Lorraine Moller

Lorraine Moller

Lorraine Moller is one of New Zealand's most successful athletes, both on the track and in the marathon. Her sporting career spans more than twenty years, but at thirty-nine she is still a top performer. She spends most of the year in the United States, where she is based in Boulder, Colorado, but she is still very much a New Zealander.

For Lorraine Moller, running has as much to do with the spirit as it has with the mind and the body.

LORRAINE MOLLER: That's something that I've learned along the way. Actually, I have a shop in Boulder called The Body Mind Connection. I started that about five years ago. I think at that time it was a metaphor for me of my own life, because I was really starting to get a grasp of how the body and mind interact. I think I needed to do that to continue to improve what I was doing, so that's been really good and I really believe that the spirit encompasses all of that. That's just my own personal philosophy that I've come to. But all of this is in the context of learning to share and to love, and to me that's the basis of anything that I do in life – and running of course has to be a part of that.

Does being spiritual mean being religious for you?

I'm not religious per se. It just hasn't been my particular path. I wasn't brought up to be religious. But I've always been interested in understanding the larger aspects of the self and my journey has been very eclectic. I love to read about different philosophies and religions and different cultures and, being a runner, I've been able to experience many different cultures. I've been to Asia, Europe and South America and getting to know people from different cultures is a great way to understand how people are so different and yet so alike. That was a remarkable discovery for me. I can see that no matter where you come from there are certain human qualities that bond us all. Running and competing in multinational events has been a wonderful way of discovering this and exploring it. In the last three Olympics it's been a very moving experience because, even though they're all there to compete against each other, it's actually a very co-operative event. Everybody comes together and everybody's putting in their share and it's according to a certain set of rules. It's the most heartwarming and wonderful experience I've ever had.

One of the other things that is so interesting is that we are told the important thing is how you do something. You strive to have this particular training programme and eat this sort of food and do these exercises and if you get A, B, C and D, then hopefully you get E. Yet, when you go to these events there are so many people of different backgrounds. They eat different foods - some people drink blood, some people are total vegetarians. There are people with different body types, they have different religions and yet they're all there doing the same thing. They're all sort of about the same, give or take a little bit. To me, the issue is the belief in yourself, and it really doesn't matter what the method is. You've got to choose methods that make sense to you. But it's the belief in them that really counts. I've explored this a lot and I've tried a lot of different things and I think it comes down to what you believe in.

You obviously must believe in yourself a great deal to run marathons?

Well, it's a funny thing. I mean, everyone to his own. I can understand people who think it must be absolutely horrible but when I'm doing it it's actually really exciting. I just love it. And it doesn't seem a long time. Other people think that to run for two and a half hours must be so very tough. But actually the best races I've done have seemed easy and the hardest races are when you're really having a hard time and you're not doing that well.

At the Olympics in Barcelona when I won the bronze medal it was so strange because you sort of get on a high. I felt really inspired but I also had such a confidence in myself. That's what carried me through. It gives you tremendous strength. It really goes hand in hand with the training. I mean, I believed in the training that I did but there were people out there who'd trained harder. There were people out there who were probably in better physical shape in some respects than me, but they couldn't get it together. Maybe because they had other things going on or they were learning different sorts of lessons to me. But I decided that it was my day and my time to put everything together that I'd learnt and to use all my past experience for my benefit. So it was great and in fact it didn't feel hard to me at all. All I knew was that I just had to get up that hill and I was going to get my medal.

I seem to remember one journalist described it as Lorraine Moller 'going over the hill and beyond it'!

Yes. You get 'over the hill' and there's always another hill to climb. It's funny how we use these expressions. I find myself starting to talking about age in a negative way. I catch myself doing it. But that's not what I want to do; I don't want to be limiting myself with concepts that don't work for me. I think life is about understanding your own belief systems. You have to remember that those are always changeable and when your ideas change then your change your world.

For me, running has been a way of understanding myself and understanding what beliefs I hold and figuring out which ones I need to change when I come up against it, and then moving on ahead. Sometimes it's more of a challenge than other times and sometimes it's difficult, but it's so rewarding if you can challenge yourself all the time and meet those challenges and move on.

Am I able to call you a 'professional' athlete?

Oh yes, that's not a problem any more. I'm a professional and proud of it.

Running is your work and your life, isn't it?

Yes it is. Being able to take prize money was one of the things that I stood up for. I think that was probably a crossroads for me. To really stand up for something I believed in. There have been a couple of times in my life when I've been asked to stand up for something I've really believed in and when I've done it it has been so rewarding. In the case of taking money it changed the face of the sport and I was a part of that. I feel really good about that. Sport has changed for so many people and now it's possible to be a professional and not get banned for life, to be a professional and compete in the Olympics.

Being banned for a life was a real possibility for you at one time, wasn't it?

I was banned and yet I never actually thought about the consequences. I never thought, 'Gosh, I might not ever be able to run again.' I'm glad I didn't think about the consequences because if I had I might not have done it. But if I hadn't taken that stand I don't think I would have felt as good about myself as I do today.

I think a lot of life is living your truth, knowing what is true within you and having the courage to live it. For me there's no other way now. If I know something's right I've got to do it, and every now and then I've got to take a deep breath and say, 'Here I go.'

How do you know what's true for you?

I think all of us can have an inner conviction – you can call it conscience if you like – about something. I think a lot of this has to do with the connection between the mind and body. We have to take time to get in touch with our inner self. I believe the inner self has all the information we need to accomplish whatever we want to accomplish in our lives. So taking time out every day in meditation or just in quiet time, just understanding our own thought processes or dreams, gives us a lot of information. All those things come from the inner self when we get in touch with our intuitive side. If we take time to do that so we have a good rapport with our inner self, then there's nothing we can't achieve. When you do that you know what is your own truth. You know what you're supposed to be doing. You know what it is to take responsibility for your own life. It means that you don't have to go and ask somebody else. You're making your own decisions. It means you have become an independent adult.

I know you're not afraid of talking about spirituality and using the word spiritual but what does spirituality mean for you? Is it the God within that you seek when you find yourself? Is there some kind of God or energy or life force and is he/she out there or inside?

Personally, for me, the concept of God is all that is, everything that exists. I believe I'm a part of it. I think all of us have access to the whole and to understanding ourselves and I believe everything is a part of that. All other people, everything that exists, even the rocks and your car or whatever, everything has that quality, that spirit.

That energy that we call spirit, you can't separate it. We're taught to think that we begin at our skins. Yet we don't. The skin is just the physical boundary but I think we can extend far beyond that. We live in this sea of thought and energy of which we're all a part and we're interacting all the time. For example, you are sitting here, we're breathing, I'm probably breathing in the air that you just breathed and so we're connected in more ways than just talking to each other and this interaction is constant.

I often hear people say so and so's a very spiritual person, but everybody is a spiritual person. Even a rock is spiritual. That's my concept of spirituality. It's all-encompassing. I don't think it's bound up in rules and regulations. I think that's one reason why I've never been able to embrace a formal religion. To me there are too many 'do nots' and 'should nots' and I don't think that's the way it is. I think we have carte blanche. Basically we have the freedom of choice to do whatever we want. I don't think we should limit ourselves. By the same token, I don't think we should live in anarchy. I think we're here to co-operate, to get on with one another, to share. We're here in relationship with everyone else. We've got to make that go smoothly. I think if you look at all life as being part of one spirit then in that case any violation against another person is also a violation against yourself. An essential belief in all the major religions is to do unto others as you would have them do unto yourself. To me, that makes perfect sense.

That's my version of God, or spirit, or whatever you like to call it – I don't think the names really matter. Often people get caught up in definitions. They argue about the definition whereas really we're all talking about the same idea.

It seems that you feel we often limit ourselves in terms of what we could achieve or who we could be.

Yes. I think a lot of that is because of guilt and shame, ideas that I think don't have any place. We should feel good about who we are. Probably one of the reasons that I haven't really liked a lot of the formal Christian religions is the idea that we're born in sin. To me that means you're guilty and shameful to begin with and I don't think that's very helpful. I believe that we're all these wonderful aspects of God. We should feel wonderful. We should be proud of that and feel proud we're human. To look upon yourself as flawed is not a good start.

I believe how much we love ourselves sets the parameters for how much we can love others. You can never love anybody any more than you can love yourself. You can never allow or accept love from anybody else any more than you love yourself. How much you love yourself to begin with sets the parameters for how you live in this world. So the first thing is learning to love yourself as much as you can.

About 1985 I met a person who said to me, 'You could really improve your running if you loved yourself more.' He said, 'I'll make you a tape that you can listen to.' But first of all he told me to say, 'I love myself.' I couldn't say it. I choked on the words. That seems terrible but I think that's a typical New Zealand upbringing. But I was willing to try anything, especially if I thought it would improve my running. Running, in a sense has got me into a lot of these things. He made me a tape and I just had to get really relaxed and then say to myself, 'I love myself.' So I promised faithfully to do it twice a day.

After three weeks I went to a race. I had always considered myself 'the best of the rest'. There were the top women runners, such as Grete Waitz, and I had always seen myself in the next rung down. So I listened to this tape and went to this race.

It was funny, because I was sitting next to Waitz in a pre-race press conference and she seemed to be getting smaller and I started to feel bigger. I could feel my shoulders coming back a little bit and I'm thinking, 'You know, there might be a way that I could win this race.' And that was the beginning. That was the first time I'd ever actually considered the possibility. Then during the race she was way out ahead. I worked my way up and I'd got into second place and I could see her up ahead. I remember thinking I could probably catch her if I wanted to. I had this moment of panic when I was actually making the decision about whether I could risk going for the win and upsetting the order of my universe. Or whether I should sit back and finish second. That would be good and that's what everyone expected, that's what I expected of myself. I knew that territory really well.

But I made the decision to catch her and as I went past her I was thinking, 'There's going to be this great fight and it's going to be really scary. I'm going to have this

173

battle.' And the funny thing was, as I went past, she waved me by. She'd actually had enough and she let me run by her. Actually, I tried to sneak past. I thought if I sneaked past then she wouldn't be upset with me. She saw me immediately and waved me by, and I went on to win the race.

I felt I owed a lot of that to the tape I'd been listening to. Because I loved myself more, I could allow myself to have more and to do better. I'm not talking about loving yourself in an arrogant way, because, when people are arrogant it's only because deep down inside they don't love themselves. Real self-love enables you to love other people better and to me that's the essence of life. In the grand old scheme of things that's what I think I'm here for. It's to learn to love more. I think that's the bottom line. Whatever way we learn to do that is the appropriate way.

I seem to remember you saying something once about being almost afraid to be a success at one stage, that we all have these fears of trying for the top, because we might be made more vulnerable, more exposed.

That's certainly been true for me at times. In my twenty years of this running thing every experience has built on the next experience. And every time you learn something different; no race is ever the same. I can't get bored with it because everything has its own signature on it.

Sometimes I think you have a theme and you work on every little aspect of it, you fine-tune different ideas.

I think it's been really good for me to go and live in the United States. I think that has enabled me to come out of my shell a lot more. Americans are a lot more self-confident, much more prepared to speak up.

Are they more encouraging, too?

Yes, in a way they are. You can ask an American, 'Do you play tennis?' They reply, 'Oh yeah, I'm really good!' Whereas a New Zealander, they might be a Stanley Cup player and yet they'll say, 'Oh, well, you know, I can hit the ball around a little bit.'

You mustn't 'skite'?

Oh absolutely. That's one of the golden rules. I think that's a really nice quality that New Zealanders have, that everybody likes to feel they're on an even level. Nobody thinks they're better than anybody else and I think that's really good. But also, as a country and as individuals, I think we could have better self-esteem.

There is always give and take in any situation. There are things I like about Americans that are really great. But New Zealand's my home and will always be home. I have enjoyed both worlds and got benefits from each of them and it's been a nice contrast for me to be able to go back and forth. I think it's a great thing to be able to live in a different culture. You see your own culture in a different way and you see yourself through different eyes and that's been really good.

You do fail sometimes, don't you? You have had what I guess you would have considered to be failures. How do you deal with those?

Well, I look back now and I don't see any failures at all. To me they're all challenges and they were all experiences and every one was valuable. In certain definitions maybe they were failures in that they didn't meet expectations at the time. If you go to a race and you try to win and don't, then you know in certain terms that's a failure. But in the greater context I think back to the Seoul Olympics. That was a difficult time because the expectation of me was so high. But it enabled me to deal with a lot of issues – the expectations of my country, the idea of success and failure. I felt I had to please everyone, that the country was relying on me, and I took that upon myself. The Olympics is such a high-stress situation anyway. You can't run a marathon with one person on your back, let alone a whole country. It's too much. So Seoul was a great experience for me because of what I learned from that.

It took me the four years to the next Olympics to be able to figure out exactly what went on and what worked for me and what didn't work for me and how I could make the situation work for me in the future. The experience of Seoul was, I think, the stepping-stone to my bronze medal in Barcelona. And I hope that Barcelona might be the stepping stone to maybe a gold medal at the next Olympics in Atlanta. We'll see.

I decided I was going to have a go at these Barcelona Olympics. So I sat down and wrote down all the things I thought I needed. I looked at the Seoul experience and all the things that didn't work for me and figured out a way to make those things work for me. A lot of that is just changing your own perception. I had to mould the situation to my benefit. One of the things I decided was to go to Barcelona and have a look at what it was like so I would be prepared, so I could have a picture in my mind of exactly what I was getting into. A year before the Games I went to Barcelona. I wanted to run over the course but I couldn't because they didn't have it set, but I got a look at the stadium. I knew what the final hill looked like because everyone had talked about that hill and seeing it took a lot of the fear out of it. I knew exactly what to expect and I could adjust my training for that and the climate and so on. So that was really valuable. I think even spending the time and the money to go and do it was an affirmation of what I wanted to do.

Then I moulded this whole idea into a wish-picture. I made this collage of things that had meaning for me and I put them all into this picture with a chocolate gold medal that I'd got from Barcelona, one of these commemorative things that I'd bought the year before, and I stuck it up the top with a picture of me with my arms in the air winning, so I could look at myself winning.

I imagined myself coming into this stadium with this big gold medal in the sky. I added a lot of other things – feathers and pictures of different things that had meaning for me, my own little personal symbols. I spent a lot of time doing this and I included my commemorative medal from the Olympic Games in Los Angeles, where I had finished fifth. That made a base for a triangle with the Olympic gold medal at the apex and on the other side I had my commemorative medal from Seoul. I saw both of those experiences as foundations for this gold medal that I was going for in Barcelona.

Then I put this picture up on my wall in my bedroom so that every day I could think about it. It was great. It's still up there, actually. I'm going to make another one for Atlanta. The gold medal's still waiting.

This may sound like a real Kiwi doubter speaking, but you were going for gold and you only got third.

It's funny because when I came into the Olympic stadium I had these mixed emotions and I wasn't sure whether I'd succeeded or failed because I was going for the gold and here I was finishing with the third, but actually I was really pleased. It was appropriate. I felt you can't do too much all at once. I'm doing it in steps and if I'd won the gold medal then I would have felt there was no place to go. I would have retired. But I don't think my time is right for retirement because there's still something else to be done. I know I can do better.

I learned so much from Barcelona and one of the things was that in some ways I had still held back a little bit. When I was visualising the race in Barcelona, which I did as a regular practice during my training, I knew that sometime in the race, and you don't know where it is, a window of opportunity opens. That's when the decisions about who's going to take the major places happen and I thought it would be somewhere in the latter stages, probably twenty or twenty-two miles. But there was a point in the race, about sixteen miles, where the race broke open. I was chasing the leaders. I remember thinking, 'No, it's too soon, I'll just hold back a little bit,' and it was in that moment where I held back that my third place was determined. My opportunity for first or second was lost and when I think back now I can pinpoint that exact moment.

Next time I won't hold back. I will go for it. So it's interesting to look back. It's not that I have any regrets because the medal I got is absolutely wonderful, but there is still an opportunity for me to improve on that, so it's great.

Journalists have already started talking about 'the wily old Lorraine Moller'. You are now thirty-eight. There is going to come a time when you will have to stop, when you will choose to stop. How long can you go on for?

I think as long as the will's still there and the body's still willing. It's not over yet for me. And I don't want other people to tell me it is when it isn't. I'm not giving up before my time. I think, like anything in life, when you're ready it happens if you're tuned in. Take John Walker. Everybody was saying he should have given up years before he did and he kept doing great. He decided in his own time.

Now, age is a limiting factor, I'm sure, but I think to begin with, thought always precedes the physical reality. The thought is the blueprint that creates what happens to us, creates our experience. And that's probably one of the biggest things I've learned through my experience with running. You get an idea and then you work towards it and you learn along the way.

I don't want to get into these thoughts about my body wearing out. My body has been recovering and repairing all the way along and there's no reason why it shouldn't keep doing it. My body responds exactly in the way I tell it to. I get out there, I can run a marathon and I set myself this idea. I know how fast I can run and what I can do and my body goes off and does it.

There will always be people who will tell you it's impossible but those are people who are not doers. They're probably sitting in their wheelchairs. I'm really only interested in what is possible. I want to always be exploring those parameters. I'm one of those people who don't like to stand in the middle, I'm always going to go to the outside edge of what's over there.

If you want to be first, if you're somebody who wants to be a leader, you want to be winning races, then you can't be a middle-of-the-pack person. You've always got to be prepared to put it out there and go that little bit extra. You're pushing the edges, and that's what I want to do. So I think it's so exciting because people are starting to think about the long term.

I'd really like to do better when I'm forty-one. To me, that's really exciting because then you know you're pushing the accepted concept of what people can do and I don't think bodies need to wear out as quickly as many people expect them to. I think people are starting to expect the wear and tear but the body follows what the mind tells it. I can see ways in which I can improve and I would like to put them into practice.

There were times when they didn't think women could run marathons and there was scientific evidence, or supposed scientific evidence, to back that up. Well, the scientific evidence changed as the people proved it wrong. I don't listen to that stuff. That was another thing I practised coming into the Olympics.

Going into the Olympic village is probably one of the hardest things to cope with. Suddenly you are in this group situation and you have to conform with the group and all the ideas of a group as a whole. You can't have things just the way you want them, and that can be really difficult. I thought, 'What do I do when I go into this village and I don't have all my support systems with me?' In my home I have all these people who believe in me and who think the way I do and support me in all aspects of what I'm doing. You go off to the Olympics and you don't have any of those and you're with this group of strange people. So I decided I'd create my own environment. I built a magic bubble around myself. It was just my own personal visualisation, but I imagined that I had this great big bubble around me and that only those things that supported me and what I was doing would penetrate that bubble. If people said things or did things that did not support what I was doing then it wouldn't penetrate my bubble. It would just fly over the top. So I walked around the village in this little bubble.

It sounds funny but it went with me everywhere. People would say things like, 'Oh, you know, I saw so and so from Australia and boy, does she look fit,' and it would just go straight over my bubble. It had nothing to do with me. There were many situations, at team meetings for example, where people would be getting really upset and things wouldn't be going right. The frustrations would be expressed and that would all go over my bubble. I'd just sit there and say to myself, 'This has nothing to do with me.' It's such an easy thing to do. It's so simple but so effective and I went to the start line and I figured even the heat didn't worry me.

You were still inside your bubble?

I was inside my bubble the whole way and when you get to the finish line then you open up your bubble and you share it with everyone. It's just great!

This interview was first broadcast on National Radio on 28 December 1993.

POSTSCRIPT
Lorraine Moller says her next major goal is to represent New Zealand in the marathon at the Olympic Games in Atlanta in August 1996. She's already training for this, running in road races in the United States and planning for 'a couple of marathons' in which she hopes to run a good qualifying time.
She believes she's becoming stronger spiritually, with a greater sense of the oneness of all life.

Neven MacEwan

Reverend 'Nev' MacEwan, former All Black, is the chaplain at Manawatu Prison. It is a job that requires him to be both firm and gentle. That seems rather appropriate, for as an All Black he was dubbed 'the gentle giant'.

As a young schoolboy, however, he had no interest in rugby. It wasn't until 'Nev' MacEwan's older brother challenged him that he thought seriously about the game.

NEVEN MacEWAN: I never had the slightest interest in rugby. In primary school I was too heavy so I had to play soccer and the only place I was any good was in goal, but I wasn't very good at that either. But both my brothers, Pat and Bill, were great rugby players and when Pat left Nelson College he said to me, 'Nev, you have to live up to the name of the MacEwans.'

So the game of rugby, initially at any rate, didn't appeal to you?

It didn't appeal to me in any way whatsoever. If you went back to Nelson and spoke to those who saw my first game when I played for Wanderers, they were just horrified when the scrum or a ruck went down there was one person who was standing bolt upright, and that was yours truly. What went on down there was too rough for me. As a boy and as a young man I was really at heart very gentle. In fact, Alex Veysey and the sporting scribes, the rugby writers worldwide, labelled me 'the gentle giant', an image I tried hard to live down. But when I look back, it was me, all right. I have always been gentle. It's very hard to come to grips with because it is not the sort of image that people like to have, particularly men.

I often tell the story that when I was a small boy I just loved nature. I loved flowers. Not the image that one likes to have of a sportsman, whatever the sport. But it is so important to know who you really are. Then you can help and encourage others to be themselves too.

Although rugby didn't initially appeal to you, you were obviously very good at it. I think you played over fifty games for the All Blacks?

I think it was about fifty-five games and twenty test matches. Yes, rugby became very important. When I first started off, a radio announcer in Nelson, Alan Patterson, came up and he said to me, 'Nev, forget all your critics. You are very good in the lineouts. You have a natural ability. Concentrate on your strengths and everything else will fall into place.' One of the things I think is important today is that every one of us is good at something, and if we encourage people to achieve at what they are good at, everything else will eventually fall into place. So often we are inclined to emphasise the things that people are not good at. They don't need to know that. They know it already.

The great thing for me was that when I left school and started playing for Wellington and then was first chosen to be an All Black I was going to be playing with my schoolboy hero, Tiny White. I wrote to him and he encouraged me and gave me pointers on how to improve my lineout work. We just practised and practised, that was my forte, and eventually all the other limitations which I had on the football field were forgotten about.

How did you feel that first time you were chosen as an All Black?

I was just over the moon. It's hard to put into words. I was just elated. There was a sense of real achievement. I had finally made it. I was also overawed by it because there were so many good players around. I don't think I really came down to earth until I ran out onto Athletic Park that cold, bleak day to play the Springboks in 1956.

Back to earth I came with a thud and discovered the reality of international rugby. It's all about pressure. But I'll never forget that. I'll never forget the tremendous times I've had with rugby. I learnt an awful lot from rugby. I have been very critical in the past, and I'm still pretty hard on rugby, but I do it to try to bring it into perspective in terms of how I see it affecting people's lives.

In what way have you been critical?

I'm critical of the expectations that are placed on players. I feel that in the past players have been exploited, been expected to perform at great cost to themselves individually. Even today there are great sacrifices and up until recently those sacrifices haven't been really recognised by the administration. Not so much in New Zealand, but the administration of the game internationally has been very slow to recognise the need to recompense the costs that players have had to pay.

What part do you think your time with the All Blacks, and it was quite a long time, had to play in the formation of you as a person, the person you have become now?

Well, rugby, like all aspects of life, has a positive and a negative. The thing about rugby and most team sports is that there are great skills to be learned and great disciplines to be learned. Life is about using skills and disciplines and learning to be responsible in every activity of our day-to-day living. In my case I was never really able to handle the adulation and the high expectations that came with rugby. I was very insecure, and unsure about the expectations that people put on me to be a 'man'.

People said, 'You would be a very good rugby player, Nev, if you were more rugged, more robust.' But it was never part of me to be that. To say to be good at something you have to do this or that puts expectations on people and sooner or later they forget who they really are. They are busily trying to be what other people want them to be and that is a dangerous area.

The positive side of rugby is the discipline. It is the responsibilities. It's knowing that if you want to have a good result you have to put a lot of hard work in to achieve it. Nothing comes easy. Nothing is without effort, and if you want something of real value there are sacrifices to be made.

During your years in the All Blacks, 'gentle Nev' was still there somewhere inside, wasn't he? What had happened to him?

He was lost. He was put aside. I started to forget who I really was and started to try to be what other people wanted me to be. It was rather like when I shared the fact that I loved flowers as a little boy and that pansies were my favourites and I got the nickname at school of 'Pansy Mac'. I never shared that thought or that aspect of my life again for years.

I think you have to sort of grow through the life's expectations that people put on individuals. People are looking for models to copy. The heroes of tomorrow have been looked at and copied and so the expectations are set. We have to be very responsible in how we handle those role models which we play. In New Zealand we have laid tremendous expectations on our heroes and when those heroes fall it can be really shattering.

Speaking of fallen heroes, that is part of the story of your life, isn't it? You were a hero, and I suppose, if we could put it this way, you fell.

I fell. It wasn't through rugby. It wasn't through circumstances. It was that I was just not at peace with myself. I was very angry with the whole world: everyone owed me something. People used to say to me, 'Nev, have a pint of beer and be a man,' so I started to drink. The reason I drank wasn't to be sociable. It wasn't because my job required it. It was because it made me feel good. It got me away from the problems, the insecurity that I had inside. It gave me the wings to fly. It gave me confidence, so I was at risk with alcohol right from the word go. Booze became part of my whole life.

Booze is not the problem. We often hear today that drugs and alcohol are the major problems in our society. We will always have alcohol. We will always have drugs. The problem lies within the person who has got completely out of control. For me, a whole series of things that happened through my life were because I just refused to come to grips or come to terms with who I was or what I was and what was going to be my lot. I hid away in myself and alcohol became a monster and my drinking brought about my downfall.

Ten years ago it all came to a head. It was as if every seed I had sown, every misdemeanour, everything that I had wheeled and dealed in, came into harvest and I had to face the music. I finished up in the courts on a charge of theft as a servant. I faced the possibility of being fined or getting the maximum for the offence that I was charged with, which was up to seven years' imprisonment. I was going to have to face the issues but I couldn't do it. I just wanted out. So I tried to commit suicide. I guess it was really a cry for help. But I finished up in Ward 5 of Palmerston North Hospital.

It was the beginning of a whole new life for me. It was the beginning of finding out who I was. It was coming to terms with who I could be, who I was created to be. But the being who I was created to be was going to be based on a deep faith that was going to come to terms with a whole new lifestyle. It was going to be the opening of a whole new work and it was in a sense a whole new beginning. It was like being born again.

Part of that was your realising and accepting that you were an alcoholic?

That was the major point. Alcoholics are great ones at denying. Everybody else is out of step, but you are okay. For me, it was the height of ridiculousness. I had attended AA meetings in the past. I had gone along as a son of an alcoholic and spoken and shared as a member with groups about what it was like to be experiencing the feelings I had as the son of an alcoholic, and particularly when that alcoholic had established AA in New Zealand. But you know, even at that early stage, all I was doing was pretending. I was saying what other people wanted to hear, not really what I was feeling inside.

I couldn't share what I was feeling. I found it difficult to come to terms with what was happening inside me. But when I came to the point of being able to say, 'My name is Nev and I am an alcoholic,' it was admitting that I had a problem and for the first time in my life I wanted to do something about it. I wanted to do it for my own reasons and to help my whole family.

Joining Alcoholics Anonymous has changed your life?

That's where it all started. At the same time some new people came into my life. You know, when you fall nobody really wants to have anything to do with you and certainly nobody wanted to have anything to do with me because I'd walked over everybody just to get what I wanted. I didn't blame anybody. I wanted to run away. But into that hopelessness and into that pit came a whole new set of people. They came and they said, 'Nev, we love you and we care for you and we're praying for you.' That just blew me away. They had something I wanted. There was something about their whole being that I was just attracted to. They had life and I sure was dead. AA and these new friends brought a dimension into my life that was lacking and so began my new beginnings and my new search and my new walk. Life continued but life had more meaning. It had a direction and a purpose. It had stability and it had security.

I guess this was a kind of religious conversion. Would you have described yourself as a religious person before? Did you ever feel earlier in your life that you were religious?

Yes, I did. I had contemplated going into the ministry earlier in my life. Certainly I had been brought up in a Christian environment – my parents had a deep faith. Nelson College was a church school so I had a real base in religion but then with the pressures of work and the lifestyle I had chosen I had turned my back on that aspect of my life and gone my own way.

What happened in this great change?

I was right at the bottom. There was just no hope. At forty-five I had just been through the courts. I had just missed by a whisper going to prison and that was but for the grace of God. There were few prospects of employment and things looked pretty bleak. I was heavily in debt with no way of repaying that debt.

Our home in Palmerston North, which I had mortgaged to the hilt, had to be sold. No matter what I had done, I didn't want my wife, Jeanette, and the children to be kicked out on the street. Yet, it had to be sold. Our solicitor said there was no way in which we could keep the home. He said our creditors wouldn't allow it and the mortgage repayments were so high that even he on his salary couldn't afford to maintain them.

'Netty' and I will always remember that painful day when we agreed to put the house on the market. But after nine months it still had not sold and somehow, miraculously, we are still living in that home. We never call it our home any more, because we know that it was only faith in God that has sustained us.

I applied for many jobs but I knew there was no opportunity for any position of responsibility. I had to start again from the bottom. The job I finally got was at Massey University as a farm labourer, drawing $125 a week gross. It was hard work. I used to come home broken, but I was learning some real basic, down-to-earth, fundamental disciplines. And being out in the open and close to nature was a deep healing process for me.

I was also learning about the spiritual dimension of life. I found that I could accept God. I think I always knew there was a God, but those people who came to visit me shared more than just that there was a God. He was alive in them. There was a vitality about them. They matched their faith with their commitment to what they were doing. So I started to look at spiritual things, while at the same time I was going to AA. The AA programme seemed to me to have it all in a nutshell. That was going to be my new religion. But I realised that it is not religion. That's man's answer to what God wants for each and every one of us.

It was when I was sharing with these beautiful Christian people that I said, 'I have come to accept God as I understand him.' But they said to me, 'Nev, you can't.' That sort of shattered me a bit and got me thinking. Then I opened my Bible and it fell open at St John's Gospel where Jesus said, 'I am the way, the truth and the life. No man comes to the Father but by me.' So the ball was back in my court again. I had to find out whether Jesus was for real, who he was and what he claimed to be. I had to either dismiss him or accept him. On the evidence that is clearly laid before us and as I did my study my verdict was that Jesus is who he claims to be.

That didn't happen overnight. It wasn't a sudden 'Damascus experience'. But I know it's for real and, as I say to the guys in prison, 'Don't let anybody tell you it's for free, because it ain't for free. It's very costly; it costs you your whole life.'

How did your prison work begin?

The last place that I wanted to be was in prison. I remember very vividly when Judge Watt passed his sentence on me and said I was not going to prison I was very relieved. But only six months later I was in prison, as the result of an invitation from an inmate who wrote to our AA group in Palmerston North. He said, 'We're having an open meeting. Would you come and be part of that open meeting?' So four of us went from Palmerston North to Kaitoke Prison just out of Wanganui for a once-only visit. It was 25 March 1980. I remember the night well because when we took off I was quite excited but on our journey across I got fearful about what was going to happen. Why did I have to lower myself to get involved in this area? When I got to the prison I began to shiver and when I went in and the doors shut behind me I started to shake uncontrollably.

I thought, 'What are these guys going to be like?' Then we came into the room where we were going to hold the meeting. I sat down and the guys came in and we started the meeting. I just couldn't get over the peace that came over me that night

Neven MacEwan

while I was in that prison. On the way back I said to the others, 'I don't know about you but I have got to go back.'

I started going back to Kaitoke Prison every Monday night, and then every Wednesday night, because an inmate said to me, 'Nev, we share in AA that higher power, but your higher power, he's someone special. Would you come and share him with us?' I have never forgotten what that 'lifer' said to me and that's what started it. I started going back to share that higher power in my life and, in a sense, I have been doing that ever since. Shortly thereafter I was appointed executive director of the Prison Fellowship of New Zealand.

A long time ago as a schoolboy you put aside that gentle part of you. Do you think you have found him again now?

I don't have to think about that one. Yes, I have found him and I realise that I have started to live out what was written years and years ago: 'the old has gone and the new has come'. I am content and I am happy with what and who I am for I know that 'although I am nothing, in Christ Jesus I am everything'. People can put expectations on me. People can put me down. People can think that I am a religious fanatic. They can put on me all the labels they like, but that doesn't affect me any more because they can't take away the peace that I have inside.

The victory is not mine. I can't take any credit for it, because it was my failing that God used, and everything that has happened I can't take any credit for. It is the story of that wonderful grace, like in that lovely song 'Amazing Grace', which I often sing. That amazing grace, that 'I once was lost but now I'm found. Was blind but now I see'. Those words have come alive for me.

As I sit down now with people, I don't ever want to be in a situation where I am judging people for what they do. I want to be able to listen to what people are feeling and to help them find the answers that lie very close to their problems. I want to sit down with people and be that gentle person, that person who I am happy to be, and help people and encourage people to be the person they really are.

This interview was first broadcast on National Radio on 24 July 1990.

POSTSCRIPT
Nev MacEwan continues to work as prison chaplain at Manawatu Prison. He says the work is very tough and sometimes he feels it is only his faith that keeps him going. But, he says, it is also very rewarding and he has learnt that you must never write people off; that deep within everybody there is the potential to succeed. His work includes helping to get ex-prisoners into employment and re-established in the community.

Shirley Smith

Lawyer Shirley Smith has been a friend of the underdog and a fighter against what she sees as injustice all her life. She has often represented gang members in court and is the widow of Dr Bill Sutch, former Secretary of Industries and Commerce, who was charged with spying in 1974, but acquitted.

Shirley Smith's sense of injustice was first aroused when she was only four and about to start going to kindergarten.

SHIRLEY SMITH: I had noticed that the schoolboys I used to see around had beautiful shiny leather bags. They wore them slung over their backs. I had been so looking forward to having one of these and when it came to the time for me to start kindergarten I said, 'When are we going to get my school bag?' But I was told, 'Oh, no, little girls don't have school bags. They carry attaché cases.' I was terribly upset. I couldn't see any reason for this at all and I created such a fuss I got my school bag and from then on I have never seen any reason why I should be differentiated against because I was a female.

That started my feminism, not only my fight against injustice. It made me realise that girls did tend to be treated differently from boys and from the moment I realised that this happened I was against it.

Your father was a Supreme Court judge, Sir David Stanley Smith. Your mother died when you were a baby and you were brought up by your grandmother until you were six years old and then your father remarried. Your father seems to have had a very strong influence on your life.

He did. My earliest memories of him were of an extremely handsome young man – black hair, blue eyes, lovely Gaelic, Celtic colouring. Our family came from Scotland. He was my hero and he remained so, I suppose, until we started to have differences of opinion when I became an adolescent, which of course is normal.

We had various encounters in which I discovered that he had some ideas about life that I didn't agree with and didn't approve of. I tended to hold out for my own point of view, which caused ructions in the family, and I can remember my dear stepmother saying to me after we had been at daggers drawn for about a fortnight, 'Shirley, dear, please apologise to your father. We can't go on like this. Look, it doesn't matter whether you're right or wrong. I'm not taking any stand on that. But please, for the sake of the family, apologise to your father.' So for her sake, and for the whole family, I apologised, but my heart was not in it.

You said once that your father found you difficult.

Yes. He decided I was the most obstinate young person he'd ever come across. This must have come out very early on, because I remember when I was still a small child he used to call me 'my little Red Fed'. I hadn't the foggiest idea what a Red Fed was. I thought perhaps it meant he thought I lived on the colour red, which I knew was an angry colour. It wasn't until I was in my teens, or even later, that I learned about the Red Federation of Labour. My dad had unfortunately been a special constable in 1913 as a young law student. So the Red Federation was very present in his mind, and that's why he called me his little Red Fed. When I discovered that this is what he meant I was terribly proud.

I would say on my father's behalf that he told me years later that he had been issued with a baton and been told to go out and help keep order down on Lambton Quay and he had seen people, strikers apparently, going in or out of Whitcoulls (Whitcombe & Tombs in those days, of course) and other special constables were beating these people on the head with their batons and Dad was so disgusted that he went home and put his baton away and didn't act as special constable any more. I was proud of him for that.

You don't have any memories of your mother at all?

No. I was only three months old when she died. It was a medical misdiagnosis. She was operated on for the wrong thing and, according to the death certificate, she died of shock. So I don't have any memories of her of my own at all. My grandmother, her mother, took me over. She was the only person available to do it. She was a widow. Her husband had died not long before my mother and she had sold her family home in Auckland. She simply took me over. Of course, she was absolutely shattered, as was my father, by my mother's death. They had been married just over a year.

My grandmother told me later on that she thought she would have gone mad if she hadn't had me to look after. We were extremely close. She was the only real mother I ever had and I adored her. And because she didn't have a home of her own any longer we used to stay in lodgings. Her favourite place in Wellington was Kenilworth, the old boarding house in Hill Street. I was very sad when that was pulled down. Or we stayed with her sister in Auckland, or relations in New Plymouth, or other relations – several families in the Waikato. So I did a lot of travelling around between three months and six years old. I used to think of the main-trunk railway as a kind of home away from home. They had a ladies' carriage that was only for mothers and children and it was staffed by a nursing sister, resplendent in white uniform in spite of all those smuts, because, of course, the trains were coal-fired in those days. She would warm bottles for the mothers and look after the children and it was a marvellous arrangement. I often think that, in the way of amenities, we are much less well off now than people used to be all those years ago.

Would you say your family was well off in your early years?

Comparatively, yes. My father was a solicitor and barrister until, I think, 1928. He mainly practised at the bar. He was in partnership with an older man to start with, and then later with his partner's son. He did extremely well at the bar and he was earning, so I was reliably informed, twice as much at the bar as what his salary became when he went on the bench. He did it, I can remember him saying, because he felt it was his duty. What Supreme Court judges were paid then is absolutely peanuts by today's standard. But compared with what other people earned at that stage it meant we were comparatively well off. The other thing was that judges were protected by law from having their salaries reduced so when everybody else was reduced during the Depression the judges weren't. So throughout the Depression we were comparatively even better off, so I was very privileged.

How did that affect your upbringing, do you think, not having to scratch for money?

I think it made me disregard money and disregard the desirability of security. Not that I've ever taken any great risks. I never had to. But I always found it hard to understand why people opted for security because it didn't have any kind of high priority for me at all. I just took it for granted, which is no doubt very unrealistic. But that's how I felt about it.

Did religion play any part in your family life?

Oh yes. I came from a family of Presbyterian ministers and Presbyterian ministers' wives. My father's father was a Presbyterian minister and his wife's brother was a Presbyterian minister, also here in Wellington. And their sons tended to be Presbyterian ministers. My father went into the law instead of the church but he had a brother in the church. I was very strongly Presbyterian, but with a sort of a gloss on it because we were not really Calvinistic. My grandfather, John Gibson Smith, was a free thinker and had in fact preceded Lloyd Geering in being tried for heresy by the church because of a book he wrote called *The Christ of the Cross*. While he was not thrown out of the church, his health deteriorated. I knew him mainly when he was acting as what they called a 'home missioner' over at Rona Bay. Before that he'd been a minister at St Andrew's on the Terrace, very prestigious. But they couldn't afford a resident minister at Rona Bay so he lived in Wellington and used to go over at weekends and perform on Saturdays and Sundays in Rona Bay.

He was a darling man and the most gorgeous man to look at. He was tall and well built and had an aquiline nose. When I knew him he had white hair and a white moustache and he was really beautiful. He also had the most beautiful nature and was a most loving person. As I say, he was a free thinker. I remember being really impressed that he came out for a picnic with us on a Good Friday. It didn't bother him that it was Good Friday.

His wife could have been an army general. She ran the family with marvellous efficiency. Managed on the very small amount of money they had and brought up seven children and relieved her husband in the traditional Scottish way of all the mundane cares of life and all the financial responsibility.

I'll never forget when I was quite small, a primary school girl, she took me one day into the matrimonial bedroom with this huge double bed and above the double bed there was a fairly small bookcase entirely taken up with small black-backed books. She said to me, and she still spoke with a Scottish accent, 'Well, Shirley, look at those books. In those I have accounted for every farthing I have spent in all the years I have been married to your grandfather.' That, of course, was enough to put me off keeping accounts for the rest of my life. I got on awfully well with her but her daughters used to say, 'She's all right with the grandchildren but you've no idea how harsh she was with us.'

My father grew up as a Bible Class boy and belonged to the Student Christian Movement. He was very much a prohibitionist at one stage. He'd apparently been prevailed upon to join the Band of Hope as a small boy and promised never to let liquor touch his lips. When he was a young man, after he had acquired his first car – a Model T Ford – he had been invited to address a prohibition meeting out at Titahi Bay. In those days it was just a little agricultural outpost. He addressed the meeting about the virtues of 'water pure and water bright' and when he came out the Model T wouldn't go. It was discovered that some wag had emptied the tank of petrol and substituted water.

He eventually got over being a prohibitionist. He used to play tennis on Saturday mornings in a foursome and afterwards they repaired to one of their houses close by. His friend persuaded him that lager was not really alcoholic, it was just a very light softdrink. So, having got that far, he tried other forms of alcoholic liquor. He was certainly no drinker, although he did drink wine with a meal and that sort of thing.

My father's faith suffered a mighty blow when my mother died because he felt that there was no rhyme or reason of any kind for my mother's death at the age of twenty-five. I think he couldn't believe in a God who could let this happen. He hardly ever went to church after that. He was not a churchgoer when I was growing up.

Did you go to church yourself?

I went to church with my stepmother. She had been brought up in the Church of England but she transferred to the Presbyterian Church when she married my father. I used to go to church with her every Sunday morning. When we moved up to Auckland for four years after my father was appointed to the bench I remember we used to go usually to either Knox Church in Parnell or to St Andrew's, I think it was, at the top of Constitution Hill. They were both fine churches with very fine preachers. I used to judge a sermon on its intellectual content and my stepmother and I used to discuss it learnedly as we came home for our Sunday dinner.

Religion was very important to me in those days. I remember my great-uncle was a very eminent Presbyterian minister. He was the Right Reverend Dr James Gibb D.D., who had been moderator of the General Assembly of the Presbyterian Church of New Zealand. He steamed me up with the importance of being a Presbyterian and not belonging to 'any of those other sects'. He'd had a stroke and was retired and living out in Seatoun and I was taken out to see him. I think I hadn't started secondary school at this stage. He was a great, impressive man physically, as well as in every other way, but here he was lying on his bed. His last words to me, as I recall, because I never saw him again, were, 'Shirley, remember that you're a Presbyterian and never give a thing to the Anglicans.' So I was terribly partisan about the Presbyterians. It doesn't sound very spiritual, does it?

What about politics? Were they discussed in your family very much?

No, we really didn't talk politics much at all. I can remember when Ramsay MacDonald became Prime Minister in England in, I think, 1924. My father, who was not a socialist or Labour man, was looking at a photograph of Ramsay MacDonald and he said, 'Well, he's got a nice face. Let's hope he'll do something.' But we really didn't talk about politics.

There was one stage, it must have been before the Depression and before he went on the bench, when Dad was thinking of going into politics. I can remember my stepmother saying to me, 'Oh, I do hope your father won't go into politics.' She said, 'Above all, he is the most honest man and you can't be honest and succeed in politics.' Whether it was her influence or not I don't know, but he never did and I'm very glad because I don't think it would have been his field. He was definitely on the side of the establishment but we didn't really talk about it.

I can remember the consternation in the family when Labour came in in 1935. I was actually overseas but I can remember my stepmother writing letters that proceeded on the basis that the whole natural order of things had been overturned. She wondered, among other things, how their wives were going to get on at Government House.

My stepmother and I didn't get on very well at the very beginning, but after a few years I suddenly had a flash of insight and enlightenment and decided she was an extremely nice woman and she and I were going to be friends. It worked out extremely well after that. She used to talk to me as a person, not just as a child.

You said once at school you were always the odd one out. How did that happen?

I wonder which school I was talking about when I said that? I was very happy at Queen Margaret's, which was my first school in Wellington. And then I had a year at St Cuthbert's in Auckland, which really wasn't long enough to get attached, and I was terribly miserable at having been taken away from Queen Margaret's. Apparently in my misery I made myself so objectionable at home that my parents decided I had to be sent away to boarding school. My father always had this extraordinary romantic idea that boarding school was good for you. If you could survive boarding school it proved you were 'worth your salt', that was his phrase. So I was sent to Nga Tawa in Marton – the Wellington Diocesan School for Girls.

I was told they sent me to a Church of England school purely on the basis that it had better playing fields than any of the other schools. They thought that what little Shirley needed was to get out in the open air and run about. I'd always been keen on games and was good at them. That did have its advantages because it was the only school in New Zealand that played lacrosse, a Canadian/Indian game. Marvellous game. It's not played anywhere in New Zealand now. Even Nga Tawa's given it up because they could never get an 'away' match – no other school played it! I never really fitted in at Nga Tawa. One reason was because I was a Presbyterian and with about three or four others I marched separately to the Presbyterian church in Marton on Sunday mornings. All the rest of the school marched to the Church of England, at least until the school got a chapel and then we had our services at the school.

There were quite often arguments about this and people used to accuse me of being a 'non-conformist', which made me furious. I said we were a completely independent branch of the church, which was set up after the Reformation. It co-existed with the Church of England, I said, and was not derivative from it. One really got hot under the collar about this kind of thing in those days. I didn't have any very good friends when I went there. I knew quite a few girls from Auckland because we were living in Auckland when I was shipped off there. I'd met them at parties, but they didn't include me. I don't know why, particularly, but they didn't and I became rather a loner. The thing is that at Nga Tawa in those days you had to be in a group. They called them 'crews' and you had to belong to a crew. If you weren't in a crew you were just non-existent. You didn't count at all. There were some rather undesirable crews, largely made up of people whom nobody else wanted, but I absolutely refused to associate myself with people in that category. This meant that eventually I simply decided to be entirely on my own. It was marvellous training, but I wasn't very happy at the time.

I found I could be self-sufficient. I found I could walk into a room full of people where nobody was going to be friendly to me and not care. Maybe I cared, but I didn't show it. And I survived, and I didn't lose my self -respect. I don't know why. Perhaps it was part of this being a little Red Fed that came out. I've always been, my father would have said, headstrong, obstinate, opinionated, determined to stick to what I believed was right. This was jolly good training in sticking up for oneself and sticking to one's guns in the teeth of what was really a pretty unpleasant and unhappy environment.

My last year was a great improvement, however, because by that time I was a prefect and head of my house. In the prefects' study there were only about six of us and we really got quite close. We were able to cook sardines on toast and stuff over a little burner and I really made friends there for the first time in my four years at Nga Tawa. I was in the school lacrosse team and my house team always won the cup, and I was in the school cricket eleven and the school star at gym. Somebody said to me once, 'You know, the reason you were tolerated was that you were good at games as well as being bright.'

Of course, being bright was the last thing. That was the other reason I didn't fit in at Nga Tawa. It was simply 'not done' to take an interest in your work. When I went there we had a headmistress from England, Miss McCall, to whom I owe an enormous debt of gratitude. She liked to run the school to some extent as a finishing school. The senior girls, the very senior girls, were allowed to wear high heels and powder to dinner in the weekend. She wanted to turn out young ladies. Most of the girls came from sheep stations. There was a sprinkling of daughters of professional people, but most of them were country girls who just weren't interested in work.

I have to be very grateful to Miss McCall because after I'd been there a couple of years she got the idea that I was somebody who she could put in for the Oxford University Entrance exam. I had just sat what we used to call Matriculation in those days – what is now University Entrance – and got through it quite well. Miss McCall had a Nga Tawa brochure that stated that girls were 'prepared for the Oxford and

Cambridge entrance exams'. It was really most misleading puffery because she had managed to send only one girl up in all her time at the school. This girl had gone to Oxford, taken a Third Class degree and married a young man who became a housemaster at Eton. They kindly asked me there for strawberries on the lawn one summer when I was at Oxford. Anyway, Miss McCall decided I was a candidate for this exam. What made it reasonable was that she had an English woman on the staff at the time, a Miss Young, who was a Cambridge classics graduate. Miss Young was prepared to take me on and prepare me for the Oxford entrance exam in Latin and Greek.

All our teachers except the domestic science one were English. They were imported from England to teach the young ladies. Of course, what we did was drive them pretty well round the bend because they'd never struck such incredibly difficult and obstreperous characters in their lives. Practically nobody ever stayed longer than their three-year contract so we had a constant turnover.

Anyway, thanks to Miss Young I did actually get in to St Hughes College, Oxford. That I owe to Nga Tawa, so my feelings about Nga Tawa are like the curate's egg, very patchy. On the whole, it was a very good experience.

Another thing I owe to Miss McCall was that while I was there she decided to have an election, a mock general election at school, to educate the girls in politics. This was really my baptism of fire in politics. She had a club that was only open to the senior school at which she announced this project. She asked girls to nominate people who would carry the banner for the different political parties. In those days we had Reform, United and the Labour Party. Well, the popular girls were put up for Reform and United. It was jolly difficult to find anyone who could be put up as a candidate for the Labour Party because, of course, nobody wanted to admit they were Labour. However, luckily, a farmer's daughter agreed to be the Labour candidate.

Then Miss McCall said (I can still see her as she stood there looking up into the far corner of the room), 'I think we shall have a communist candidate. Now, who will you put up as a communist candidate?' Well, of course, nobody would put up anybody as a communist candidate. That would be an absolutely deadly insult. And nobody would have accepted it, so, having got absolutely no response after several tries, she said, 'Well, I shall have to choose.' So again, she looked up into the corner of the room, then she swung round and pointed at me. I had only just joined this club. I'd only just got into the senior school. And she said, 'We shall have Shirley Smith as the communist candidate.'

It was a joke. Everybody thought this was going to be a great laugh and I'm sure she did too. I didn't know anything about communism at all. So I wrote to my father and said, 'What on earth am I going to say? The girls won't stand for my cutting off the royal family's heads.' He wrote back and said, 'Well, you can make the Prince of Wales a commercial traveller. He's very good at that sort of thing, travelling around the world. He didn't have much else to offer, so, after drawing a blank everywhere, I went to see Miss McCall. I said to her, 'Look, you've made me the communist candidate. I know nothing about communism. You've got to give me something to read.' She saw the justice of this and out of her shelf she pulled two small books. I think one was a Home University library book. I'm not sure what the other was, but they were books in which people who were not particularly sympathetic towards communism had set out what they understood it to be.

I borrowed and read these books and I was convinced. I thought, this is wonderful. This is absolutely marvellous. This is rational. It is designed to produce what the world needs and distribute it in the fairest possible way without any kind of racial prejudice or sexual prejudice. Women are treated equally, money is to be put into education and health and it's all for the best, the best of all possible worlds. I thought, this is the answer!

We all had to make at least one speech to the whole school during our campaign. We had to choose a lieutenant and I asked the head of my house to be my lieutenant and the dear girl actually agreed. She was marvellous. We chose colours and put up posters. The other girls who were candidates were not at all keen on making speeches. They each had to make one and they said something along the lines that their fathers had suggested during the campaign. But I, having read these books, put up a notice saying the communist candidate would address the school at 7.30am before breakfast on such and such a day. I had boned up on what I wanted to say and I didn't have a single note. I stood there and delivered my speech and made quite an impression.

When it came to the actual election the Reform and United girls each got about thirty-odd votes. I can't remember who came top. The Labour candidate got about thirteen or something like that. I got eleven and I was thrilled to bits. I had thought perhaps I'd get about three.

Miss McCall got the local MP, who was of course a conservative, to come and announce the results and preside over the evening when the whole thing was wound up in the school. We didn't have a proper hall: it was the school gym. Each of us had to make a speech when the results were announced. So the others got up and said something very public school and old school tie-ish, like, you know, 'Well, I congratulate the winner. No doubt the best man has won. I'm sure the country will do well under her.' The winner made a graceful speech saying, 'Thank you for your votes and we'll do our best for the country.'

Then it came to me. I thought, I'm not going along with this guff. So I got up and I said, 'I don't think the best man *has* won.' (Of course we never thought of saying the best woman in those days!) I said, 'I think it's a disaster for the country.' And I proceeded to hold forth on why it was a disaster for the country and why they should have put me in. There were interjections from the floor and I had to answer lots of questions and objections and there was a lot of heckling.

I remember Josie, my second-in-command, looking up – she was really quite committed at this stage – as if to say, 'Can you really answer that one?' But I had an answer for everything. I don't know how. I was inspired. I didn't care if I was bottom of the poll. I felt I was cock of the walk. The local MP had been asked to announce the order of merit in speaking. So the dear man gets up and says, 'The order of merit in speaking is the order of the poll reversed.'

As we were going down from the platform I found myself side by side with him on the step and he said to me, 'Of course, you don't believe a word of it, do you?' I said, 'Of course I do, every word.' His jaw dropped and he looked absolutely shattered.

When I went up to Oxford I didn't immediately plunge into anything political, but there was quite a strong, very left-wing group in the college and I got friendly with them. I didn't want to get organisational at that point. I wanted to get on with my work and, of course, enjoy the fun and games I was having. However, the Spanish Civil War started very shortly after I went up to Oxford. We all felt terribly deeply about that. It was also the time of the rise of Hitler and Mussolini. We all thought the Soviet Union was the 'one great white hope', you see, or 'red hope' – the only real opposition to Hitler, the only power that could possibly stand up against him.

We had a Conservative government in England, which was waffling and com- promising. When Czechoslovakia was sold down the river that was just too painful for words. I was won over by the line of argument that everybody who could contribute anything to try to save the world from war had to get into it. We really felt this was the watershed. I've always thought the 1930s were the watershed. Either we stop Hitler now, we stop without a world war, or we have a world war and God knows what will happen. And look what has happened to the world. We were quite right. But of course with all our efforts we didn't stop the war.

I joined the Communist Party, I think, in the summer term after I had sat my first public examination. I was an Oxford University party member, which was, perhaps, a bit different from some other party groups. The person I admired enormously was a party organiser who was not a university man, who had the name of Abe Lazarus. He had given up his entire life to working for the party and lived on the smell of an oily rag. He was utterly devoted and dedicated and I thought I'd never be unselfish enough to live like that. But I thought that was the ideal. I don't know what happened to him. But then, of course, the young men were going off to fight in the Spanish Civil War. It was a very idealistic time. We were in it because we felt we'd got to fight against the forces of evil and we really thought that the Soviet Union represented the forces of light, which of course it should have been. The trouble is that every system is run by fallible human beings and I don't think any revolution has survived without being betrayed by the people involved in it. It's always happened. It was a period of slow disillusionment, I suppose.

I came back to New Zealand towards the end of '39 after the war had broken out. My final exams in Oxford had been in June '39 and by that time, of course, the Soviet Union had made its treaty with Hitler. That was a frightful blow to all of us. It was very hard to understand, but it did come home to us that the western powers would be quite happy to have Nazi Germany and Soviet Union exhaust themselves fighting each other as long as the west could keep out of it, and they were prepared to give away Czechoslovakia, Spain or whatever in order to keep out of it. You couldn't blame the Soviet Union for opting out of it and saying, 'We're not going to carry the ball on our own against Hitler, so we'll make a non-aggression treaty with him and see how we cope with the resulting situation.' It was still pretty hard for us to swallow but I think that is really what happened and it was a great, great pity.

What do you feel about communism now?

I still feel that the theory I first learnt about at school is good but I don't think that human beings are capable of putting it into effect. At least, experience since the war seems to show this.

When you married your husband, Bill Sutch, in 1944, you were still a communist sympathiser, however. This must have presented some difficulties for him in his career.

Only one that I know about, and that was when he was in line for the appointment as Secretary of the Department of Industries and Commerce. This was all rather secret and, even at this stage, I can't talk about it freely. A friend of Bill's leaked to him that I was the snag. So I took steps that I promised faithfully to the person who arranged it for me that I would never talk about, so I can't tell you what I did. But it was arranged that I should talk to somebody and explain to them exactly the history of my membership of the Communist Party, when it ceased, and what my present attitudes were. I didn't compromise anything I believed in. I simply told them the story straight. I didn't crawl or anything like that. That was accepted as satisfactory and Bill was appointed to the position.

Some people see Bill Sutch as one of the greatest New Zealanders; others see him as a traitor who got away with it. You must have some strong feelings about that.

You won't be surprised to hear that I agree with the first opinion you voiced. He certainly wasn't a traitor who got away with it. He was the last person to be a traitor and I'm only too happy that, in fact, justice was done. It so easily might not have been. He wished to see New Zealand prosper and do well. He was devoted to the idea of developing all our people and their skills and their abilities, and turning New Zealand into a wonderful small nation in the South Pacific to be an example to the world again as it once was. He was the quintessential patriot.

It was in New York, when your husband was there with New Zealand's United Nations delegation, that you began to have ideas again about becoming a lawyer was it not? I say 'again' because at secondary school you had expressed interest in doing law but your father thought it was no place for a lady.

That's right. I had become interested in law because Dad always used to come home to lunch. When I was at home in the holidays he would talk about his cases. He would go over what had happened in court in the morning and ask us what our views were. If it was a traffic accident he would use the cutlery on the table to set up the intersection, with napkin rings for the cars. I thought it was fascinating and I said, 'Dad, I would like to be a lawyer.' He was really quite shocked. He said, 'Oh no, it is no career for a lady. It is much too sordid.' So I put it out of my head. It must have been the only time, I imagine, when I didn't stick to an idea of my own and bowed to his views.

I never thought about it again until Bill and I were in New York and the United Nations used to put on lectures for their staff, and their wives and families could go. I went to a lecture given by a woman lawyer from the Status of Women Commission. She stood up there on the platform. I can still see her in my mind's eye – a slim figure in a black suit who proceeded to speak in a most competent and fluent manner. What her subject was I have no idea. I didn't really take it in at the time because I was so fixated on looking at this slim figure in her black suit. And I said to myself, 'You are a lawyer. If you can do it, I can.'

When we got back to New Zealand I found that my young brother's best friend, whom I had known as a troublesome little boy, was not only a lawyer but a partner in his father's firm. I thought, 'If he can do it, so can I.' So in that first year – it was 1951 – I suggested to my husband and various people that I might study for a law degree. Nobody thought it was a good idea. I was advised against it by everyone, so I dropped it. That was a miserable year. I had nothing to do except housework and the cooking, which I didn't get around to much because I was so depressed. I think it was an early case of 'suburban neurosis'. I was so depressed I could hardly move myself to do anything. If I had made the beds by lunchtime I thought I had achieved half a day's work. I got a strange feeling. I don't know when it arose, but I thought, somebody is going to walk into this room and look around and I'll be there and they'll say, 'Where is Shirley?' because I will have become so insubstantial. I will have faded into the wallpaper. I thought, I've got to do something about this. So the next year I didn't discuss it with anybody, not even my husband, I just went up to the university and enrolled. I only told them when it was a fait accompli.

I enjoyed the law course enormously, much more than I had expected to. I just loved it. And Bill was very good and supportive and very proud of me when I passed exams.

After your husband's death you became well known as a lawyer acting for gang members. How did that happen?

I think the beginning of it was when I met Dennis O'Reilly. He was running a house in Epuni Street for young Polynesians who had run away from home. We didn't have names like 'street kids' then. I think it was my law clerk, George Rosenberg, who introduced me to Dennis. Dennis's boys were always getting into trouble and he would ask us to act for them, which we did. Then he got a big old house in Newtown that had been a boarding house. He was allowed to take it over and make it a home for his people, who were all Black Power. So from then on we were acting for Black Power.

George and I took a whole series of cases over a couple of years that I am very proud of, really, because we won every single one of them – not by any sleight of hand, just by seeing their cases were properly put.

The trouble was they never paid a cent, even though some of them were in good jobs – concrete and demolition jobs and things like that. I complained to Dennis and he said, 'I was talking to one of them the other night and saying he had got to pay you and he said, "But I was found not guilty. What have I got to pay for? I haven't done anything wrong." He's got a point,' said Dennis.

I never said we wouldn't act for them on that basis, but my secretary got angry and one day when Dennis rang up she said, 'Dennis, go away. You don't pay. We don't want you.' I was furious when I heard about it.

Then in 1980 there was a big fracas between Black Power and the Mongrel Mob outside the District Court. I was rung up by 'Big Charlie', who was the leader of the Porirua Mongrel Mob. I didn't know him personally, but he rang me up and said, 'Shirley, I have got fifteen of my boys in the police cells. Will you go down and see what you can do for them?' I said, 'Okay.' As I went down into the police cells a cry went up, 'Shirley, your children need you!' Well, how can you resist that sort of thing?

Every now and then some of the boys I know have been involved in something pretty nasty, but on the whole they get involved in things that result from having too much to drink. I talk to them one to one, on a person-to-person basis, as a fellow human being who is just as good as I am, and we get on fine. They know I put everything I can into doing well for them in court. I can't win every time, and quite often they don't deserve to win. Often I am just making a plea for mitigation, I am not really defending them. But they know they can rely on me to do my best for them. Their wives, girlfriends, mothers and fathers, everybody knows who I am. If I turn up on the doorstep somebody says, 'Oh, it's the lawyer' and there is a cup of tea and a biscuit immediately and everybody clusters around.

I am not to be congratulated for what I do. I am just grateful that I have discovered these marvellous people. If other people would treat them on the same sort of basis, I think they would find that they were very much rewarded. The trouble is, you see, they expect to be rejected. They expect contempt and hostility and when they get it they fire up immediately. They are on the defensive and then all the ugly behaviour you read about will come out, or it is likely to. But the way people react to them is counter-productive. If people could only learn to give everybody the benefit of the doubt to start with, basically, no matter what they look like, there is a human being in there.

You have said of yourself, 'I have been a rebel since I was born.' What is it that you are rebelling against?

Anything that does not seem to me to be right. Anything that doesn't seem to stack up for me. Of course, from my earliest years that has included an awful lot of conventional behaviour, or things that people conform to, just because other people do them. Unless I could see a reason for doing it, I wasn't prepared to do it. But I haven't so much rebelled against conventions as disregarded them if I didn't think they had a sensible basis.

You have, I think, a very strong sense of purpose, a sense of direction in your life. Where do you think this has come from?

I think it is genetic to start with. It must be. I come from a very high-principled, strong-willed, determined Presbyterian family. Most of the members knew perfectly well what was right according to their lights, and they were going to stick with them, come hell or high water. That came from my father's family. From my mother's family I got a lot of love. I don't mean I didn't get a lot of love from my father's family, but my mother's family were my close family during the first six years of my life when I was living with my grandmother. I spent most of my time with her family. She had married a widower with four children so she had four stepchildren. We never regarded the 'step' as significant in any way at all, or the fact that I was only a half-cousin, not a real cousin. Those cousins were really my brothers and sisters. They were about my own age. They were the ones I spent time with when I was little. I got a lot of support from them. I think it is terribly important for children to feel they are loved and secure.

The adults would tell me about my wonderful mother. So, although I had never known her, I grew up cherishing the knowledge that I had a wonderful mother and I visualised her, idealised her. I was also very lucky to have an extremely intelligent and very kind stepmother with whom I got on extremely well.

I suppose one is simply the result of all these influences: first of all the genes that one inherits, and then all the influences that one has had in childhood. I have sometimes wondered why I have always been so clear in my idea about what I thought was the right thing to do. I know sometimes I have been wrong. I can see quite clearly when I have been wrong and some of the beliefs I have held very firmly have sometimes turned out to be dross rather than gold, particularly in the political arena.

I have sometimes been disappointed in people, but as you can see from what I have said about my clients, I still always hope for the best in people and I am often rewarded. I have been very thankful that I have always had a clear idea of myself and the kind of person I am. I know what is right for me to do and what would be wrong for me to do. I have never had any doubt about this sort of thing. And if I have done wrong I will acknowledge it. I have no doubt about that, either. But I don't go around carrying a lot of guilt forever. All you can do is admit you have been wrong and take it from there – try not to make that mistake again. Try to learn the lessons that life teaches you. How sententious I sound! But make something out of whatever happens. Learn from it. One never stops learning. That's an old bromide too, but it's true.

This interview was first broadcast on National Radio on 18 January 1989.

POSTSCRIPT
In early 1995 Shirley Smith was voted an honorary life member of the Wellington District Law Society. She says that although she has retired from the law, she hasn't retired from life.

Shirley Smith

Keri Kaa

Keri Kaa

Keri Kaa is senior lecturer in Maori studies at the Wellington College of Education. She is also a writer, composer and community worker.

She comes from a family of thirteen, many of whom have had a high profile in Maoridom and the wider community. Keri Kaa was number eleven in the family.

KERI KAA: Also reared with us were two grandchildren, one of whom is my whangai, the one I nurtured. I suppose, in Pakeha terms, he is my adopted son. There were also a number of foster children. Before it became fashionable to be a matua whangai my father had foster children from Social Welfare homes whose families had sort of departed or fallen to bits. So I grew up in this very big, noisy household where there was not much privacy for children. So we all tend to be very gregarious but are in fact intensely private people because survival in that sort of hurly-burly was to do with privacy being in your head.

Quite a number of your family are leaders in the Maori community. Your brothers and sisters, they're, as you said, gregarious; they are leaders in all sorts of areas of the community, aren't they?

Oh, that's really the fulfilment of a prophesy when my mother's mother was a young girl. She would have only been about sixteen and the only daughter and her parents lived at a place called Whakato Manutuke, which, as you know, was then a Ringatu stronghold. My grandmother's father was, I suppose, a lieutenant in Te Kooti's group of followers and Te Kooti was visiting at the time. In the photographs I've seen of my grandmother, she is wearing bright beautiful clothes. They look Edwardian. There were little bows and sort of white collars and things.

She was a small, frail woman – a frail girl, really – and she was supposed to go back to a church boarding school and Te Kooti said to her father, 'Don't send her back because if you do she will die. I suppose he sensed that it was spiritually not the place for her to be. Her father said, 'What do I do with her?' and Te Kooti said, 'Marry her off.' Her father said, 'But she's so frail-looking, who would want to marry her?' Also visiting at the time was this man from a place in Wairoa. He was there visiting his sixteen-year-old son. And Te Kooti pointed to the son and said, 'There, at the gate, that young man.' Because he knew the family trees, you see.

Then they arranged the marriage and the story was that she would give birth to twelve. I don't know if you understand the significance of the number twelve in the

Ringatu Church but Te Kooti said, 'One of that twelve will marry and will also produce another twelve, whose voices will be heard,' and that's us.

That's your family?

Yes. You see my mother had twelve children. There are thirteen of us, but our father had another son so he's number thirteen. Our mother, herself, gave birth to twelve. She told us the story a long time ago and keeps on telling it in the way the old people talk. They retell the stories so that you don't forget and so at different periods of your life you begin to understand the significance and the symbolism.

I never understood the symbolism until I went to see a cousin in Gisborne who comes from a very strong Ringatu background, a woman called Rose Pere. I was waiting outside her office and I said to her secretary, 'Tell Mrs Pere I'm here.' And the secretary said, 'Who shall I say is here?' So I told her my name and I thought it was very funny that she went in and told her that I had arrived and was told to shut the door. I thought, that's very odd, but perhaps she's tidying up her office the way some people do before they let guests in.

So I waited and I waited for a long time. It was probably about fifteen minutes, and suddenly the door opened rather dramatically and the secretary stepped out and said, 'You may go in now.' And when I got to the door Rose greeted me in Maori and said to me, 'Haere mai te tekau ko ma rua!' (Welcome the twelve!) And I thought, this is really weird. She always says this to me. There's one of me, and she always greets me as though there are twelve. But it's because she knows the story of my background and these family details.

There's also the fact that an important date for the Ringatu Church is the first of July. It was declared by Te Kooti. I was born on the first of July. So there's a whole lot of all that caught up in my family background.

Your father was an Anglican clergyman, wasn't he?

Yes. He was a farmer before that, a farmer who really wanted to be, or I suppose should have been, an academic. He was scholarly by nature. His hobby, for instance, was learning whakapapa, reams of it, because he worked as a licensed interpreter in the land courts. He read voraciously, as did a lot of the old people of that generation. If you heard them speaking and were in another room you'd have thought it was a troop of rather well-educated English people. In that sense he and his generation were very English. He could recite Gray's *Elegy*, all the verses, and he recited a lot of poetry to us.

I used to go with him on the parish rounds. He was ordained when he was about fifty and he always said he realised that he should really have been an office worker

– I suppose in today's terminology a kind of bureaucrat. But his passions were for the traditional history, the whakapapa, for cricket, and for haka.

A lot of our own particular appreciation for literature and poetry came from him. He had been educated at St Stephen's School in Parnell, the original St Stephen's up in Judges Bay, and the things they had to learn were totally removed from the sort of village life they had – Latin, conjugating verbs and things. Yet our father and his brothers were immensely proud of the knowledge, the body of Pakeha knowledge, they had acquired. And of course they used it to great advantage. I sometimes wonder what they would think of the current unrest now regarding Maori people going and learning about things that are not anything to do with farming, because they viewed things quite differently then. They would find some of the rhetoric now, and some of the attitudes, quite disturbing.

What about your own schooling? I understand you have some mixed feelings about your education at Queen Victoria College?

Oh yes, I do. Especially after twenty-five years of being in the classroom as a teacher myself. I saw some pretty good teaching and some not-so-good teaching. A lot of the time at school we weren't allowed to think for ourselves. We were very organised. We lived a very ordered life, though not as cloistered as nuns. But in some things Queen Victoria opened a lot of doors for us. It was the first time we'd ever seen ballet. We were taken to the ballet and the poor staff would have to put up with us, you know, 'tippy-toeing' around the corridors. We were trying to pirouette around the place and looking like horses! We were also taken to see the Singing Boys of Mexico and the Vienna Boys' Choir. In that sense we had a very good introduction, I suppose, to western culture. But there were one or two things I had qualms about. When I became a teacher and understood what had happened to us educationally that made me determined to be a good teacher and not repeat the sort of mistakes that I suffered. It was okay for me because I could stick up for myself. But there were a number of kids coming through with me who had no means of speaking up.

What would you call a good teacher? What's the mark of a good teacher?

Someone who is organised, who is warm and doesn't put kids down and who is an inspiration. At my school during my second two years I can think of only four people like that.

That you would consider to be good teachers and a model for you?

Yes. One in particular I based myself on – a man called Haoni Waititi. He was tough but he was on about excellence – he's the man they named the marae after, the

Haoni Waititi Marae. He was also dying, and in his classes we always felt this sense of urgency and it wasn't until some years later that we realised why. He was then in the throes of publishing his textbook, *Te Rangatahi*. I was in his guinea-pig class of third formers, all those of us at the four boarding schools at that time. I still have the original books that he made for us. He made his books out of those registers that accountants used.

He was an inspiration. He believed in excellence and he was very disciplined and also a very good musician. One of my memories of him was hearing him play the piano at boarding school. Sometimes we would hear the school piano going in the school hall. He was always known to everyone as 'sir', largely because he was the only male on the staff. The pupils would say, 'Oh, sir's in the hall. And he would play, four hours a night – just play. What we didn't know, but the staff all knew, was that when his illness was at its worst and the pain was at its most unbearable he would go to a piano and just lose himself in his music.

Back home, you went to church?

We had no choice but to go. We lived opposite the church. We went to the village Sunday School. I don't know whether you've even been to Samoa or the Cook Islands, but Sunday is a very tapu day and of course the bells go at dawn and off you go. When I was in Rarotonga last year I just lay in bed and burst out laughing because it reminded me of my childhood. It's interesting how over three decades that has all changed. At Sunday School we won the prizes for the best attendance. What people didn't realise was we had no choice but to go, with our mother shooing us along. And then she would wait outside the church with a stick or threats. We had karakia every Sunday night, a full service, all in Maori.

I'd never ever sighted the words of the general thanksgiving until I went to Queen Vic. We just knew from memory the way the Ringatu people do and one day in the chapel I was busy poring through this book and I saw this prayer and started reading it and thought, 'I know this.' It wasn't until the end that I realised what I'd learnt from constant repetition as a small child was in fact a general thanksgiving.

We would always have church in the sitting room and we had to kneel down and lean our elbows on a chair – it's hilarious when I think about it – and then we'd all pray with our backs to each other and when we had brothers away in the army, like in the K-Force and the Malay Force, there would always be prayers for them.

What do you feel about the traditional church, the church institution, now?

The church, or the Anglican Church, which is the one I know about, seems to be in a state of confusion. I'm not sure whether it's at the crossroads and whether it's going anywhere. I used to be a very devout Anglican and then I went off the church. I think everybody goes through this period. You begin to question what the priest is on about and what the bishop's on about and whether the liturgy is really the church's mission statement and whether the way the church is administered and its practices are meaningful to your life. So I simply departed for a few years.

But the curious thing was that whenever I went home I just automatically went to church. That's the way our village is set up: there's the church, the school and the marae, and there was a village shop. So I automatically go to church because that's the sort of gathering place. The thing I like about being a Maori is that we're very ecumenical. We trot off to the Mormon services. My only hope every time I trot off is that at least the service might be conducted in Maori. But it's not always so.

After a period away from the church I've gone back again. I've joined an Anglican church group. We're in a curious position – we have a Pakeha parish that has been revived, but the service is Maori, as is the vicar. He was looking for a parish and they were looking for a priest and he took us along with him.

It's a curious thing to us that the English people brought the Gospel here. That's my little joke, really. They said, 'Look, you naughty natives, put away all your pagan gods and worship the one true God.' I suppose it's a cynical view of mine that in 1990 we don't see many very shining examples of Pakeha people worshipping their one true God, but we are still there. I think a lot of people in general have taken a fair hammering all round, spiritually and economically.

A lot of people have just given up, but we keep going to church. I keep going to church because it's the only place I can escape to for an hour where the phone doesn't ring and people can't phone me and I have time in which to think and reflect upon the week. The only thing that worries me is that people are always wanting me to show them how to run Sunday School because I have a lot of experience running a Sunday School. They want me to come and sing in the choir because I had many years of singing in the St Mary's Cathedral choir. I don't want any of that any more. I just want to have a time in the week when spiritually I can think my way through a number of things and get my head together.

A number of Maori people have told me they believe that the Gospel was here before the missionaries came.

Oh, yes. We knew of God but we used another name. You know all this debate at the Lambeth Conference about sexism within the Anglican Church? We have no problem with that. To us it's E Te Matua, the parent. We don't say whether it's a 'he' or a 'she'.

Sometimes for a bit of fun in church we will call out, because we have this tradition in our village of dialogue between priest and people. I read a book about it and I was in hysterics and I showed it to my mother. She laughed and she said this had always been so in this village, that the priest would say things and he would receive a challenge from the congregation. We still do that. It's just the way we do things.

There's a part in the intercessions in the Anglican Church that says, 'Let us pray for all men everywhere.' One day I yelled out, 'And what about the women?' The whole congregation looked around and the priest, who was my cousin, was standing with his back to us at the altar. I could see his shoulders heaving with laughter and he said, 'Let us pray for all women everywhere.' So I said, 'Kia ora.' I think the church needs a great kick now and then. It needs to be reminded.

Would you call yourself a feminist?

Well, I suppose, if you want to hang a label on me, yes, I don't mind that label. But you see I came from a very strong line of women. In Ngati Porou all our great houses are named after women and many of the rangatira families are descended from females. It seems to me women have always had a very powerful, upfront role. Our best orators have been women. Women in leadership are the norm to me. So when I'm living in another tribal area like this one I have to make the adjustment and remind myself we are not at home. In my mother's own tribe, you see, she and her sisters were a very powerful force in their family and they were articulate.

On a lot of marae you'll find that women actually are, I suppose, the keepers of the faith and the knowledge. In other tribal areas you might not see them in a very upfront role but they are there. When I grew up as a child they were there, upfront. They had plenty to say and they frequently shoved the men aside. I saw Tarati shut up a whole queue of men because she outranked them in the whakapapa and she preceded them onto the marae. One of them was my grandfather and he couldn't do a thing because she came from a senior line of descent. None of the men would challenge her because they didn't have the right to. That, for me, was the norm.

So I grew up with the whole notion of the feminist movement but we didn't call it that. I think people confuse it with the idea of western feminism, the stuff that Gloria Steinem and Germaine Greer and all those women were into. That should never be confused with the mana of Maori women, because I think that's imposing on it another cultural grid. We are on about a different kaupapa.

What would you say is your greatest joy? What gives you the greatest joy or happiness?

Oh, a lot of things. My family, sometimes. Some very good close friends. Listening to music. I have eclectic tastes in music. Going to the movies. Walking. All sorts of things. A good book. A great argument with somebody. Lots of things interest me. And sometimes just being left to myself.

This interview was first broadcast on National Radio on 6 August 1990.

POSTSCRIPT
These days Keri Kaa continues to go to church services, but only when she's able to fit them into her busy life, and when and where the mood takes her. She particularly enjoys what she describes as 'the more intimate services on the marae'.
She recalls a requiem mass on the marae when her young nephew died.

KERI KAA: We buried him on New Year's Day, and we had this communion service at East Cape under the stars on New Year's Eve. It was a beautiful still night and the moon was rising up over the sea. It was the first time for a long time that I had felt a spiritual sense of communion.

Keri Kaa feels that things are continuing to change and grow in her life. Among other things this year, she is doing some work towards a Masters degree in education. She says that is a very good academic discipline:

I am having to come to terms with new ideas, new philosophies about education. It is a good shake-up for the old grey cells. What the old people say about learning is that there is no end to it. So you shouldn't think just because you've turned forty or fifty you should stop going to school.

As a teacher in Maori studies, Keri Kaa feels she simply teaches what she is good at, what she knows, which is language, customs and history. She has an interest in the traditional dance forms, in the haka as performed by women and men, in poi dancing and action songs. She also composes and writes poetry in Maori and English. Keri Kaa has a particular interest in where the traditional dance form sits in the contemporary dance framework and is at present engaged as a co-director of a theatre event that will combine Maori dance and singing with Celtic traditions. Regarding moves by Maori women to claim greater recognition of their contribution within Maoridom, Keri Kaa believes:

It's a jolly good thing and it's a bit late. We have been a bit slow about that. I think it is time that the Maori men acknowledged that the Maori women, that we, have made a difference. I think they have to make that acknowledgement without any malice or fear.

The real leadership is coming from Maori women and it always has, but it has never been publicly acknowledged. That's the huge push that people such as Mira Szaszy and her followers are making. I know that there is a team of key Maori women who would like to propose an alternative to the fiscal envelope. They are very high-powered Maori women and they can see that what is currently on offer now is a social and economic disaster. So politicians had better take great note of what they are on about.

There are Maori women with mana and with years of back-breaking work behind the scenes, and the nurturing and the parenting, and politicians should listen to them.

Bruce Stewart

Bruce Stewart

Bruce Stewart has done many things. He's been a deer culler, builder, cabaret singer and prison inmate. He's also a writer and the founder of Tapu Te Ranga Marae in Wellington, where he works with disadvantaged Maori and Pakeha young people.

Son of a Pakeha father and a Maori mother, Bruce Stewart first became conscious of his Maori side on his first day at school.

BRUCE STEWART: The kids came around me at playtime and they were pointing at me and calling me, 'Maori, Maori, Maori.' I was devastated. I ran home crying to my mum that I was not a Maori. And my mum told me I was a Maori, 'cos Mummy's a Maori'.

For years and years I never wanted to be a Maori. I tried very hard to be a Pakeha: I learned all the Pakeha things, I went through a long period of talking posh like some of my Pakeha aunties and uncles. I did very well at sport and academic things and I got liked. There were Maori, but I never mixed with them. I mixed with Pakeha, and I got a real kick when they used to talk to me about 'Maoris'. They used to say, 'Aw, Maoris are this and Maoris are that' and I thought, well, I'm just the same as them. There's no difference.

But I kept my mother hidden. I did quite well when I went on, academically. But I would never show up at any prizegiving ceremonies, because I'd have to show my mum and I didn't want my mum to be seen. My mum knew, but she didn't say anything. She just loved me.

That meant a lot to me. My mother was so quiet and so loving even when she was under enormous pressure. I found out lots of other things about Mum. She decided to marry a Pakeha because of what she went through as a little girl. She decided her kids would be half-castes. They would perhaps marry Pakehas so they'd have a better chance of survival.

She knew that the path she was on was a difficult path. She had a Pakeha husband and she never spoke one word of Maori. She didn't even say 'kia ora'. She never talked about Maori things. Just sometimes, she would pull out some tatty photographs and say, 'Now this is your uncle George, he's a gentleman, this one. And this one here is your Uncle Taira. And this is my dad, and this is my mum.' But that happened only very rarely.

My mum died when I was seventeen. I became very bitter and angry and I completely changed. I suppose if things hadn't happened along the way (I ended up in jail, eventually) I would have headed something like an IRA gang, but a Maori version – fighting a kind of a guerrilla warfare. It worries me that there might be others around with the same thoughts.

But I think the tide has changed. Now it's quite a big deal in some ways to be Maori. But to me it's kind of watered down. I started looking for the truth after my mum died. I started looking at Maori things. I went to my people and I found a lot of them drunk. Whenever I looked for my uncles I could go straight to the pub any day of the week just about and they'd be there.

On the marae I had expected people to live together and do their gardens together and work together and share and it was all laughing. This is how I read about it in books. Because that time when I thought I was a Pakeha I was also a closet Maori. I used to read things and try to imagine that my mum was a great Maori princess. In actual fact, she was pretty low-born and so am I. In fact I'm even lower-born in some Maori circles because my father is a Pakeha. But as I got to know about Maori things I started to look behind the talk and started to look for other things. Like, I knew about the younger son or the younger-born woman or man, but there were lots of stories about a lot of them doing very well, making their own mana, making their own story. And I thought, well, that's for me. I'm a nobody but I've got a chance of doing well too. Look at Tane. Tane was a nobody. He was right down the list. But he did some wonderful things and I thought, well, there's a chance for a low-born like me.

I get really upset when the negative side of whakapapa (that's our genealogy) is used to support 'what a big deal I am and who I came from'. In fact, I find that Maori are great snobs. They talk about Pakeha being whakahihi – stuck up. But Maori would leave them for dead.

While I was in prison I read an article by Cliff Whiting in a magazine called *Te Ao Hou*. It said the marae is your economic base. The marae is your spiritual base. The marae is your art gallery. It's your museum, your kindergarten, your university, it's everything. And I thought, wow, that'll do me. I don't need much more than that to last me the rest of my life. I wanted a place, you know, that would have those qualities. And so I started. I only had $25 when I got released, which doesn't last long when you come out of prison after a fairly long sentence. Your chances of being prime minister, you know, are fairly slim. So you have to make your own way.

A lot of my friends started getting straight back into the big stuff. Now a lot of them are dead. I was in the Mr Asia gang – I was one of the starters of that. But I decided to give it all away and get into another kind of life.

I started seeking, looking for things. I've always had that. I've always tried very, very hard at everything I've believed in – a kind of obsession or single-mindedness.

Sometimes I've suddenly found it was all bullshit. Then I just put on my parachute and jump out of the plane and pull the ripcord. I just leave the whole lot behind and start on something new. I've done that lots of times.

Once I don't believe in anything I can't take even one step. But as long as I believe in it I can do it even without wages, like now. I've been here sixteen years. I don't get paid. I work seven days a week, all sorts of hours, and I love it. I just love it. It's very fulfilling; it's a joy. I get a real buzz out of it, and other people come along and they get a buzz out of it too, and I get a buzz off their buzz. And we have thousands of people come here, about seven or eight thousand a year. They come and stay and I get a buzz out of it and so I keep going. I love it.

That time in prison was quite crucial, wasn't it, in turning things around for you?

Yeah. It isn't for most people. Most people get all their contacts in prison and set up their whole network. I hated it so much, and I hated the system so much, but it gave me time, time for nourishment – self-nourishment – and that was a word I didn't know then. I know it now. I've had times when I've just had to get away and get some self-nourishment. Not retreat, just sort of build myself up again. That's happened a lot from my writing. I start writing and suddenly I uncover layers. I don't know why it happens. I just uncover some layers in me and then suddenly I've written something and I can't believe I wrote it, you know. There it is. I didn't even believe it when I started and yet there it is. It just turns up on the page and I go running to Cathy and say, 'Look at this!' That's happened to me a lot. I live a very busy life, far too busy, and if I had any choice now I'd want more lonely hours. I really thirst for the discipline in the loneliness, and when I've had the nourishment I want more.

Recently Cathy and I had a break, the first break we'd had for five years, and took three days off. We went around this lake up in the centre of the North Island. There's a track about sixteen kilometres long right around this lake and it's very beautiful. It was just one of those magic days and there were lots of native birds. We stopped to have the lunch we'd prepared. We were quite weary, but bouncy still.

It was about the middle of the day and there were ducks and swans, and birds up in the bush, and the waves were sort of lapping the shore – it was too big for words. We didn't say a word. Cathy and I just quietly ate our sandwiches and we were part of it. It's happened before in my life – some time when you're part of something very big and universal. You're just conscious of something. I don't know what it is, I can't explain it – I don't even really want to try. We weren't a big part of it. We were just a little part of a great big thing. And we were enjoying it.

Then suddenly out of the blue came this guy on this sort of motorbike thing that goes on water and he went straight through the ducks. Then he saw us and started showing off how good he was on it and it just shattered us. It was such an intrusion on this magic moment.

As I think back to that magic moment now, you know, none of it went to school, none of it had any special training. It was just going by itself. It was just all working. And I think in those magic moments there's a feeling that you're touching on something that works all by itself. It works for Cathy with her Irish background, and for me with my predominantly Maori background.

I've got some Scot in me as well, but I'm becoming closer to my Maori side, very close, and I see more and more that the Maori is tied to nature, that the whole of the story is about nature and working in harmony with nature. For me the word 'truth' has been replaced by the word 'harmony'. I just love this word, you know. You're just in harmony with everything. You're just part of it all. I don't believe we're the boss.

In Maori we have lots of gods, or deities, if you like. One of them, one of the senior ones is Tumatauenga. Tumatauenga is the god of war, the destroyer. He's the male personality and he's also the originator of man – mankind that is, the human race – and it's quite something that he's the destroyer. It doesn't matter what he destroys, whether it's positive or negative, he just loves destroying. But also from Tumatauenga came matauranga – the knowledge. The word is from the same root. The knowledge can build up or destroy. The knowledge can be positive or negative and that's what I see the more I look at our mythology.

Thank god we don't have a hell. And we don't have the devil. But they came under pressure from Christian groups to have a devil so they made one up and called him whero. He doesn't exist in the old mythology. I don't want a whero. We do have some very tricky gods.

I love the idea of tapu and noa, the male and the female in balance, in harmony. And the Sky Father is not on top of the Earth Mother – they are alongside each other. Somehow artists always have this guy always on top of the woman. But they are alongside and they complement each other; the one's not greater than the other and we need that today in our families. I mean, this is a living thing. I believe it. I know it's metaphorical. I know all that. But it'll do me, that software. It'll do me. It's the two in balance.

I love the idea of whanau. The whole thing is set up to be a family. Everything is related and when the first botanists came here to name all the plants, they found that everything was already named. Our people knew every stream and every creek and everything had a name. People by and large lived in harmony with nature.

The other way is wanting to take nature to bits. Like the boy with a clock. He puts it back together and there's lots left over, a handful of bits, but the clock seems to go, sort of, you know.

Here we have a lot of technology, but we try to be very careful about what we do. So we built this great big place here from the wastes of the city. We hardly ever buy new things. Old buildings that are pulled down, we use them. We recycle them, make things out of them. It takes us years and years. I heard someone say, 'He's been on that job for sixteen years and it might go for another sixteen!' Meanwhile there's life and there's hope. I think my quest has always been there, this looking for the answer.

You were a Christian at one time, weren't you?

I was a devout Christian. But then I started asking questions. One of the things that worried me a lot was about my ancestors going to hell. I wanted to know how you could have a hell, *and* a loving God. That troubled me a lot but I was told not to worry. And I asked questions about nature. I've always been close to nature, but there wasn't much about nature in this teaching. But I was told that was kind of earthy thinking – a lower kind of thinking. 'You're above that,' I was told. 'You've got to get your mind up.' Those things niggled away at my faith.

Then I started to think about how the Maori were ripped off by the church and I started turning against Christianity. I became very bitter. I learned how, in the name of truth, they slaughtered all these people and children – culling heretics. That got me very angry and I became quite aggressive towards Christianity.

But there were other things, like for instance the word 'utu'. I always thought it meant revenge and I always thought it was one of the most powerful things in Maori. I had all these thoughts of revenge. If any Pakeha did something to me, I'd bring revenge down on them. Then I learned that the word had been redefined by the missionaries. In fact the word meant – and there's quite a lot of proof for it – that you get what you deserve. And so if you sow positive things, you get positive things and if you sow negative things you reap negative things.

That brings me back to this thing called the wairua. It's sort of hard to explain. It's a kind of a force. It could be the cause of cause and effect. I realised you don't have to go out and actually be the right of arm of utu. It just happens by itself so you don't have to worry too much about it. That's been quite a change in my life, and it's only happened quite recently.

I don't believe any more in this idea that someone is watching you all the time. When I was first a Christian I believed there was a little hole at the back of the church and if I shined my shoes really well and I poked them right out in front things would go well for me. We did the car up, too. I thought if we always parked out in front of the church God could see that straight through the window, and he could see my shoes and I'd go down well. I actually believed that. I don't now. I believe that it all goes by itself. We're just a part of it, we live with it and that's nature. The mythology is a way of explaining it. There are some things I can't understand behind the veil, but the mythology is a way of saying that behind the veil is okay.

These stories give me a way to live by. Like the story of Tane. When he was born it was all in darkness but Tane said, 'Hey, there's a better life than this. There's something missing here. We've got no light in here. It's dark. These two parents of ours – I want to separate them.' They said, 'You can't, you're too young. That's the big boys' job.' Tane had a lot going against him. They tried and they couldn't, and he tried and he could. Because he always knew what he was doing. Tane believed in what he was doing. And it happened and there was light. And the two became in balance, in harmony.

I started to think of me and my many periods of darkness. There is a way out. There is light at the end of the tunnel. The story of Tane is not just a quaint myth but something you can practise. You can practise it every day. It doesn't matter whether it's an actual truth or not. I know it's a metaphor, but it's a metaphor that works for me.

It's in the form of a story but it has a deep meaning for you?

Yeah. The stories are there to help us make another effort. These ones work for me and I feel we've all got our software and it goes in some computers and doesn't go in others.

For years and years I thought I was in charge of things. I don't know where I got the information from, but I really believed I was in charge. I was the boss. And that's not harmony. The Maori say that a stone has its own mauri life force. They don't say human beings have more mauri than the stone. Everything has a life force. We just need to be in harmony with that.

Sometimes I take too much. I've got the ability because I've got hands and because the others haven't got hands I can grab. Then I'm grabbing too much. I'm grabbing more than my share. I'm out of harmony. When we have a buffet meal here I watch all the greedies getting in first. They're usually boys or men and they're grabbing armfuls of food. There's something not in harmony there. And I worry about things that happen back in their homes to put them out of harmony.

Harmony is bringing the children up to embrace everything else, to realise that you can't cut down the trees. You just can't go and slaughter a tree – you're slaughtering a life force. They were here before us, great trees. You picked up the dead wood for the fire and if by chance you had to cut down a tree you worked it out with the tree. And it might take months. 'Can't be done this afternoon, sorry.' It could take months of talking and consultation with the tree before you could cut it down, and that's a kind of harmony.

You used to be a very successful deer culler. What do you feel about that now?

I'm vegetarian now. I can't eat red meat. I was brought up on three feeds a day of meat. I was brought up cutting sheep's throats and knocking off cattle. I used to shoot a couple of thousand deer a year. No one told me, no one preached to me. I just felt it was out of harmony, you know. When I was on the farm there was blood everywhere and the lambs wandered around crying, covered in blood. A few of them died. Some of the sheep didn't mother again and all this sort of business and I thought, God, I don't want to be part of this!

I was brought up in it. I was brought up hunting great trophies. People came to my father's house from miles around to see this famous stag head. What a man! That was the height of masculinity, to shoot a stag like that! I went out shooting for 30 years and I was determined to beat my dad. Then I was determined to beat everyone in the world. And one day I thought, this is bloody stupid, so I just jumped and pulled the parachute chord.

In the ordinary way of hunting meat you just went out and got a feed and brought it home to the family. But this was far different – we were chasing round mountains for months and months. Hiring aeroplanes and everything just to get ahead, to say, I'm the greatest hunter and therefore the best man.' That's what it was saying. So I changed, and that's part of the progress. In fact, I've still got all the stag heads and I don't know what to do with them. I feel a bit embarrassed about them. But I dare say they'll end up in a museum or something like that. It's just part of what I went through – part of my growing. I worry when I see people stop growing, though. If we could just follow through, keep following it, it will iron itself out.

Do you feel you are now more in harmony, at peace, with yourself and your world?

I'm a lot better. I still keep seeking, though. Some of the 'bogies' come up every now and again. I've become much more peaceful, but then some bureaucrat comes along and flashes his credentials and says I'm this and I'm that and then stomps all over something that's sacred to me. It's happened here very recently, you know. And I have ideas of flying back to my past. It actually pops into my head. More than that, it pops into my mouth. All this talk about what you believe and suddenly in a few seconds it can all be demolished. 'You're not out of the woods yet, you know. You've got a way to go yet!' Every now and again it raises its ugly head. It can happen in an instant. It's much harder to be a builder. The trouble with us is we come from this warrior stock. Fearless warriors. I know it's in my genes. It's pretty frightening and destructive.

Some people try to work into the Maori beliefs the idea of good versus evil. It's not that at all. It's about being in harmony. I don't believe the female side represents darkness and the other side is the good side. It's not. In Maori the light and the darkness are compatible with each other, they work it out. We have a meeting house here and one side of the house is male. That's the tapu side. One side of the house is noa. That's the female side. But both sides of the house lean against each other. The tapu cannot keep standing unless the female, the noa, is standing too. They're leaning on each other. If one side falls down the other falls down too. I love it. I love that concept. It's the harmony.

We've recently come into a big block of land here. It's fifty acres, roughly. We're going to turn it all into native bush. We're going to put a fence around it to keep the predators out and we want to bring the birds back. It's years since we've seen tui here. It's not whether the Pakeha have done it or whether Maori have done it. That's not important. We've got to do it together and, strangely enough, there's more Pakeha coming out of the woodwork to help with this project. They're coming from everywhere, beautiful Pakeha coming out. And our Maori have got to work through a fair bit of stuff here. And yet it's right there in our software. There's very few of our people want to stand up. But it will come.

What do you think about the future – about relationships between Maori and Pakeha?

I'm very hopeful. There are a lot of people riding on certain tickets causing trouble. But I'm very hopeful. It's gone a long way and where it's particularly hopeful is among the children. There's not a lot of hope for the big ones. Some of the big ones can't see or bend but the 'littlies' come here. This little Pakeha girl with big wide blue eyes said to me in all innocence a while ago, 'Mr Stewart, where do you keep all the rottweilers?' She'd been told or maybe seen snippets on TV that Maori have rottweilers and they keep them at the marae and they rip kids, people, to bits. And I said, 'Oh, we haven't got any here, you know.' We believe that one of the things we have to offer the Pakeha kids is to tell them, and we believe it too, that this is their marae as well. I think there should be one in every district, if not every street – a community centre that people use and share.

I think the biggest thing in Maori that attracted me was sharing. 'What's yours is yours and what's yours is mine and what's mine is yours.' There is some kind of purity in this sharing. Yet, what I was taught at school was completely different. I was taught that the winner takes everything. The first prize, you get the lot. There's a second prize and a third prize but it's the first prize, that's the big prize. And a whole lot of people miss out. So I learned that. There's still a lot of the old thinking in me, unfortunately.

I'm hopeful when I see sharing among the children. It's happening in schools and it's wonderful. A great time is coming because of the young ones. We are learning to share and I feel that I have something to share with them, too, about the harmony, about just sitting quiet among the trees, just listening and looking and not rushing around all the time. We don't need a great skateboard or a bike that can go anywhere or a horse or a motorbike. We can just stop and listen sometimes.

This interview was first broadcast on National Radio on 15 June 1991.

Alison Gray

Alison Gray is a sociologist and a writer and is also well known for her work in the field of oral history. Her best-known books include 'The Smith Women', 'The Jones Men' and 'Springs in My Heels – Stories about Women and Change'.

Alison Gray grew up in a family where there were strong rules about what was considered appropriate behaviour.

ALISON GRAY: It was an exuberant and warm family, lots of noise and fun. My mother came from a family that was much more genteel. They aspired to gentility and had quite strong rules about what was seemly and what was appropriate. When I went to my father's parents' golden wedding, which I enjoyed, people did skits and performed but there was a very clear message from my mother that this was not really an okay thing to do. Women didn't behave like this. It was unseemly, almost to the point of being 'tarty'.

Mum was the strongest person in our house. You were expected to be seemly, to be appropriate at all times. Anger was something you didn't show. You didn't show feelings of any kind in excess. So that was a really important thing for me, growing up. I realised later it not only restrains you in terms of self-expression but it also puts limits on ideas and limits on artistic ideas. My parents' idea of good art was the Kelliher art exhibition, Gilbert and Sullivan, that kind of thing, and I remember feeling guilty that I liked Picasso. This was 'pretentious' and pretension was something that wasn't approved of.

You actually felt guilty when you behaved in this unseemly fashion?

Yes, I felt guilty. I felt I was somehow trying to put down the family or think that I was better. I found it a very confusing message as a child. The other important thing for me was that I was the third child in a family of six but I was also the third child in less than three years. I was trying to get attention and my mother was trying to cope and survive and obviously those two things didn't match very well. The last thing she wanted was someone trying to get noticed.

That puzzlement over how to be myself and how to get noticed caused a lot of problems in my family. I was always being labelled as the one who was different or trying to be different.

This 'unseemliness', did it extend to expressing warmth and love as well?

It certainly did. You didn't show or express feelings. When my brother-in-law died several years ago my mother was very proud that my sister didn't cry at her husband's funeral. It wasn't okay to show any feelings. You got over your grief very quickly if you had it and you didn't show it. That was good behaviour. Similarly, you didn't whoop and roar and holler in joy around the house. This was not nice either. You were just very, very controlled and you didn't share any kind of problem with anyone outside the family. Things were kept tight inside the family and because we had six children in our house we actually weren't encouraged to bring kids home to play. There were always heaps of us around so there was a very close, tight, insular, inward-looking family, a bit scared that what was happening in the outside world might contaminate us and give us daring ideas.

In many New Zealand families there seem to be rules about 'skiting', showing off or boasting. For some people the family is the only place where you can 'skite', but in others you can't even do that.

Skiting or showing off was definitely not on at all; it was jumped on very quickly. My parents had six children. They didn't have a lot of money and they had this dilemma about whether they treated us all the same, even though we were very different. They decided to treat us all the same, which meant we all had to try to act the same. So if one did well in some area, nothing too much could be made of it because the others hadn't all done well in that area. So there was this lack of reward for the child who had done well; no one got too much attention or too much notice. They tried to balance things out and, of course, the cost of that is quite high.

What was the cost for you?

The cost for me was that I never got a sense of when I'd won approval. I talked later with my sisters about it and they felt the same. We were continually wondering what it was that would get you a word of praise. So you made more and more effort academically or, if you were sporty-minded, you would do more at sport. But no matter what we did, we didn't actually get that word that said you're wonderful, so we kept driving ourselves harder and harder in the hope that we might. When my father was dying I was sitting with him, and I don't think he quite realised that it was me, and he said, 'You know, we treated all our children exactly the same. We didn't praise any of them so they wouldn't get swollen heads. We made this agreement that we wouldn't praise them.'

There was a time when it suddenly clicked with me that no matter what I did I was never going to get praise because it would have broken this rule. I might have got a swollen head.

It suddenly made sense and it was an enormous relief to me that I didn't have to keep doing more degrees or whatever it was to get approval because I realised that I would never get it. In some ways it was too late because I had three children by then, but I realised what my parents' philosophy had been all their lives.

So you came to a time when you no longer needed their approval? Did you replace it with anything?

By then I was an adult in my thirties with children. I was a solo parent and I had to work. I had to try to learn to like myself better and not seek other people's approval and I haven't actually achieved that totally. When people say I've done something really well that's great, but I only half believe them. I think they're just saying it to be nice to me. It's a very hard lesson to learn. It's one I'd like to feel a lot more at peace with. It's hard to take compliments when you didn't grow up with any at all. It's very difficult.

When did you decide you were okay ?

I don't know that I have. I still worry that I'm not a good mother, that my writing's not up to scratch or that I might have hurt somebody unintentionally. I don't lie awake at night thinking how great I am.

Another thing that contributed to who I am is that my parents had a very, very strong emphasis on education. That's one of the positive things they did. They did lots of positive things – I don't want to make them sound ogres. They certainly had strong values that they believed in and acted on with integrity and one was education. So, although we lived in a small house with no car and no fridge and we were scraping up threepences to go to Brownies and things, they sent my eldest sister and my brother and me to private schools. This was an amazing shock to me. I got there and discovered that there were people who came from a world I never even knew existed. They had farms and cars and all this kind of thing and I suddenly realised that class existed in New Zealand. The school itself was physically beautiful and we did fencing and archery as our sports. There was lots of art, which was wonderful for me, and I really enjoyed the beautiful aspect of it. I've never lost that interest in art. But at the same time I felt totally out of place because I was this person who couldn't go to birthday parties when I was invited because I had no way of getting there or getting home because my parents didn't have a car.

We moved when I was at secondary school and I went to Wellington Girls' College and the very first day I was there I saw two girls physically fighting in the basement. This absolutely devastated me and I realised that there was yet another group of people and I didn't belong in that group either, and I had this strong sense of there being layers and groups of people. I was very puzzled about where I fitted into those different groups; also about what made up the groups. How did you get into one group rather than another group? Was it money, was it brains, was it artistic ability or sporting ability or where your family lived or what ethnic group they came from?

So these issues contributed to a sense of displacement. I didn't feel that comfortable in my own family, in fact I felt quite alienated there. They all thought I was a bit pretentious because I liked the wrong artists and liked jazz, so I felt quite lonely in my own family. I also felt displaced socially about where I fitted in a group and where my family fitted. My mother's messages were very clear: our family was heading for the proper kind of middle-classness. This was important. There were some people we couldn't play with because they were not quite 'up to snuff', and there were others she was a bit envious of, I think, and considered that's where we should have belonged if only things had been a bit different. So there was a constant question of where I fitted in. I suppose I've never quite sorted that out.

There seem to be these polarities, don't there – recognising your sense of difference and recognising where you fit in?

That's right. I think everybody struggles with that to some extent and that some people work it out more easily and more quickly than others. I think that, along with that sense of difference is an enormous desire to belong, an enormous desire to fit in and just be one of the gang. At school you wanted to be one of the group and not the outsider and you wanted to have a group who shared interests and artistic ideas and intellectual ideas. It was really important to me to have that but I had to go outside my own family to find it and that felt like a betrayal.

Did you feel that you were being disloyal in some way?

Yes. I was being disloyal to my family's beliefs, to my family. The message I got from my parents was that the family was the most important factor in my life and it was. I depended on them and hoped to get a sense of love and support from them and the fact that I didn't get it and tended to search for it elsewhere did seem like a betrayal. I think everyone has that dream that their family's a safe haven and the one place where they can go to get unconditional love. But it didn't feel like that to me. It was definitely conditional on obeying the rules.

Did religion play any part in your family's life?

Our family was reasonably religious in the sense that we all went to Sunday School in an Anglican church. My mother was Anglican, quite strongly so. My father had grown up Presbyterian and at one stage he'd considered being a Presbyterian minister but he opted to become a school teacher instead. So we all went off to Sunday School with our threepences and put them in the plate and went to church and to communion as I got older. Bible Class played quite an important part in my life simply because in those days that was the main social setting. We had Bible Class dances on Friday night, which were a great attraction. We starched our petticoats and things and went along. It was a safe place where we could go on Friday nights and meet other people. The religious side was quite important but I knew a lot it was the social interaction.

I went to Old St Paul's in Wellington, which is an incredibly beautiful church and I just loved the feeling inside it, the wonderful peaceful quiet. It's full of spirituality. It's warm. It has that lovely timber, stained-glass windows, and I just love the music that goes along with the church and fills it. It emanates from an organ you can't see; it sort of appears from nowhere and fills the church with this lovely sound. And there's the light through the windows. So I went there for that. That was a very important place for me to go. It was quiet and peaceful, and legitimate as well.

But the church thing stopped quite abruptly, and quite sadly in a way. It happened when I was about fourteen. I used to sing in the choir and we were singing away and I suddenly listened to the words that I was singing and thought, 'This is nonsense. I don't actually believe this stuff.' It was quite remarkable. And I could never regain it. I could never quite believe in it again. It was about God being up in heaven, a physical God, and people resurrecting, and life after death and I couldn't believe that something that came from Israel 2000 years ago would have relevance to me in New Zealand in a literal sense.

I just thought, 'This is bizarre,' and I never recovered from that kind of mind-blowing experience one day when I was about fourteen. The literal words we sang and the sermon and this Jesus person didn't actually relate to me at all, and it just went. I got really quite upset about it because I desperately wanted to have a kind of faith that was structured and focused in a building and in a ritual. That was quite a devastating loss, really, and I don't quite know why it happened, but it was definitely an intellectual thing that destroyed it.

Have you replaced it with anything else?

Oh yes, definitely. One of the great pleasures has been finding that spirituality continues regardless of the intellectual framework within which it's structured. It's been replaced over the last twenty years with a sense of a much wider universe. I think as I've got more in touch with the physical land, through going out and exploring it, and also art and music, I've realised there's an enormous kind of shared joyfulness and a shared ongoingness of life. There's the great sturdiness of mountains and rocks when you're standing upon them. They've been there forever. They're going to be there forever. They're kind of brave and the rivers wear them down and another bit builds up and there's an ongoing life force that we're just part of, really. I feel most at peace when I'm outdoors and feeling part of something that's a lot bigger. It's very strong and empowering to feel part of something that's going to keep going forever. I don't feel quite as small and useless.

So you fit in there with nature?

Yes. There's an enormous dignity about nature, really, and it's also strong. There are hurricanes and earthquakes and yet it keeps going; it shifts and moves and it's never stable but it keeps going for centuries and centuries, for thousands and thousands of years. And it will give you support. You can eat off it, live off it, sleep in it, and it will encompass you. It just keeps going. It's good.

One of the major turning points in your life, I understand, was a very serious accident in the 1970s.

Yes. It changed me dramatically. I had a major car accident in 1976 and my three young children were in the car with me. They were aged about six, four and three, I think, at the time. We were driving along and it was appalling weather and I was very ill. I was also leaving my marriage. I often wonder when people talk about accidents whether they are caused by such a combination of circumstances. We spun out in the road and hit another car. No one was killed but we were all injured, quite seriously.

That experience and the long months of recuperating changed my life. I realised life can go *snap* like that in ten seconds – the ten seconds it takes to slam into another car. And I remember, as the car spun out of control and I knew the accident was going to happen, I spent two seconds thinking, 'This is it, this is the end of my life.' It was quite calm, really. I was quite surprised. And it wasn't the end of my life - I woke up. Well, I didn't quite wake up. I was lying in Taihape Hospital with a lot of people round me and it was quite dark and I can remember their voices getting more and more anxious and stressed out and one of them saying, 'It's too late, she's gone, she's gone.' Someone else would say, 'No, no,' and in my little head I'm saying, 'No, no, I'm still here. It's all right. Keep going, keep going, I'm still here.' But apparently they couldn't hear me.

Fortunately they did keep going and they flew us all off in helicopters to Wanganui Hospital. I just had that sense when someone else had given up. I thought, 'Well, I could give up, really.' It didn't seem that bad, not too difficult and not at all scary, and I didn't see any great figures of light as people are supposed to. It was just quiet and dark and peaceful. I think that was a real turning point, a sense that life can stop at any moment and that I had actually said, 'No, I'm still here and I'm going to hang on,' and I did. So that's an odd spiritual experience, I suppose, in a way.

I didn't see any angels or anything like that, but I did have an enormous sense of peacefulness and I think I reached a kind of rock-bottom where there is a will to live. One of the most difficult things in my life is that I've always struggled with the will to live. I've always kind of thought of suicide as a way out, and it's often been an option that I've explored more or less seriously. I'm often puzzled about why we're here and I was quite surprised that I did want to keep going. There was this interesting realisation that deep down in everyone is this kind of affirmation about living, but I have great empathy with people who don't actually make that statement and decide not to carry on.

Why do you think we are here?

I'm still not sure why we're here and I still have crises when I think, 'What's the point? Why are we here?' I suppose the only way for me is not to ask that question too much, really. It's just to *do*. I don't think we're here for any great purpose other than that. I mean, why are trees here and why are ants here and why are mosquitoes here? (I often ask that question, why are mosquitoes here?) But each one is fulfilling a life-span of enjoying being on this planet, I think, and trying to do it as well and as carefully as possible. I don't know why we're here and it puzzles me and sometimes disturbs me so deeply that I have to change my line of thought and think about something else.

How did your life change after the accident?

Well, a number of things combined. My marriage had just ended. I had these three young children and I knew I had to earn a living to support them. But I came increasingly aware of individual people who are out there when you're ready. For instance, I was working at Victoria University at the time, and the one and only marvellous Jim Robb, who was professor there, quietly made sure that I was able to work in a way that enabled me to manage my children and keep a job. So my life was changed by a recognition of other people's enormous generosity and goodwill.

People were just superb to me and my three children while we were recuperating. We'd been at Playcentre in Kelburn. The whole Kelburn community came round with food and things for the children, who were immobilised for a couple of months with plasters up to their necks. They were only small and there was an enormous

Alison Gray

outpouring of goodwill and I suddenly had a real sense of community. There were people there who cared, who cared about me. In fact, it was so moving and the food was so good I actually didn't really want to get well, but I did. And I think it gave me a real sense of wanting to work with other people and appreciate them.

I decided to go for it. I decided life is very short. Your life might end at any minute. You'd better jolly well make sure you're doing what you want to do and take risks. So since then I've taken risks that I probably would have hesitated about before. I thought, 'You've got nothing to lose, go for it!' So I have done more things since that moment in 1976 than I probably have done in the rest of my life put together.

I've taken a lot more physical risks. I think I'd already begun that journey with a friend (again, there are people out there when you're ready for them) who persuaded me that I could actually go tramping with my three small children and we could climb mountains and so on. So I took a deep breath and was amazed that I actually did it, with support. I continued to go along that line of exploring physically in the outdoors. I took a mountaineering course and was absolutely exhilarated by it. I later met other people who persuaded me to try other things.

I travelled. I decided I wanted to see more of the world – that was one excitement. I also took risks with work. I'd never had a really permanent job but the university people were marvellously supportive of me. They were always finding me one-year contracts so that I was able to bring up my kids and be home for them after school. But in the end I felt really burnt out. I felt I'd been teaching a long time and didn't think I was getting much feedback so one year I actually took the risk and left university.

I did a year's research on teenagers, which I thoroughly enjoyed. I set up my own business and that was quite scary, really, not knowing whether I was going to get enough work. But we've survived, we've survived very well. It's been lots and lots of fun. I took risks with relationships and risks with friendships and explored new ideas such as the women's movement, which was a marvellous new challenge for me.

Just kind of going for it, I think, so if I want to do something, I do it. The worst thing that can happen is that you'll fail. The very worst in the outdoors is that you'll get killed. I never actually thought about that because by nature I'm so cautious and timid that I'm not actually likely to put myself in that situation, but also I knew from that accident that even if you do, so what? You know in the end that isn't the worst possible thing, and because I've always been ambivalent about why we're here anyway I thought, if you die, well, you die, that's it, really. So that kind of freed me up from worrying all the time about what the worst was going to be.

225

Taking risks involves entering your fears. When you take a risk what is it that you're afraid might happen?

I still live with my fears and I still wonder why I actually put myself in the positions I do, because I still get really quite frightened about doing things. I'm afraid of making a fool of myself and I have my mother sitting on my shoulder saying, 'Don't be so silly. People your age don't behave like that.'

I'm still afraid people won't like me. And there's that real need to remain part of the community. There's the fear of not having enough food to eat, which was the situation when we were first on our own, the kids and I. And there were often times when we didn't think we quite had enough. But we did get there so I don't think that's a real fear. I think there's probably the fear physically outdoors of being hurt. When I ride my mountain bike I'm afraid I'll fall off and it will actually hurt. And sometimes I actually get tired of trying new things, too. I want to be nurtured a bit rather than constantly pushing frontiers for myself. I still think I'm seeking approval of some sort and I've got no idea who it's from, which is interesting, isn't it? There's obviously something in me that keeps me trying new things and I don't know who for, or quite why I do that.

One of the risks you've taken is to write books, both fiction and non-fiction. You're sticking your neck out a bit, aren't you, when you write?

That's right. The other risk is in my work. When I do research reports that are commissioned pieces of work, I still feel anxious that people will not be satisfied with my work. I really want to try to do a good job and I'm anxious that they should feel it is done satisfactorily. But I'm not sure why I choose to take on writing books, which are completely off my own bat and which, of course, I don't necessarily earn a large income from. That seems pure masochism in some ways. But I'm interested in exploring. I'm very curious about how other people manage their relationships, given that parts of mine have been quite difficult to manage. Part of it is to understand my own life better and that drives me to ask other people how they manage their lives, which is behind such books as *Mothers and Daughters* and *Springs in My Heels* and *Teenagers*.

The fiction is an extension of that and I find that really scary. I find I've been contemplating writing more and I've actually decided to have a rest and not push myself for a while. It is scary and I have a real admiration for people who do it because you've got to make it all up from scratch. And there are a hundred thousand critics out there waiting to jump on you. It's quite a damning society, I think. But also for me it's the ultimate challenge in overcoming those rules that I grew up with that you don't do anything unseemly. I think novels should be decidedly unseemly. I think they should explore the edges and the barriers and do things that are really imaginative. However, I still find it is probably one.of the last frontiers for me, to let my own imagination go and really take that intellectual and imaginative and creative and artistic risk. It's kind of like the last barrier. I don't feel that I've got that many physical barriers I want to overcome any more. I feel I've taken enough scary risks and pushed myself and feel good about that. But the intellectual, imaginative one – I'd love to take a real risk there.

You do make yourself very vulnerable, don't you, when you are being creative, when you're trying out new things and pushing the barriers? So many people have written poetry that's hidden away in drawers somewhere and they've never let anybody else hear it or read it because they'd expose themselves to rejection.

Yes. I think that fear of rejection in fiction still inhibits me from doing it. I've applied a couple of times for grants for fiction and not got them and felt, well, that must mean I'm absolutely useless as a fiction writer and I'm not meant to do it and I'm hopeless. And I take those things to heart more. It's almost like I don't want to try and push that boundary. I'm looking for a reason not to try it and yet I know it's a kind of last thing I really do want to experiment in. I don't know why we push ourselves into areas where we end up feeling vulnerable. I think maybe I want to explore the limits, explore the heights and depths and there's only one way to do it and that's to try.

Someone suggested to me that she was afraid of success, of going for the top, because there is a great risk of failure.

Yes, the risk of not doing something well is quite inhibiting. I think of all the books there are in the world and I think, who needs another one? Maybe I haven't got anything to say or I won't say it properly and people will be critical. But if you're going to always spend your life only wanting to do the best thing ever, you're not going to ever do anything. You need to start.

Is everybody creative? In a sense we are creating our own life story, aren't we?

Oh yes. I think everybody is. One of the great excitements of interviewing people for the books I have done is that I discover behind every door in every suburb in every city and in every town is a really interesting person. I've never felt the need to go and interview important or famous people because I know every single person has an interesting story that is not only revealing about themselves, but adds something to my life and informs and excites and instructs me. I think people greatly underestimate the value of creativity, the value of their life stories, the value of what

227

we together can pool. We pool our life stories and share our experiences. I think that's what we need more of – more sharing of everyday life experiences, and feeling that even though you might feel you are alone and not coping, you're actually normal.

It's tremendously reassuring when you share your life story to hear others say, 'Oh, I know that feeling' or 'I know what that feels like – particularly about being scared.'

That's right. Being scared and also wondering why you do it, really. I can remember once when I was out tramping with some friends and we were climbing Mount Hikurangi up in the East Cape. The mist suddenly swirled in while we were up at the top – it's quite rocky up there. You've got to climb across a kind of crevice and go round these rocks and for some reason I turned round and they'd all gone. They'd obviously seen the mist coming and wisely turned back, so I was left alone up there. I can remember my heart thumping against my chest and asking myself, 'Will I get back over these rocks?' My hands got a bit shaky. Of course I did, but it was a real sense of both ultimate fear and the ultimate achievement. It was also the sense of being part of nature and finding it's challenging but it's also supportive.

I've often talked to people in other countries about where they feel most comfortable. And there are some people who feel comfortable on the plains and some people who are hill people and so on, and a friend in Australia said she found New Zealand landscape too hostile and too challenging. I believe it is challenging but I don't think it's hostile. I think it just needs to be treated with respect and care and time and caution. I think that's a good model for treating other people, really. It has enormous rewards for the degree of challenge.

For me, I suppose, that's what spirituality is about. It's a model of how you should treat other people. Other people are challenging, but they're not hostile. You need to treat them with respect, love and care and they'll actually reward you in terms of the effort you put in.

This interview was first broadcast on National Radio on 18 January 1994.

Greg Newbold

In 1975 Greg Newbold was given a seven-and-a-half-year sentence for dealing in drugs. He was eventually to spend five and a half years in Paremoremo and Hautu prisons.

While in prison he studied for a Master of Arts degree. Since his release he has become a specialist in prisons and penal policy and is now a senior lecturer in sociology at the University of Canterbury.

The year 1975 was a major turning point in his life. In his book 'The Big Huey', which was written about his experiences in prison, he described that year as starting off one of the best years in his life but ending as one of the worst.

GREG NEWBOLD: I had no commitments. As a result of my dealing in drugs, for the first time in my life I had plenty of money. I had a motorbike and everything I needed. I was leading an exciting life and also using heroin. Heroin is a great security blanket. When you're using heroin, if you've got plenty of it then you feel incredibly secure. My life was pretty fast and I was really enjoying it.

But it was also the worst year in your life?

Yeah. It was a great year until about July. Then on 25 July I was arrested for offering to sell heroin in a big drug bust that ended up with me being sent to prison. The police came smashing through the windows and doors with their baseball bats, screaming and yelling, with dogs and guns and stuff and chucking everyone around. The house turned from a scene of tranquillity, where we were just sitting around listening to music, to absolute bedlam in the space of a couple of minutes. There were about fifteen policemen in plain clothes, and at that point my life completely exploded.

You were both a drug taker and a drug dealer, weren't you? When did you first get into drugs?

I was getting into marijuana before I went to university. As soon as I left school I was using marijuana. I'd been intending to use marijuana ever since I was twelve, ever since I'd first heard about it. I'd been trying to find it, wondering what it was like and thinking it'd be incredibly exciting, but I didn't actually get into contact with anyone who could get me any marijuana until I was in the Fire Brigade after I left school.

What was the attraction of drugs?

I've always been an experimenter. I've always liked taking risks and I think that's what it was. I read in the *Reader's Digest* about the hippies in 1961 and '62, how they used drugs and all the terrible things drugs did to people. As soon as I heard that I thought, that's for me!

What was your family background?

It was sort of stable, initially quite poor but my dad worked hard and we eventually became, I guess, middle-class North Shore. The marriage broke up when I was about twelve and I lived with my mother. They both used to drink quite heavily. My dad was always very stable and my mum was always very unstable. I don't think that affected us very much because all my brothers and my sister, who had the same sort of background as me, turned out far more conservative than I am.

I noticed you dedicated your book, 'The Big Huey', to your family. Did they stick by you throughout?

Yeah. They stuck by me wonderfully. My mum and my dad always used to visit me in jail. When I was in Paremoremo Mum would come out one week and Dad would come out the following week, without fail. Then when I went down to Hautu, down near Turangi, Mum would visit me one month, and Dad would visit me the next month. I can never repay that. It's something that means a hell of a lot to you.

So you were arrested in 1975. What happened then? You were taken to Mount Eden, weren't you?

Yeah. It was sort of like out of the blue. I was sort of plucked out of society, just *ping*, like that. It's just like if you have an accident or you get seriously injured. It just happened. I was in jail and I didn't come out. I was denied bail and for the next five and a half years I was just gone and all my affairs, my flat and everything, were just left undone. My family cleared all that up too – shifted my gear out of my place and jacked me up a lawyer. They used to bring me changes of clothes, because when you're on remand you don't get changes of clothes. You have to get someone to bring you fresh underpants, a toothbrush. Everything has to be brought up for you and I was on remand for five and a half months, I think it was.

We were locked up more or less twenty hours a day. We got two hours' exercise in the morning and two hours' exercise in the afternoon before trial and sentencing.

So what's it like being locked up all that time? From freedom to prison just like that?

You're really just marking time because remand time doesn't come off your sentence, or it didn't at the time. They take it more into account these days. But it meant that you were just doing nothing. There were no facilities whatsoever offered to remand prisoners. There was no recreation. There was no education. There was nothing. You didn't get movies; most of the time most of them had no radios. There was nothing except the companionship of the others and the other long-termers. The other long-term remandees became your friends and I made some really good friends among them.

Terry Clark was one of them, actually, the 'Mr Asia' guy. And there were a couple of other guys up there who were on long-term remands and ended up doing long sentences and we formed a sort of a clique. I actually look back quite fondly on my remand time, even though most of the time it was just pure boredom.

What's your attitude to drugs now?

I still don't see anything wrong with marijuana. I think it should be legalised. It's a matter of personal choice as far as I'm concerned, and I think victimising marijuana users is a bit like victimising homosexuals – what they do doesn't harm anybody else. But as far as hard drugs are concerned, I'm right against it. I'm right against heroin, I'm right against cocaine. I'm against addictive compounds in general. I'm against cigarette smoking as well, for the same reason.

You said at the time, I think, that you felt that the money you were making compensated for the risks you were taking. You didn't seem to have any guilt about being a drug dealer?

No. None at all. At the time I was involved in the drug-using, drug-dealing subculture and that was our life. I was twenty-two years old. Everyone was doing what I was doing, and the other thing about it was that drug use was glamorised in the songs of the day. Lou Reed was singing about heroin and actually going through the motions of shooting up on stage. He used to wrap the microphone chord around his arm. It seemed to me to be the glamorous thing to do. Mick Jagger sang the song 'Brown Sugar', which was about morphine. The Beatles were always singing about LSD. So drugs were really glamorous at that time and we who were using them didn't see anything wrong with it at all. Using and dealing. If you use, you've got to deal. You can't be a user and not be a dealer because it's far too expensive.

So you ended up in Mount Eden. When you were first locked up and that door clanked shut what were your feelings?

I was absolutely devastated. I mean, it was like being locked in a fridge. I just couldn't believe it. I couldn't believe that a place like that existed. I'd never been in contact with anything of that nature and Mount Eden Prison is nearly 100 years old. It is built like an old castle, an old gothic castle, inside. It's absolutely incredible. I had seen pictures of those kinds of institutions – like the dungeons of the Middle Ages. But I didn't think anything like that existed in Auckland, in New Zealand society, and I was absolutely stunned. I couldn't believe that we were actually going to be locked up in those cells. I thought it must have been the storeroom or something.

What about your future? Did you think you were going to be found guilty?

No. I expected I would be found not guilty. In depositions the evidence the police had against me was incredibly weak. The police almost let me go because there was nothing really there. They knew I was guilty because of a statement that one of the co-defenders had made, but he wasn't going to take the stand, so they couldn't question him about it. So they got a policeman to stand up and do what they call a 'verbal'. The policeman, a detective, stood up and verballed me, and for about half an hour he told lies about a conversation it was alleged he'd overheard me having. At trial it was proven, virtually without a doubt, that he was lying because he could not have heard anything from where he said he was hiding, which was four hundred yards away from where the meeting took place. But the jury found me guilty nonetheless, which really shocked me. They believed that policeman.

But you were guilty, were you?

I was guilty all right, but I was convicted on false evidence. Without that false evidence I would never have been convicted.

What do you feel about that now? Your sense of guilt, if I can call it that, about being a drug dealer and having to suffer for it?

I have sort of mixed feelings. I still don't feel guilty about it because I know that at the time I didn't feel I was doing anything wrong. I wouldn't do it now because I now think it's wrong, but I don't feel guilty about doing it then. I didn't think it was wrong and, therefore, I wasn't acting against my conscience. It's just that my conscience has changed.

As far as the prison sentence is concerned, well, it changed my life completely. I think it's almost certain that if I hadn't gone to jail I would have got more heavily involved. I would have got involved with Terry Clark, who knew me. I didn't know him but he knew me. He was eyeing me up, thinking about including me in one of his schemes. So things would have turned out very differently for me. I think it was probably providential for me to get busted that time. I mean, I've managed to make something out of it and if I hadn't been nicked I probably would have gone the other way. I would probably have got a bad habit and maybe been killed or landed up in some jail in England or something like that.

You say it was providential. Do you believe in providence? Do you believe in a higher power or anything like that?

No, I don't. I'm a devout atheist. But I still think it was luck, it was actually good luck that I got busted.

When you say you're a 'devout atheist' what does that mean?

Oh, just that I am a confirmed atheist. I totally renounce any belief whatsoever in any higher power. I don't believe there is any such thing.

So where does power lie?

I think my own power lies in my own head. I think I'm the complete master of my own destiny in that sense. I don't believe there's any higher authority that directs me or directs world events.

How do you think you should you use that power? Your own power?

For myself. I place a premium on honesty, actually. Honesty's the most important thing to me. Someone asked me the other day whether I thought intellect was the greatest quality a human being could possess and I said, 'No way.' Some of the most intellectual people are also the most dishonest and horrible people I've ever met. I think honesty is the most important thing and that has really wide ramifications. It's not just telling the truth. It means being honest with yourself about yourself and being honest to other people about yourself, which can sometimes offend people. People quite often don't like honesty and you do have to temper it with compassion, I mean you don't want to go and tell someone that you really hate them. Compassion comes into it as well – empathy and all the rest of it. But I think honesty is the main thing for me.

But it does involve caring for other people as well?

Yeah. Definitely caring for other people. Empathising with other people. Being a Christian. I'm not a Christian, but the Christian ethic – and the Marxist ethic for that matter, they're pretty similar. Just a basic sense of humanity I think.

How did you get on practising those ethics in prison? Or did you?

In jail the big thing was community, the inmate community, and so a really powerful ethic developed at Paremoremo, and at Hautu when I was there, too. What mattered was what was good for the community, the inmate community. It was all for one and one for all. Even if pursuing that ethic caused you to serve more time or have to serve some time in solitary confinement, provided what you did was for the good of the community, then that was what should be done. That was the fundamental of it. Thinking about other people and not thinking about yourself. That's where that honesty thing was strengthened for me.

When you were in Mount Eden I believe you had your first experience of trying to battle for somebody else, for better conditions, and getting into trouble.

That's right. One of my co-offenders was locked up unjustly and I had this sense of justice. I was naive but I did what I thought was the right thing – at the time. I wrote a letter to my lawyer, and got caught. I was trying to right an injustice. He'd been locked up in a cell with no clothes on all lunchtime in the middle of winter.

And you got in trouble because of that?

Yeah, I got stuck in solitary confinement over that. I was absolutely devastated. I'd only been in jail two weeks and there I was in solitary. If you walk into Mount Eden Prison and you think the standard cells are bad, man, wait until you get down to solitary. There things are really rough. I wouldn't worry about it now because I'm used to it and I know what to expect. But these cells are subterranean, they're dungeon cells underneath the ground. There's nothing in them. Nothing in them except a tiny dim filament bulb so it's always sort of semi-dark. There's no bedding. There's just a plastic sheet on the floor and a piss pot and a water jug and that's it. And they'll give you a Bible or, if you're lucky they might give you some other sort of a book to read, if you can read in that dark. At night you get your bed but they take it away in the morning. And, by the time your food comes down, it's cold. They give you a broken plastic knife and fork to eat it with. When you're not used to being locked up and you're put on your own for seven days, they call it the 'go slow', because time goes real slow in solitary.

What were they trying to do to you?

Oh, it's punishment, passive punishment. They lock you up in solitary until you cool off, let you think about it for a while. And the more solitary you do the less of a punishment it becomes.

So you were found guilty and sentenced to seven and a half years. Then you were transferred to Paremoremo?

Yeah. I was put into 'Classification'. It's different now, but at the time Classification was for people serving two years or more. You would go to Paremoremo to be assessed and you would be watched for a number of weeks to see how you were reacting to your imprisonment. To see whether you were aggressive, whether you were passive, whether you were compliant, whether you were rebellious. And then a report would be made and you'd front up to the classification board – the superintendent, welfare officer, psychologist, your divisional officer and so on. And they would decide. They would speak with you, ask you which institution you'd prefer to go to, and a decision would be made about where you would be transferred to or whether you would be sent over to the standard blocks and stay at Paremoremo.

I got classified initially to Paparoa Prison in Christchurch but I stayed so long in Classification that I applied to be transferred over to A Block in the standard blocks. Having reached A Block, because I was doing a long time, I elected to remain there for the next two and a half years, basically so that I could study.

And you did your MA in A Block?

Yeah. Well, at Paremoremo, because there's not much work available and it's difficult to get guys to do any work anyway because they haven't really got any incentive, they're really happy if somebody is going to do something constructive. So it's easy for somebody to get full-time study. I applied for full-time studies and I got it after six months. That meant I was able to apply myself completely to what I was doing, which was to do a research project on the social organisation of inmates at Paremoremo Prison, a maximum-security prison. I think it's the only one that has ever been done in the world, actually, a study on inmate society by an inmate in maximum security.

Before you were sent to A Block, you said you were quite a long time in Classification.

Yeah. I was there eight months. I wasn't used to being locked up, of course. I'd spent twenty hours a day locked up in remand and then I spent about 20 hours a day locked up in Classification as well. Well, that was around ten months of pretty well solid lock-up and my head started going a bit funny. I felt I was going round the bend, actually. It was a physical thing. I can remember sitting in my cell and feeling my head turning somersaults. God, it was a terrible feeling. It was just like living death. And I was like living death. I would get up and I would feel I had anaesthetic in my brain. I'd never had a feeling like that before and I can understand why they've had so many suicides up there. You're just not there.

So I went and saw the chief officer. They are compassionate, you know, those guys up there in Paremoremo. They were maximum-security administrators and they were tough guys, but the senior administration were bloody compassionate men as well. They knew. They could see when a guy was in trouble and they saw it straight away with me and just shot me straight over to A Block.

This was the result of your being locked up for long periods, that you felt you were going round the bend?

Being locked up for a long period, and also the social tensions in the place. Locked up with a bunch of yahoos, lots of people cutting their wrists, like being in an asylum. The big guys bashing up the little guys. The guys who were in for child molesting getting smashed up all the time. Fights all the time. Tension all the time. People screaming and yelling and threatening each other. It was just a madhouse, absolute chaos socially. And it really spooked my brain up.

Is it still like that in Classification as far as you know?

Classification has been dispensed with. They've changed to a segregation unit. They've needed to have a segregation block because the conditions over in the standard blocks, which were very stable when I was there, became destabilised when the gangs took over. So did the maximum-security prison itself, as well.

Parts of it became like Classification, with a lot of guys and a total lack of solidarity and commitment. The gangs buggered it up, particularly the Mongrel Mob. The Head Hunters and the Black Power weren't such a big problem but the Mob are now over in D Block. The administration moved them over to D Block because of their destabilising effect on the institution.

I've met lots of individual Mongrel Mob guys who are really nice people, but as a group, boy, they're anarchists, you know. Just no commitment to anybody else except the gang itself, which is a bad thing in a jail. We always used to say inmates first, gang second. But the Mongrel Mob switched that round and said Mongrel Mob first and everybody else second. That really screwed up the solidarity.

Your time in Paremoremo was quite stable, relatively speaking, was it?

It was very stable. There was a close-knit society that was really supportive of its members. Particularly in its relationships with the administration, the inmate society was well organised and stable. There were conflicts between inmates all the time, of course, and that was a constant source of tension, but there was an underlying stability to the whole regime, and an underlying predictability from day to day about what was going to happen or what to expect. I built up some very powerful friendships in Paremoremo with people who are still close friends to this day.

What was the attitude to prison officers?

Our attitude towards prison officers at Paremoremo was that they were there to do a job and their job was to lock us up at night and to see that we got fed and that was it. Our attitude was that prison officers should do that job and nothing more and leave the inmates to organise themselves. And by and large they did that. They understood that. We were on first-name terms with the prison officers up there, and they were on first-name terms with us, because we were locked up for a long time, week after week and month after month. So you got to know them and get on first-name terms. But we didn't acknowledge the right of prison officers to interfere with inmate politics.

What we did was our business and what they did was their business. For us, the whole concept of rehabilitation was just trash. We didn't want to be rehabilitated. The prison officers were just there to run the jail and as far as rehabilitation was concerned it followed the same rule. 'I'm doing my lag and I'm getting out. I don't want any interference from prison officers.' And that was the way it was in maximum security.

Is rehabilitation in prisons an unrealistic dream?

Yeah. I think it is. Most inmates reject it. We used to make jokes about it. Those inmates who do accept it do so because it's a means of making their lags a bit easier. All the research indicates that rehabilitative efforts taken in prisons don't produce significant results. But that doesn't mean that prisons should be tough places. You're in prison *as* punishment, not *for* punishment, and being in prison is a punishment.

In prison facilities have to be made available for those inmates who want to make use of them – things like education facilities, a gymnasium and those sorts of things. So that inmates don't just stagnate and rot while they're in prison. Welfare services perform two main functions in prison. First of all, they keep the inmates occupied and in doing so they help prevent rebellion. They keep the jail on a stable plane. The other thing they do is provide the wherewithal for those inmates who do want to do something with their time in jail, as I did with my studies and as others have done with learning a trade or a skill. Some people are able to make use of that.

Would you say you're hard or soft on prisons now?

Oh, I'm pretty hard-line, I think. I wouldn't consider myself a liberal as far as the prisons are concerned. I believe that prisons basically are punitive agents and cannot pretend to be anything more than an agency of punishment. But, within the context of punishment, you have to make things available so that people who want to make a new life for themselves when they get out are able to do so. You don't force it on people. If you try to force people into rehabilitation they'll rebel against it. But if they want to do it they can do it. Jack Hobson, who was the superintendent at Paremoremo, used to say prisons don't rehabilitate people. People rehabilitate themselves. And that's really the truth of it. The jail is not particularly effective as a deterrent. It's not particularly effective as a reformative agency either, but it's the best thing we can come up with.

This is society's way of punishing people who do wrong in their lives?

That's right. I think some people can be deterred from crime by punishment. A lot of white-collar offenders would, for example. The corporate thieves, the corporate criminals who steal a hell of a lot more money every year. I think it's been estimated they steal fifty times more dollars every year than the burglars and the thieves. They are people who weigh up the consequences of their actions before they commit them and they could be deterred by long periods of imprisonment. But under the present law they are not sent to prison. They are treated very softly. They sometimes take people's entire life savings and yet they're seldom regarded as criminals and treated with the degree of severity of someone who went and pointed a gun at somebody or broke into someone's house and pinched their video.

You went from Paremoremo to Hautu Prison Camp, a minimum-security prison. Was that quite a different kind of regime?

Yeah. The strange thing about minimum security is that it's minimum security/maximum discipline, whereas Paremoremo was maximum security/minimum discipline. I found that difficult to accommodate. I had come from a relaxed regime in maximum security to one where inmates were treated like kids, really. Suddenly you found people were giving you orders and exercising their authority, sometimes unwisely and unfairly.

But you had to put up with it or else you were sent back to medium security. The conditions in minimum security are pretty good. The work was great: you were outside all the time putting up fences, digging ditches, working in the bush. It's a very healthy lifestyle in minimum security.

We used to go down the creek, knock trout on the head with slashers and cook them up at lunchtime. We'd go out and bring back a bucketful of blackberries and pinch a whole lot of stuff from the food stores and make up huge blackberry pies. We lived like kings a lot of the time in minimum security.

It wouldn't have been difficult to escape, would it? Did the thought ever occur to you?

No, never. It was a ridiculous idea, escaping. Nobody escapes in New Zealand and gets away. I do know one person who got away. But, hell's bells, where do you go to? Go down the South Island or somewhere? You're going to get picked up sooner or later. And if you get picked up, well, then you're back in jail and you get an extension of your sentence – six months' extension or something. So no, I never ever contemplated escaping. I knew that the only way to escape completely would be to leave New Zealand. You'd have to go to Australia or further afield and never come home again. I'd rather do my lag.

Get it over with?

Yeah, you get your lag over with. If you haven't got any family over here, no roots, then I can't see any reason why you wouldn't want to escape and leave the country completely. But if you have roots here, like I had the family and a possible career, well, there's no point in escaping.

I gather you found things far more difficult in Hautu than you did in Paremoremo. Why was that?

That was because of the authority structure. I've always been a person who doesn't like taking orders. I don't mind taking orders from people who I believe are competent to give them but when people seem to exercise their authority just for the sake of it, or they abuse their authority or do things that I believe are unjust, I find it very difficult to accept. I had the same problem at school, actually. We had a very autocratic headmaster and I ended up getting kicked out simply because I just don't like people who wave authority around like a big stick. So that's what happened in Hautu. It really got my back up and I rebelled against it and spent a lot of time fighting against the authority structures down there, fighting against autocracy.

What was going on inside your head at that time? You seem to be like some other people I know who hate bullies, for instance, and almost deliberately pick a fight with them. Has that been your experience?

I wouldn't pick a fight with a bully, but if a bully picks a fight with me I wouldn't normally back down from it. It was the same thing in a more removed sense in jail. If someone exercises or attempts to exercise their authority over me unfairly then I'll rebel against it. It's a sort of altruistic thing with me. I got involved with the anti-Springbok tour protest, even though I hadn't been out of jail long. It was '81 and I'd only been out a year. I was still on parole, but I got deeply involved with the Springbok tour protest because I felt passionately that the Springboks shouldn't be here. I was prepared to take some quite considerable risks to demonstrate my opposition to it.

Being on parole would make it much more risky than for other people, wouldn't it?

It wouldn't have looked too good for me. It's a different type of offence, but it wouldn't have done me any good given that I'd been not long out of jail. But I told my probation officer I was going to protest and could get arrested – he was a rugby supporter. He knew the way I felt and respected it, and he said, 'Just take it easy if you can.'

At Hautu I understand one of the differences from Paremoremo was that the rules kept changing. It just seemed to be one of the ways in which power was used.

Yes, that happens in most jails but not at Paremoremo. The administration make rules and change rules and exercise rules as they see fit and you get rules changing from officer to officer, from shift to shift. You get one officer changing his application of rules from day to day and from inmate to inmate. That really gets my back up: prison officers who happen to have a pet dislike for someone and put them on charge for something that everyone else is getting away with.

It's injustice that really pushes your buttons, isn't it?

It really brasses me off and I always end up in the gun in those sort of situations.

What is it going on to make you feel so strongly about injustice?

I don't know. I think it's a basic concept that a lot of people have. I think everybody feels it but some people react and some people don't. Some people can bow their heads to injustice and rationalise it in some way but I can't. I don't compromise very easily. That's probably why I've never been married. I set down, this is right and this is wrong, and if it's right I'll go this way, if it's wrong I'll go that way, and that's it.

When you were in prison you seemed to be, well, fairly controlled as far as physical fights were concerned. You rarely got involved in fights, did you?

That's right. I did I get into a couple of fights. I bashed a guy up once for pinching my shampoo or something. But I believe if you live by the sword you die by the sword. For me, fighting is always the last resort. It's not something I take lightly – I would only do it as a last resort. I've got verbal skills. I was a debater at Paremoremo. I don't punch first and talk later. I talk first and then I would fight later if I had to.

There was a time, though, when you were quite rebellious at Hautu?

Yeah. It started off quite smoothly and I was keeping a diary. I was intending to write a book when I got out. Lots of people talk about it but I was going to do it, so

Greg Newbold

I kept these diaries and I used to smuggle them out; in fact I was smuggling diaries out of jail for the whole time I was there. Then finally this bloody diary got sprung. On the first day, my first page, my very first sentence, I called the superintendent a Pommie four-letter word and of course he read it and I was really in trouble. He had an army background. He knew how to ride people and that's what he did. From that point on he just tried to crush me. That caused me to react the opposite way and so I was sometimes so tense I had a headache all day – just tension, just waiting for the next thing to happen, knowing that I would have to react to it and wondering what the consequences of my reaction would be.

There was a period when a whole bunch of us were reacting against that superintendent. We were sort of committing acts of sabotage around the jail. For instance, one of the guys blew up the paint shop. He poured, I think it was forty or eighty gallons of turps over the floor and put a little time-bomb in there.

Another prison officer, he was a bad officer, a bad screw, everyone hated him. We slashed his tyres and put sugar in his petrol tank and eventually threw a bucket of shit over it.

There were a few other incidents. Once I sabotaged all the locks in the jail. Jammed matchsticks up inside all the padlocks in the jail so that they couldn't lock us up that night. Things like that. Schemes that we'd come up with. If they did something to us we'd all get together and plan our retaliation.

There are both good and bad prison officers, are there not?

Oh yeah. The majority of prison officers are just doing their job and they want to have an easy day. They want to get on with the inmates. They want to get on with their superiors and eat their lunch. They want to get their pay and go home. But there were some who were bucking for power, who were bucking for promotion and who really went out of their way, from our point of view, to make our lives miserable. From their point of view they were exercising as much authority as they had and sometimes exercising more authority than they had. That's a small minority, though.

At the other end of the scale there is also a small minority of prison officers who are true humanitarians who really can empathise with inmates, who can understand inmates, who get on well with inmates and who perform a really marvellous service as far as inmates are concerned.

I've said a good prison officer is worth ten welfare officers, and there were prison officers like that at Paremoremo, especially among the senior administration. And there were prison officers at Hautu in the rank and file staff who were bloody good people, really nice guys, and we recognised it.

How long did you spend at Hautu?

I was there for about two and a half years. I got a period of work parole after that.

It must be hard when you're getting towards the end of your sentence. You must be frustrated and impatient to get out?

Towards the end of my sentence was a very tense time for me because I'd gone through this period of about twelve to eighteen months when I was *persona non grata*, when my cell was getting tipped out all the time, when I was being searched all the time. The superintendent had directed the prison officers to put pressure on me and I was under this constant pressure, pressure, pressure.

Then about six months before my date for release the Mongrel Mob was going to have a strike over an issue that I thought was unjustified. I knew some of the main guys in the Mob and they were good guys and I liked them and I went and talked to them. I got the whole Mob in this prison cell on the morning of the strike and I just said to them, just explained to them, why it was illogical for them to take the action that they were planning, why they really didn't have justice on their side, why it was a bad idea to go ahead with the strike. If they wanted to strike over a real issue I would have supported them but on this particular issue they had no justice. And I managed to talk them out of it.

The prison officers all thought that I was organising them and when everyone went back to work and the word got round that I'd sort of talked them out of the strike the administration took that as a sign that I'd done them a favour. Which I hadn't. I'd done the Mongrel Mob a favour. I was moved into a good job, which, of course, made it look bad for me. It looked like I had compromised myself but I hadn't.

Anyway, for the last six months I was actually okay. Suddenly I was okay and they started hammering my mate instead. My best mate, he was stuck in the position that I'd been in. They had to have someone to scapegoat, so he became the scapegoat and I became the good guy. But all that time I knew that I was on a very fine edge. I knew it would be easy for me to fall off or get pushed off by something. The superintendent was always testing me, trying to make me react. He'd drive around in his car and wave at guys, you know, and expect you to wave back, that sort of shit. There's no way I was going to wave to him, like, you know, here comes my mate. You've got to keep this distance. You don't say goodnight to screws when they're locking you up: 'Goodnight and thanks for locking me up' sort of thing.

I remember they had these old policemen's shoes from the police force. The police had changed their shoes so we got all the old shoes and they tried to make us wear them when we went to the parole board. Now, to call someone a policeman in jail, that's fighting talk. There are no more words needed if you call someone a policeman. And to make us wear policemen's shoes to the parole board was just the worst possible thing they could do. So we refused to wear them. Those were the kinds of things that can make you into a bad guy again, you see. So it was pretty tense that last six months. I had to keep my integrity and my honour and all that intact, but I was copping all this stuff. It was pretty tense, but I managed to get through it.

Eventually you were released. It was a sort of a two-stage affair, wasn't it? You initially went on work parole. What is that?

I left the jail and went up to Auckland and I had to report to the work parole. It was a house in Mount Eden. Just a big house with about eight guys in it. We used to go out to work during the day and we'd have to come back in by six o'clock at night. Then we'd have tea and we could muck around. On weekends we would be allowed out from Saturday morning until Sunday night and that was just great.

It was brilliant earning money. We had to pay board. We got $20 to spend and the rest of the money went into a bank account. If there's any rehabilitation in the prison system that's when it happens. That's when it starts. When you're actually working in the community, saving money and living in a fairly sort of normal environment like an extended family. There was a warden and his wife, who were like your mum and dad, and all us inmates. About six or eight of us. We all got on well, we got nice meals, were well treated and it was pretty good.

Was it also a difficult time since, in a sense, you were free yet not free?

It was very, very difficult. You'd got to come back at night and you're just revved up and you'd want to go out. You're like a dog let off the chain. You really want to go for it but you can't so you've just got to keep it quiet. Quite a few guys abused it. A lot of them got caught and sent back to jail. It's a big temptation. It's like being a kid in a lolly shop and not being able to touch any of the lollies, you know. But we had the weekends and they were pretty good.

So there came a time when you were officially released or discharged. Can you remember your feelings when that happened?

Yeah. A great sense of release and of relief. I was released, released from jail. It was over! It was great, like a huge weight off my shoulders, and the most important thing from my point of view was self-determination. Once again I could make my own decisions. Once again there was nobody standing over me telling what to bloody do all the time. That's the thing I really hated. I hate authority and something I really detest is not being able to make my own decisions. That's one reason I live by myself, you know. I just love it. I love being on my own and being able to make my own decisions.

So you're free again. You have to make some decisions about the rest of your life. Is there a temptation to go back into crime in some sort of way again, or is it all clear and you know you're never going to go back again?

You know you never *want* to go back again, but that's different from never going back again. I know there was a time after I got out when I was running close to the wind. I got involved in a couple of things and I used drugs again. The first thing I did when I got out was score some smack, actually. I had a taste within half an hour. Within half an hour of hitting Auckland I had a needle in my arm.

You start trying to pick up the threads from where you left off five years before. So I started doing that, but there came a time when I knew I was going to have to make a decision one way or the other. I was real lucky from that point view because I got a job. A guy called Bernie Brown, who's an associate professor of law at Auckland University, got me a job in the law faculty doing research on prisoners' rights. That sort of got my foot back in the door of the university. And when I was there I met a guy called Bill Hodge, who's also an associate professor up there.

I'd done a lot of running when I was in jail, just around the football field, but I used to win the running races. And Bill said, 'Come out for a run.' He started taking me out on these runs, about twenty-mile runs up the Waitakeres, and building me up. He said I should run a marathon. And I can remember one night when I was at this place I was offered a syringe with some cloudy liquid in it, which was a mixture of morphine and cocaine – a beautiful cocktail – but I had this twenty-mile run with Bill the next morning. And I thought, either I use this bloody dope or I go for the run. There's no way I can do both, because I'll be too buggered tomorrow morning to run twenty miles if I have a taste of this stuff, and I decided that I was going to go running. I really decided that. I couldn't face Bill.

So he had a hell of an impact because he really took me under his wing. When someone takes you under their wing and helps you out you can't just sort of spit in his face. I couldn't let him down so I said, 'Right, that's it. I'm going to go running.' So I turned down this taste and I went out running with Bill the next day. I told him and he's an American and he said, 'Well, you would have been a real dumb ass if you'd done that.'

That support is absolutely crucial at that time, isn't it? For every prisoner.

It's crucial. It really is. To have people who are prepared to go to bat for you. First of all it was Bernie and then it was Bill. Bill stood by me, just like my dad. He became like a big brother to me and stood by me for years after that. People like Bernie and Bill, they're sort of a really powerful crutch for you initially, and a sort of moral force as well.

I have tried to do the same with mates of mine when they've got out. Bill and me, we'd get guys and try to get them out and get them running but it doesn't usually work. Bill thought because we had a success with me that it would work with other people as well, but it hasn't always been that way. Quite often we'd be dealing with guys who had longer histories of offending than I ever had.

And you've become something of a fitness nut now. Would you call yourself a fitness nut?

No, I wouldn't call myself a fitness nut. It's not fitness as such. Some people would call me a fitness nut but I wouldn't because I know lots of people who are like me and we're not all nuts. But yeah, I started running marathons and I was boxing for a while too when I first got out. Then I started doing triathlons. I've done quite a few triathlons. I will always keep training anyway, I think, as long as I can stand upright.

So you went back to university. What happened then?

I went back to varsity and I got a scholarship. I got First Class honours for my Masters thesis and I won a scholarship so I went to Auckland University and studied the history of the maximum-security prison for six years – really a history of prison administration in New Zealand. It took me a long time. The scholarship only lasted three years. I was lucky, because I published *The Big Huey* in 1982 and that got me some royalties. It also got me some credibility with the Justice Department, which is something I needed to continue to get access to the information that I wanted.

I also got a job as a stunt man on films and that's where my principal finance came from, actually. I was only doing minor stunt work but I liked the work and it paid extremely well. I worked on about six feature films, like *Mutiny on the Bounty*, *The Savage Islands*, and some Chinese kung fu movies.

What's minor stunt work?

You have fights and you get thrown over tables and you jump through glass windows, fall off trucks, get blown up or have sword fight and sometimes get cut, you know.

Doesn't sound very minor to me!

Well, as opposed to falling out of an aeroplane or driving a car under a bus or something. The specialist guys do that. But we were with a group and the leader of our group was real good and for the rest of us the main thing was just keeping your head in a tight situation. Things like getting shot, having explosive charges over you and they blow you up. You might have to fall ten feet and land on the ground and not show that you're hurt.

So at university you started studying for your PhD?

Yeah. I got the PhD in 1987 and then got it published under the title *Punishment and Politics*. I was out of work then for eighteen months. I had some part-time teaching but I didn't have anything permanent. It took me a long time, but eventually I got the Canterbury job and I came down here to teach sociology. It's a good job. I was so happy when I got it. Never having had a proper job or a proper income, suddenly to get a decent salary coming in every month was really something. It made a big improvement in my life.

You've become quite an expert in the prisons, in penal policy. This means you're still involved in this area. I would have thought that maybe you would like to forget about it all and do something quite different.

No, it's not just something that I am involved with. It's now my profession. It's something I know a hell of a lot about and I get on with guys who have been in jail because I have something in common with them. And I don't have any problem with that at all.

At the moment I'm on the board of trustees of the Salisbury Street Foundation in Christchurch, which is a post-release facility for guys when they get out of jail, and I'm really enjoying being involved with that particular organisation and being able to contribute to the programme.

You've said that you are a totally different person from the one who went into jail so many years ago. What are the principal differences, do you think?

Well, I'm older. I'm more street-wise. I'm not as naive as I was before and also, after being in jail, I'm probably less compromising than I was. I'm less compromising with my own values, but probably more accepting of people who are different from me. When you are in prison you have to accept all sorts of people you might not like – you might not want to be associated with certain types of offenders, for example. But at the same time you've got to live with them. And you realise that, even though they may have been labelled such and such a type of offender, they're still a human being underneath it all. Like the Mongrel Mob, for example. When you get to know the guys in the Mongrel Mob individually they're ordinary human beings just like everyone else.

So you become a lot more circumspect. A lot more philosophical as well, I think, about the world and about people. I used to have a lot of time to think about these kinds of things when I was in prison. And those lessons that you learn, the things that you work out in your head, you never really forget.

So what would you say is your philosophy for life now?

Being honest is a big thing with me. It's always been big and it's even bigger now since I got out. I feel strongly about personal integrity, being decent and fair with other people. An important thing for me also is enjoying life. When you get out of jail there are lots of things which you appreciate that you have never appreciated before, like tranquillity and beauty and all the neat things that New Zealand's got, things that you were brought up with but you were quite blasé about.

When you're locked up in a sort of concrete pen for a few years, when you're deprived of these things, you start to wonder about the beauty of those aspects of life that you never really noticed before.

We used to look out of the cell block windows at Paremoremo, and at night you could just get a glimpse of the trees and the grass up on the hills of Albany. And when there was a beautiful sunset about three or four of us would look out that window and think, wouldn't we like to be out there, you know. Sometimes when the wind was blowing in the right direction you could just get the smell of the grass or the smell of the pine trees and that was really magic. And you always thought when I get out, boy, I am going to savour those things.

I still do. I love it down here in Christchurch, I just love it. Getting up early in the morning, in the winter and in the summer. I get up at half past five. It's still dark but I get on my bike and I'm up the top of the Port Hills on that summit road, a long way above sea level, right up high. You feel like you're the king of the world up on the top of those hills and you can see for miles and you're totally alone. The city's way below you. There's Lyttelton Harbour on the other side, and the sun's coming up behind the other horizon. There's snow on the Alps and it turns pink and the sky and then all the hills turn pink and it's just amazing. It just blows you away. There's little rabbits running around and birds singing. It's just terrific, and that's the sort of a thing I don't think I'd be able to appreciate as fully as I do now if I hadn't been locked up for a couple of years and deprived of it.

This interview was first broadcast on National Radio on 16 January 1990.

My Story

In writing this afterword, which tells something of my own personal story, I am responding to suggestions from my publishers, Ros Henry and David Elworthy, from friends and from people I've interviewed who have become my friends. They have said, 'We want to know, who is Neville Glasgow? What about your story?'

My own search for meaning has traversed many different paths. It began in my childhood. I was a dreamer, a 'bookworm', a child who was intensely curious, always asking, 'Why?' My parents' exasperation was expressed in the phrase 'little boys are made to be seen, not heard'. This was used on many occasions as I attempted to join in the adult conversations. Another response I got to my frequent questions ('What's that for?' or 'What are you making?') was, 'It's a wigwam for a goose's bridle.' That floored me!

But I also had questions about what I saw as injustices, things that didn't seem to fit, or seemed to me to be unfair. Why was my father sometimes caring and at other times physically brutal? I had many thrashings, sometimes with a stick around my legs, sometimes with the strap that hung behind the door; sometimes I was punched in the head or thrown across the room.

I'm not saying that my experience was all that unusual. I fear it was all too common in those days. But it's only in the last few years that I have recognised that I was a physically abused child and how that has affected my view of life and what it means.

Yet, I could be proud of my father. He worked hard to provide for my mother and the family during the Depression years. He became a dairy factory manager, a position of some status in the small country towns of the Waikato and King Country where I spent my boyhood and adolescence. He taught me many practical things and he could be very funny. He was a practical joker and loved reciting poetry and telling stories.

My mother was far less volatile, very much occupied with running the home, feeding the family – three boys and one girl – and stretching the household budget, but I don't remember her talking very much. She lived in Dad's shadow. I knew she cared for me. She sang songs to me at bedtime which I can still remember, but she wasn't a 'touching' or 'cuddly' person. Her part in the family discipline was to say, 'Wait until your father gets home.' My brothers and I would wait in fear, wondering what sort of mood our father would be in when he came home from work.

I suppose in the simple black and white terms of my childhood my question was, 'Do my parents love me or hate me?' Sometimes it seemed one answer and then the other. I felt I was receiving a double message.

It was this double message, I think, that set me on the search for meaning. What is life all about? Is it an unhappy world or a happy world? Is life about love, warmth, excitement and feeling good, or is it about fear, hurt, anger, rejection and feeling bad? How can you make sense of a world like this? I saw it in very black and white, either/or terms. It had to be one or the other.

My religious upbringing didn't give me any clear answers either. I grew up in a family which, I suppose you could say, wasn't strong on religion but was strong on the concept of sin. One of the family rules was, 'Never play cards on Sunday.' All sorts of activities were seen as 'sinful', and when I hurt myself, stubbed my toe for instance, while doing something naughty I would be told, 'That's God punishing you!'

Being sent to Sunday School in my early childhood was also a form of punishment. I'd much rather have been playing outside. I did admire some of my Sunday School teachers, however. Despite much of the theology of the time, which reinforced my feelings of being 'bad' or 'unloveable', they showed me in their lives that love that the Christian message is supposed to be about.

But in religion as in life I was receiving a double message. On the one hand I was singing 'Jesus loves me', while on the other the devil was waiting to tempt me. God wasn't much better. He was waiting to pounce on me and punish me for my transgressions.

That confusion and that feeling of being a victim stayed with me for many years. It probably provided the motivation for my early attempts to do something about my situation by linking up with conservative churches and groups, which, although they confirmed my feelings of being a victim or a sinner, also offered me a way out: 'Believe in the Lord Jesus Christ and you will be saved.'

Being 'saved' wasn't all that simple either. It also meant subscribing to particular rules and forms of behaviour and belief that today I find unbelievable. One was the doctrine of original sin, which claims that even little babies are born 'bad', that all humans are innately evil and can only be saved from the consequences of their lives and actions by believing what the Bible says, or what the church says it says. This doctrine has been responsible for the misery and suffering of millions of good people. And not only fundamentalists preach this doctrine: it's still there in all sorts of subtle ways in mainstream Christian denominations as well. I believe it is an utter travesty of what Jesus was on about.

To me the message of Jesus is encapsulated in his words about loving your neighbour as yourself. Jesus is telling us to love our*selves*! – not only ourselves, of course, but quite definitely ourselves.

I was in my forties before I accepted that I was loveable. It suddenly came to me that I was worthwhile. I wrote it down on a piece of paper that I still have: 'I am a good person. I don't have to be anybody. I am!' And for the first time in my life I really believed it.

For years I had imagined if I could only find the right way to live, if I cared for other people, obeyed the right rules, behaved in the right way, believed the right beliefs, I might find a place where I would be a victim no longer, where I couldn't be hurt any more.

I know now that experiences of pain, suffering, deprivation and depression can be some of the most important times in helping us to find meaning in our lives. This is not to say we should deliberately seek out pain and suffering. But they are part of the price we pay for being human, for having the capacity to think and talk about our experiences, to choose what our attitude or response shall be, to wonder 'Why?' and seek to find meaning in the painful things that happen to us.

This is not to deny that times of joy, celebration and exaltation can also help us to find meaning. 'Follow your bliss!' says mythologist Joseph Campbell, and I couldn't agree with him more.

For me, the need to find meaning in my life is urgent, never very far away, particularly during black periods of depression that descend on me, sometimes quite inexplicably. Those times have provided me with some of my greatest tests, yet they have often also been my greatest source of inspiration.

I bear the psychological label 'depressive'. Perhaps another label for a depressive could be 'victim', because when you are depressed, deeply depressed, you feel you are a victim. You see yourself pressed down, weighed down by the world, your life, your circumstances, with no choices and no energy to fight your way out of the smothering blackness that seems to surround you. It's only when you cast off the role of the victim and reach out for the light again that you can begin to be healed. But it isn't easy.

I have suffered recurring bouts of depression since my early twenties: deep dark plunges into a black hole with sometimes only a pinpoint of light to show the way out or tell me that there is a way of escape. Sometimes it's terribly difficult to hang on, to continue to fight, to continue to believe that you are not going to be like this for the rest of your life.

There have been times when suicide has seemed a realistic option; when it has seemed the only way to stop the pain. It's hard to describe the pain, but if someone you love has suddenly died or you have been rejected by someone you desperately wanted to love you, you will have experienced something similar. You feel there is literally nothing left to live for; that your life no longer has any sort of meaning or purpose.

I've had to accept that my depression is partly genetic. It has been described as 'endogenous', or arising from chemical disturbances within the brain. It is partly the result of early childhood experiences and is also triggered by my immediate circumstances and my reaction or response to them.

Do I have any choices? Yes, I do. I can use medication and I can seek help from a counsellor or psychotherapist. I can accept the love of my wife and family who continue to love, accept and support me, even when I am going through one of my black periods. They are very important to me in what I sometimes see as a battle to keep my sanity and stay alive.

But finally I have to deal with what is essentially my own attitude, how I look at life in general and how I look at my own life. I have to exercise what has been described as 'the last of the human freedoms', the right to choose our attitude in a given set of circumstances. When all else appears to fail, when everything around me seems to be crumbling, or I feel I'm drowning in the darkness that surrounds me, something says to me, 'You have the right to choose your attitude and no one and no thing can take that away from you. You, and only you, can give this experience 'meaning'.

I can illustrate what I'm saying by sharing with you what was probably the blackest period of my life. In the late 1960s I was a Presbyterian minister in my first parish in a provincial New Zealand city. It was a very large and poor parish. Much of the area it covered was in low-cost housing and there were plenty of social problems. That was partly what had attracted me. I saw myself following in the steps of Jesus – the 'man for others' – preaching the Gospel, bringing hope to the hopeless, helping the poor and fighting for the common good.

I knew the parish was very divided in its theological views and that my predecessor had been very conservative and a preacher in the 'hell-fire' tradition. He had left behind a large band of enthusiasts. Yet I felt I could bridge the theological gap and bring people together as my own background was religiously conservative. I thought I could 'speak their language', even though my approach by then was more liberal.

Unfortunately for me, this was also the period when the views of Professor Lloyd Geering, then principal of Knox Theological College, were dividing not only the Presbyterian Church but the country as a whole.

My attitude was that we should at least give Lloyd Geering's views a fair hearing. I tried to explain what I thought he was saying and stated, 'The heretics of today may well be the prophets of tomorrow!' This was the last straw for my conservative parishioners. In hindsight I can see how, in my enthusiasm, I had tried to move too fast with too many changes in the parish. This had also contributed to the suspicion and anger that was now directed towards me.

I received a lot of hate mail. People would come around to my house and shout abuse on the doorstep. I was even accosted on the street by a man who grabbed my jacket and spat out his accusation, 'You're the minister who agrees with Professor Geering!' Some ministers of other denominations wrote letters to the newspaper saying I was not worthy to be a minister. Some of my conservative parishioners formed a prayer group to 'pray me out of the parish'. Their prayers were answered.

Under this barrage of hate, coupled with a demanding schedule of social work and near seven-day weeks I collapsed physically and mentally and was admitted as a voluntary patient to a psychiatric hospital.

On my first night there I tossed and turned and moaned as I tried to cope with what was happening to me. In the middle of the night I was told I was disturbing the other patients and put in a locked cell (that is the only way I can describe it). The rest of the night I lay awake, my ears filled with the shouts and screams of a nearby patient. 'My God,' I thought, 'I must be really mad!'

A voice inside my head told me, 'This is hell, your hell, and this is what it's like.' Yet I also thought of *A Pilgrim's Progress* and how the pilgrim does win through in the end. When I looked around I saw only blackness. I looked up and in my imagination I saw a long way off a tiny pinpoint of light. It gave me hope – somehow, some day, all this would make sense. It all seemed meaningless, but some day I would walk out into the light again and once again my life would have meaning and purpose.

And it has. There were long months of struggle. I was so heavily drugged I thought I was in the hospital for only two weeks but it was six. I could only shuffle around like an old man.

Gradually I began to fight back. (One of the strong motivations for me was the smell of stale urine in the toilets next to the ward I was in.) My journey out of hell wasn't easy, particularly as initially I had to go back and stand in the pulpit and preach to my congregation, many of whom hated me. That was one of the hardest things I have had to do in my life.

Eventually it became clear that for my health and that of my family I should be shifted to a more accepting parish. This came to pass and I spent a couple of happy years working alongside a warm and supportive minister in a team ministry.

After a time, however, doubts about the church and its ministry and my place within it were began to make themselves felt. I was becoming increasingly frustrated with what I saw as the church's unwillingness to change its structures and its language to meet the needs of people. I was also having theological doubts about the nature of God and what it means to have faith. 'Has God made us in his image, or do we make him (or her) in our own image? Is he/she really an imaginative and symbolic expression of our concern to find meaning in our lives? Is faith or spirituality more about psychology than theology?'

My son, who had been seven years old when I suffered my 'breakdown', began to exhibit some disturbing behaviour. This finally tipped the balance and I decided it was about time I gave my family greater consideration. I left the ministry and began work as a radio and television journalist in the old NZBC. After twenty-five years in broadcasting I believe I have found my niche.

The experience in that 'cell' in the psychiatric hospital – my 'dark night of the soul' – was a major turning point in my life. I discovered that I could live through hell and come out alive. I could dare to believe that my life has meaning and purpose. Nothing and no one can take away from me my right to choose my attitude to whatever is going on in my life, no matter how meaningless it might seem.

Something, someone, called me out of the darkness and into the light. Some people would call it God. Some might see it as the action of the energy or life force within me; others might say it was simply the organism fighting to stay alive. But the call has to be answered. It is *my* response, how I look at life and how I live my life (the two are inextricably intertwined) that gives my life meaning.

If my life is a story, who is the story-teller? Who or what decides who I shall be and how I shall live my life? My genes? Circumstances? The environment? My early childhood? My relationships with other people? Some kind of God, out there in the depths of existence or within me?

I believe that ultimately I am the one who tells my story. I am the one who gives meaning to my life. I am responsible for my own healing and I am the one who must exercise the freedom and responsibility of being human in living out my response to that most wonderful gift, the gift of life.

Neville Glasgow

Directions

The *Directions* radio interviews are broadcast on
National Radio in summer and winter series.
Details regarding specific dates and interviewees
are published in the *Listener*.
Information about the series is available from
Replay Radio, Box 123, Wellington. Cassette
copies of the programmes may be purchased
at a cost of $20.